When Britain Ruled the Philippines 1762-1764

The Story of the 18th Century British Invasion of the Philippines During the Seven Years War

By

Shirley Fish

This book is a work of non-fiction. The events and situations are true.

© 2003 by Shirley Fish. All rights reserved.

No part of this book may be reproduced, stored in a retrieval system, or transmitted by any means, electronic, mechanical, photocopying, recording, or otherwise, without written permission from the author.

ISBN: 1-4107-1068-8 (e-book)
ISBN: 1-4107-1069-6 (Paperback)
ISBN: 1-4107-1070-X (Dust Jacket)

Library of Congress Control Number: 2003090028

This book is printed on acid free paper.

Printed in the United States of America
Bloomington, IN

1stBooks - rev. 11/15/05

Contents

Introduction vii

Chapter One: An Invasion Takes Shape 1

Chapter Two: Preparations for the Invasion Begin in India 17

Chapter Three: Spain's Contentious Colony 31

Chapter Four: The Endless Cycle of Conflicts 55

Chapter Five: Spanish Manila 70

Chapter Six: Manila's Neglected Military Defenses 87

Chapter Seven: The British Invasion of Manila 105

Chapter Eight: The Seizure and Looting of Manila 125

Chapter Nine: The Troubled British Government of Manila and Cavite 139

Chapter Ten: The Filipino and Chinese Supporters of the British .. 160

Chapter Eleven: Colony Returned to Spain 169

Chapter Twelve: Following the Money 179

Epilogue 191

Reference Notes 199

Bibliography 209

Acknowledgment and Author's Note

When I arrived in Manila in 1995, I became interested in the fascinating history of the Philippines. After looking through many history books written in the Philippines by various historians, I was amazed to see that almost all of these individuals devoted only a minimal amount of space to the British invasion and occupation of the archipelago in 1762 to 1764. The invasion was part of a broader campaign launched by the Admiralty in England against Spain and was a direct result of the ongoing Seven Year's War – the world's first world war. I thought that this was an important part of Filipino history, which had basically been ignored by the historians in the Philippines. Intrigued by the lack of information available concerning this momentous event, I began researching the activities of the British Royal Navy and Army during the 18th century, in London and in Manila, to find out the true story behind the invasion. Thus, what appears here is a result of my four years of researching the story.

So many individuals have offered assistance or have been of some help to me in the process of putting this book together. I would like to thank the staff at the British Library/India Office Library in London and the Public Records Office at Kew for their friendly and valuable assistance. In the Philippines, I would like to thank the employees of the Filipinas Heritage Library Makati, Metro Manila, for their courteous, friendly and extensive assistance. Lastly, I would like to thank my husband Ian Fish, for his support, dedication and patience in helping to finalize the manuscript, as well as endlessly reading chapter after chapter as the book progressed.

INTRODUCTION

The Spaniards in Manila had been confident that they could fend off an attack by one of the many Asian countries surrounding the archipelago, but they never expected that an invasion would be launched against them by Britain. Consequently, when the British forces sailed into Manila Bay in September 1762, they found that they were hopelessly unprepared to defend the colony.

After the two-year occupation of the Philippines, the territories seized by the British were returned to the Spaniards at the end of the Seven Year's War. Even though a peace treaty was signed between Britain, France and Spain in early 1763, the Philippines was not mentioned in the document, as England had not received news of the capture of the archipelago. Conversely, the commanders of the military campaign were unawares of the signing of the treaty by the three warring European powers. As a consequence, they remained in control of the Asian possession until 1764 when the seized territories were returned to Spain. The Spaniards continued to control the archipelago until 1898 when they lost the country during the Spanish-American War to the United States.

But what ultimately triggered the animosities between England, France and Spain, which in turn led to the Seven Year's War between the three countries and to eventually the Philippines becoming a part of the world's first war? For the answer to that question, it is necessary to go back in time and briefly review the history of the conflicts between the three European powers which were long-standing and had their origins decades before the advent of the Seven Years War.

The War of the Spanish Succession 1701-1714

The first major conflict of the eighteenth century erupted in Europe after the Spanish Hapsburg king, Charles II, died in 1700. The fact that he had been childless led to an ongoing concern as to who would be his successor. Debates regarding this issue began as early as 1699 when two other Hapsburg monarchs both made claims to the Spanish throne. Louis XIV of France, insisted that the Spanish crown and territories be turned over to his grandson, Philip V, who was also the great-grandson of Philip IV of Spain. Also claiming the throne on behalf of his grandson, Charles (later known as Emperor Charles VI) was the Austrian Emperor Leopold.

Before his death, Charles II selected his grandson Philip V as his successor, and this was a move, which was heartily welcomed by Louis XIV. He accepted the Spanish throne on behalf of his grandson. However, Philip's ascension to the Spanish Empire was not welcomed news in England and Austria. The disagreement with Philip's ascension to the Spanish throne led to the War of the Spanish Succession.

The succession issue became the main source of conflict, as the French monarch, Louis XIV had long been contemplating an ambitious plan to combine the royal houses of Bourbon France and Spain and thus, creating a powerful empire. With his grandson on the throne, Louis XIV was well on his way to turning his dream into a reality.

The decision by Charles II to leave the Spanish throne to his grandson was angrily objected to by England, Austria and the United Provinces of the Netherlands. They had argued that the unification of Spain and France under one realm, as envisioned by Louis XIV, was completely unacceptable as it would undermine the balance of power in Europe. Clearly, it was thought, Louis XIV would be in a position to manipulate his young grandson, the newly installed Spanish king, and his actions could affect the entire course of events on the Continent. England, France and the United Provinces equally objected to a possible union of Hapsburg Austria and Spain.

As a result of the succession disputes and in an effort to curtail Louis XIV's ambitious plans, England, Austria and the United Provinces joined forces and became allied in a war against France. The German State of Bavaria, as well as Portugal and Savoy, were allies of France. After a number of battles, England eventually retreated from the war as very little had been accomplished by 1711.

Simultaneous to the Spanish succession war in Europe, friction arose between the colonies of Britain and France in North America. The battles between both countries were the early stages of a struggle for the possession of America. The conflicts began with frontier disputes and led to the Queen Anne War of 1701-13. The war ended with the signing of the Treaties of Utrecht (1713), Rastatt and Baden (1714).

Under the terms of the treaty, the Spanish Netherlands, Milan, Naples and Sardinia were ceded to Austria, while Gibraltar and Minorca were turned over to England. Sicily was surrendered to Savoy. In North America, France ceded Nova Scotia and Newfoundland to England. Additionally, as part of the conditions of the treaty, the new king of Spain, Philip was recognized as the legitimate heir to Charles II. He, in turn, renounced his claim to the French throne. But what proved most controversial in the treaty and which would lead to further conflicts between the two countries, were the commercial concessions granted to England.

England was granted a monopoly to provide slaves to the Spanish colonies in the West Indies. Known as the *Asiento*, this and the fact that England was also allowed to send vessels to the Americas where she could engage in trade, became two annoying sources of continuous irritation to Spain. While the concessions proved most beneficial to England and her designs towards becoming a major commercial power in the Americas, they also meant that Spain was slowly losing control of her colonies.

Spanish merchants were also apprehensive with the terms of the treaty, as their once exclusive Spanish colonies in the Americas were suddenly opened to British encroachments, as well as the dreaded contraband activities. To the dismayed Spaniards, the colonies which had become a source of revenue with silver continuously flowing into the peninsula from their settlements in the Americas and with all sorts of trade goods available, had suddenly opened a door to the British they would have preferred keeping shut. The Spaniards had become the dominant force in the Americas, but although trade concessions were reluctantly extended to the British, the Spaniards endeavored to at least ensure the safety and security of their lucrative Manila-Acapulco galleon trade.

In an attempt to prevent any outside intervention in this profitable trade, new restrictions were imposed upon the galleons which, in turn, led to further conflicts between the Spanish merchants in Spain and the Manila-based investors whose cargoes and livelihood depended on the continuous success of the galleon trade. Another blow to Spain was the fact that she had ceded her territories of Gibraltar and Minorca to the British as part of the conditions of the treaty.

During an interlude of thirty years after the signing of the treaty, Spain and England enjoyed a relatively peaceful period. Spain still faced a number of difficulties mainly revolving around the trade concessions granted to the English as they were still exceedingly suspicious of England's intentions in the Americas.

This led to the Spanish practice of overtaking British vessels sailing into American waters and sending aboard a search party. The search was conducted in an attempt to uncover any contraband activities the English were clandestinely carrying out in the Americas.

Another area of contention concerned the navigational rights extended to England as her ships sailed in and around Spain's colonies in the Americas. This conflict led to another war between Spain and England and this became known as the Spanish War.

The Spanish War 1739-1748

During the years of 1714 to 1739, the Spaniards were continuously attempting to revise the Treaty of Utrecht. The Italian wife of the Spanish King, Philip V, Elizabeth Farnese, spearheaded the attempts to alter the treaty. She strongly objected to the terms contained within it and made every effort to regain territories ceded to England, France and Austria. In particular, she was most anxious to recover the Spanish territories of Gibraltar, Minorca and the Italian States for her sons.

An alliance was established between England, Holland and France in 1716 in an effort to derail Farnese's persistence in altering the treaty. The three allies were determined to maintain a balance of power in Europe, which was established through the treaty. The Duke of Orleans of France added his support to the alliance as the treaty affirmed his ascension to the French throne, which had been threatened anew by Philip V.

In 1717, the Emperor of Austria had also joined the alliance to uphold the terms of the treaty as well as to ensure the succession of his young daughter, Maria Theresa, to the Austrian throne upon his death. As a woman she was not considered eligible as a candidate for the throne, but her father the emperor set into motion his plans to install his daughter as his successor. Consequently, with England, France, Holland and now Austria forming a quadruple alliance, the much sought after balance of power in Europe was maintained until 1739 when Farnese's attempts to modify the treaty were successful in that her efforts led to the Spanish War of 1739.

Angered by the trade concessions granted to England and the loss of so many territories ceded to England, France and Austria, conflict between Spain and England inevitably led to combat and harassment of the British on the high seas. As British vessels were continuously searched and English merchants manhandled, these events led to episodes such as the *Jenkins' Ear* affair. Back in England, outrage was growing against Spain. The *Jenkins' Ear* incident of 1731, had been reported to the members of the House of Commons indicating that a ship's master by the name of Robert Jenkins had been attacked by the Spaniards during one of their ship searches. The Spaniards had cut off Jenkins' ear as he was suspected of conducting illegal smuggling activities. By this time, the British government had exhausted all attempts to prevent the Spaniards from searching their vessels and had no recourse but to declare war against Spain in 1739.

Britain launched a number of sea attacks against Spain's settlements by positioning their ships in the Caribbean and in the Pacific in an attempt to destroy trade in her colonies. Additionally, the action was an attempt to expand the trade concessions they already had in the Americas, as well as to gain, if possible, prize money by plundering Spanish vessels and their possessions.

Vice Admiral Edward Vernon, aboard his flagship, was ordered to attack the Spanish settlements of Porto Bello, in Panama, as well as to take the city of Cartagena in Columbia. At the same time, George Anson, the forty-three year old captain of the *HMS Centurion*, was on his way to the Caribbean where he was ordered to join forces with Vernon. Anson was in command of the *Centurion* for two years in the Americas and in the East Indies where he was able to circumnavigate the globe as well as capturing a Spanish galleon.

The English effort in the Caribbean to undermine Spanish control and communications in her territories in the Americas was largely unsuccessful. Vernon failed in his attempt to capture Cartagena, and although he attacked Porto Bello in Panama, he was unable to secure the Isthmus of Panama as he was instructed to do so by the Admiralty.

War of the Austrian Succession 1740-48

The deaths in 1740 of the Hapsburg Emperor Charles VI of Austria and Frederick William I of Prussia, led to another war over territories and succession. Charles, not having a male heir, had selected as his successor, his young and politically inexperienced twenty-three year old daughter, Maria Theresa. But as women were ineligible to ascend to the throne, Charles's decision led to another succession dispute in Europe. Knowing that his daughter faced an uphill road as his successor, Charles had attempted before he died to smooth the road ahead for his daughter's ascension to the Austrian throne and claim to the Hapsburg territories. Consequently, to ensure the peaceful transition of the monarchy, he had established a legally binding document known as the *Pragmatic Sanction*.

The Pragmatic Sanction had been accepted by other European powers agreeing to Maria Theresa's ascension to the Austrian throne. But the uncertainty created by Charles's death, provided Austria's enemies with the incentive to claim Hapsburg territories as their own. These succession and territorial disputes led to the war. Maria Theresa's ascension to the throne was brought into question by the Elector of Bavaria (later Emperor Charles VII), Augustus III of Poland and Saxony and Philip V of Spain, while Frederick II of Prussia claimed part of the Austrian territory, Silesia. England, still at war with Spain, became allied with Austria as did Holland and Sardinia, and Saxony later on also threw in her support of Austria. The allies of Prussia were France, Spain and Bavaria.

In the background, Elizabeth Farnese of Spain was still demanding the return of Milan to the Spaniards, while the French king, Louis XV, was determined to destroy the Hapsburgs. As France and Spain were allied, in an endeavor to further his aims, he became allied to Frederick of Prussia. Consequently, Louis XV and Frederick II were against Francis of Lorraine becoming emperor of Austria. War erupted between Austria and Prussia, as Frederick invaded and took the territory of Silesia. The Treaty of Breslau formalized that the territory was now Prussia's – whereupon as he no longer needed his allies, he disengaged himself from them.

Without needing to concern herself with Prussia, Maria Theresa sent her armies into Germany where she was able to successfully oust the French. This victory worried Frederick and he again entered the war requesting that Maria Theresa sign a new document, the Treaty of Dresden, reaffirming that Silesia did indeed belong to Prussia. Meanwhile, the British during this time, were providing sea power in the Mediterranean and assisting in the defense of Milan which had been invaded by the French and Spanish.

Despite the fact that England was still embroiled in conflicts with Spain, France proved to be the greater threat to her. As the antagonism grew between France and Britain, the question over the Austrian succession became secondary, as both countries were determined to become the greater commercial power in North America, the Caribbean and in India. France eventually declared war against England in 1744.

In 1748, the Treaty of Aix-la-Chapelle ended the European segment of the war. Maria Theresa recognized Prussia's claim to Silesia and her husband, Francis of Lorraine, became emperor. The French returned Madras to the British in exchange for their settlement of Louisburg in Canada, as well as evacuating the Netherlands. Parma was returned to Spain while Austria retained Milan.

The Seven Year's War 1756-1763

While the Seven Years War was fought in four worldwide arenas: Europe, North America, the Caribbean and in Asia, it was mainly a continuation of the colonial rivalries between Britain and France. Both countries vied for commercial supremacy and territorial gains. The European battles under the Seven Years War banner, paled in comparison to the conflicts and open warfare Britain and France fought on land and sea. When the conflicts ended with the Treaty of Paris in 1763, Britain was clearly the victor and on her way towards becoming a vast and powerful *British Empire*.

However, in Europe, the war had begun over the issue once again of the territory of Silesia. Both Austria and Prussia claimed this territory as theirs. During the earlier War of the Austrian Succession, Prussia had invaded Silesia and in the Treaty of Dresden, her hold on the territory was formalized with Austria's consent. But by 1756, Maria Theresa of Austria was determined to regain her lost territory and was irritated with England for having convinced her to surrender Silesia to Prussia in the first place.

Consequently, the Seven Years War, had its origins in Europe where renewed hostilities between Austria and Prussia led to open warfare and dragged other European countries into the conflict. Allied to Austria, was France, Russia, Sweden, Saxony and Spain. Britain and Hanover sided with Prussia.

With both Austria and Prussia also vying for supremacy in Germany, the war began when Prussia invaded Saxony in 1756. Other battles took place at Bohemia and Leuthen (1757), Zorndorf (1758), Kunersdorf and Maxen (1759). During the course of the European war, England was at first only able to assist her allies financially, as she was unprepared for war. This changed under the leadership of the British statesman, William Pitt, the First Earl of Chatham (1708-1778), who came to control the British government and her military.

In Europe, Pitt's government provided Prussia with extensive support, both financial and with military assistance on land and at sea. The victory at Minden in 1759 was led by the Prussian, Ferdinand of Brunswick, who was appointed to lead the offensive by Pitt. This was followed by sending his commanders Boscawen and Hawke to blockade Toulon and Brest and prevent a possible French invasion of England or the sending of assistance to French Canada. Boscawen destroyed a French fleet bound for Brest, off Lagos, while Hawke, sat in wait for the French at Brest where he intercepted another French fleet and destroyed them at Quiberon Bay.

In North America, the conflicts between the British and the French occurred during the same time frame as the Seven Years War, and they came to be known as the *French and Indian Wars*. The French controlled territories in New France (Canada) extending from Quebec, in the north, to Louisiana and the Gulf of Mexico. While the British controlled the Eastern seaboard, her settlers in the Atlantic states were continuously attempting to spread westward beyond the Ohio Valley, which was then located in French territory.

The French had constructed a series of defensive forts forming a barrier to protect this region and keep out the colonists. However, the British knew that they had no choice but to oust the French if they had any hopes of spreading across the country and settling new lands. Major General James Wolfe, in Canada, was victorious in wresting control of Quebec from the French in September 1760.

Meanwhile, Florida was controlled by Spain, as was most of the west including Texas and California, Mexico, Central and South America except for Brazil, which was a Portuguese possession. The Caribbean was a hodgepodge of possessions belonging to the British, French and Spanish, but even there, they were engaged in commercial rivalries. Although the British colonies in the West Indies were not as rich as those of the French, it was not especially interested in taking other islands as it feared a reduction in the price of sugar if further territories in the region were seized.

In India, the British trade company was successful in its conflicts with their French counterparts at Plassey in 1757 and then again at Masulipatan and Wandiwash in 1758. In 1761, they captured the French settlement of Pondicherry. This ended France's plans of becoming a powerhouse in the sub-continent. The victories, on the other hand, had established the British East India Company as the supreme mercantile and foreign power in India.

With the ascension of George III to the British throne, he sought peace rather than a prolonged continuation of the war. However, Prime Minister Pitt was strenuously in support a continuation of the war. He could clearly see that in time Spain would come to the aid of France and even suggested that an attack be launched against the Spaniards to minimize the threat to Britain. But the Cabinet and the king did not agree with Pitt and he was dismissed. Nevertheless, Pitt's fears turned into a reality when Spain became allied to France and declared war against Britain in January 1762.

Prime Minister Bute and Lord Anson of the Admiralty in London put into motion the plans for the campaigns against Havana and Manila. The British government declared war against Spain and sent a fleet to capture Havana. In India, another fleet was organized by Brigadier General William Draper, in charge of the military and Rear Admiral Samuel Cornish leading the naval side of the offensive against the Philippines.

Chapter One
An Invasion Takes Shape

"Whereas, we have found it necessary to declare war against Spain, and nothing can tend so much to the effectually annoying and distressing our enemies as attempts on their colonies and settlements in the different parts of the world; and we judging that a successful attack made by our forces in the East Indies on the Spanish settlement of Manila in the Philippine Islands would be greatly for the advantage of our trading subjects in those parts, and would at the same time give a very sensible blow to the commerce of Spain." [1]

King George III

One of the more obscure and least understood historical events of the eighteenth century was the British invasion of the Philippines in 1762. Although the country of more than seven thousand islands had been periodically engaged in conflicts with the Dutch, Chinese and Muslims during the sixteenth and seventeenth centuries, the British attack was the first time Spain's sovereignty in the archipelago was successfully challenged by a European power.

As a Spanish possession, the archipelago had been reluctantly drawn into the war as part of a plan launched by the British Admiralty in London and approved by King George III to attack Spanish and French settlements in North America and Asia. The invasion took place during the latter stages of the Seven Year's War, which began in 1756 and concluded in 1763. Peace talks were already underway between Britain and France in 1761-62, and it was just a matter of months before a treaty would be hammered out between Britain, France and Spain. But an event occurred which was to ultimately affect the Philippines. The war, which began over a succession issue in Europe, had escalated into a continuation of colonial rivalries between Britain and France. This led to fierce battles being fought between the two countries in Europe, North America and in India in an attempt to gain new territories and commercial supremacy.

Spain managed to maintain her neutrality throughout the entire period of conflict, but during the latter months before the war's conclusion, she became allied to France. On 15 August 1761, an exhausted France, still reeling after having lost many ships and troops to the British in North America and in India, turned to Spain for its support. When the Spaniards

Shirley Fish

signed the *Family Pact* with France, due mainly to the royal ties that bound the two countries to each other, Spain, had in turn, become Britain's enemy.

King Charles III of Spain decided on the Spanish-Franco alliance. Signing the agreement with the French King, Louis XV, the pact indicated that both countries would come to the defense of the other if required. Spain's entrance into the conflict was viewed as being quite a pointless move. As Spain had much to lose and little to gain by aligning herself to France so late in the war, the decision succeeded in placing the country in a very dangerous situation.

By the end of 1761, Spain had achieved a certain level of prosperity in the Americas, and it was presumed that this was also the case in her Asian colony of the Philippines. While her American possessions provided the peninsular Spaniards with a continuous flow of silver helping to invigorate her ailing economy, the Philippines on the other hand, was almost completely neglected by Spain and its colonial government in Manila. For the few Spaniards living in the Philippines, only the Manila-Acapulco galleon trade mattered or prospered. Nevertheless, by remaining outside the disputes between France and Britain, she was able to concentrate on strengthening her overseas territories and in particular, her colonies in the Americas. It was therefore, absolutely necessary to maintain her neutrality if she was to hold onto her prized settlements in the Americas and in Asia without suffering huge losses a war would surely extract from her Royal Treasury.

At the same time, Britain was on the verge of becoming an all encompassing empire and naval power in the world. She had achieved numerous successes in North America and in India, which had, in turn, infused the British people with a new sense of patriotism and invincibility. With Spain's alliance to France, the British government and the East India Company realized that a new opportunity had come about to exploit and gain greater commercial concessions, as well as new territories. Spain was clearly vulnerable to Britain's military designs and possibly an attack or an invasion of her settlements.

Thus, the British government wasted little time and had rapidly seized upon the opportunity to encroach upon Spain's territories. The main objective in the Philippines was the retention of the island of Mindanao once a peace treaty was signed. With this in mind, Britain declared war against Spain on 4 January 1762. The Spaniards, upon hearing the news, reacted by issuing their own declaration of war against Britain later that same month on 18 January.

Events moved quickly after the declaration of war was announced. On a cold winter's day in London, the British government and officials of the Admiralty convened a Secret Committee meeting on 6 January 1762. Under discussion were the war measures to be enacted against Spain and France. Attending the meeting were George Anson, the First Lord of the Admiralty; Lord Ligonier, Commander-in-Chief of the British Army; Grenville, the Duke of Devonshire (Lord Chamberlain); Duke of Newcastle (First Lord of the Treasury); the Earl of Egremont (Secretary of State for the Southern Department), and the Earl of Bute (Prime Minister).

At the meeting, Lord Anson announced his plan to attack the very heart of Spain's possessions in the Americas, namely Havana, and possibly the French settlements in Louisiana. In the bustling city of Havana, luxurious cargoes and silver arrived periodically from Mexico and the other Spanish possessions in South America for re-shipment to Spain. Anson's plan was quickly approved and later, while they continued discussing the upcoming campaign, the Earl of Egremont introduced a proposal suggested by Colonel William Draper to attack the Philippines. Draper was then in London where he was serving as a Chief of Staff and involved in the planning stages of a military campaign against the French settlement of Belle Isle.

The Earl of Egremont later wrote of the decision to strike against the Spanish possession of the Philippines where he mentioned that the offensive would be of some benefit to the East India Company. He stated that, *"a successful attack on Manila, the capital of Luconia* (Luzon) *one of the Philippine islands, would not only greatly annoy and distress the enemy in that part of the world, but would also considerably contribute to the security and perhaps to the extension of the East India Company's trade."* [2]

As the military campaign would depend upon the participation of the East India Company's ships and troops in Madras, Lord Anson had already discussed the matter with Laurance Sullivan, Chairman of the East India Company in London. He had requested their cooperation in the venture during the latter months of 1761. This, in turn, led to a meeting between Sullivan and the Court of Directors of the East India Company on 30 December 1761, where he explained the proposed expedition.

The Court of Directors agreed to the enterprise, as they had expressed an interest in permanently retaining the island of Mindanao at the end of the war. However, soon after an initial agreement was reached to cooperate with the British government's plan to invade the Philippines, several of the Company's directors became uneasy with the idea of attacking the archipelago. They could not envision any clear cut benefits for the Company and also worried about the safety of their settlements in India, which could be attacked by their enemies in the region if they provided ships and troops for the enterprise.

Lord Anson asked Colonel William Draper in late 1761 to formulate a plan for the invasion. In his report to Lord Anson, he described in detail how the invasion could be carried out, as well as providing an explanation of the various benefits to be derived by the British government and the East India Company once Manila and Cavite, the initial targets, had been seized.

According to Draper, the plan called for the cooperation and support of the East India Company's ships and soldiers in Madras, working together with the British Royal Navy ships and military already based there. These had been sent out to protect the Company's settlements in India. Draper's own regiment of foot soldiers, the 79th, was stationed in Madras and he suggested that they could be employed in the military campaign.

He also thought that the Philippines was completely vulnerable to attack. As the distance was so great between the archipelago and Mexico, where the viceroy's office was situated and to which Manila reported and was administered, the Spaniards could not have had enough time to send out reinforcements to defend the colony. Draper was confident that the invasion could be smoothly launched and successfully carried out saying, *"If the expedition is carried on briskly Manila can hardly be reinforced from America, from whence alone it can receive succours."* [3]

Brigadier General William Draper

As the man whose proposed plan was enacted upon and led to the invasion of the Philippines, Colonel William Draper was an adventurous individual who was possibly after what he viewed as an opportune and a potentially profitable military campaign. As Draper came from an affluent family, he was born with a silver spoon in his mouth so to speak in Bristol, England in 1721. His father, Ingleby Draper, was a wealthy customs officer. His grandfather, William Draper, was a squire in Berwick, where he was remembered for his fondness for fox hunting. An uncle, Charles Draper, was a captain in the Dragoons (horse soldiers).

Draper received his earliest education at the Bristol Grammar School and then as he grew towards manhood at Eton and King's College, Cambridge in 1740. At Cambridge, he received a Bachelors Degree in 1744 and became a fellow of the College. Later, he received a Masters Degree. For a period of time, he was contentedly employed as a teacher at King's College, but he soon became bored with the everyday routine of university life and yearned for a change. His search for adventure, led to his seeking out a career in the military. Even though he was originally destined to follow a career in the church, he instead accepted an appointment to serve in Lord Henry Beauclerk's foot regiment.

This was followed by a stint in the 48th foot and where he later served at Culloden in May 1746. He was then appointed to the position of an adjutant in the Duke of Cumberland's regiment the 1st Foot Guards. In January 1747, he traveled to Flanders where he served as a lieutenant and then as a captain of the 20th Regiment by 1749. While serving under the Duke of Marlborough in 1756, he married his first wife Caroline, the daughter of Lord William Beauclerk who was the brother of his first commander.

By November 1757, he was ordered to raise a foot regiment of 1,000 soldiers for service in the East Indies. The military unit became known as the 79th Regiment. He arrived in Madras in 1758 and while there, he fought in the Anglo-French Wars. Then in command of the royal troops, he was involved in the defense against the French during the siege of Fort St. George.

As his reputation grew and he became well known for bravery in battle, he rose through the ranks and was eventually elevated to the position of colonel in 1760. For the proposed military campaign against Belle Isle during the Seven Year's War, he was temporarily promoted to the rank of Brigadier General. As the mission was postponed, he returned to his rank as a colonel. He was once again elevated to the rank of Brigadier General for the Philippine expedition in June 1762 by George III.

At the age of forty-one, Draper had already had his share of adventure as a military man. As a participant in the military campaigns against the French in India, he had managed to survive intact. Given this premise, one can only assume that the Spanish-Franco alliance provided him with an opportunity he could not pass up. If successful, he could have had enough money to live comfortably in England a very wealthy man. But career-wise, seizing the Philippines from the Spaniards could lead to an elevation in his status within the military hierarchy and to royal recognition for his achievements in Asia. No doubt, Draper had carefully reviewed the pros and cons of the expedition and how he might personally gain by commanding the venture.

With a sense of confidence, Draper was able to easily mingle amongst the highest echelons of English society. This, no doubt, enabled him to associate with individuals such as Lord Anson and the Earl of Egremont, for how else could he otherwise propose such a fantastic plan to invade the Philippines if he had been just an ordinary man on the street. He clearly had access to the corridors of power in England and in India, and those powerful associations enabled him to introduce his plan to the most prominent officials of the land. When he did, they had eagerly embraced the invasion scheme.

It is interesting to note that prior to his arrival in England and while still based at Madras, Draper had at one point traveled to Canton on sick leave. At the Chinese port city, he received first-hand reports concerning the state of affairs in the Philippines. It was then that he first became aware of the seriously undermanned Spanish military garrisons. He also learned of how mismanaged the colonial government was run by the Spaniards. He realized that the Spanish colony could be easily captured and used as a device to later negotiate with Spain for trade concessions and territories in the archipelago and more importantly to gain prize money.

A Secretive Asian Colony

During the mid-eighteenth century, the Philippines was considered to be one of the wealthiest countries in Asia. Its wealth was, however, a closely guarded secret. As European nations were not allowed to trade at Manila or at any of the other Spanish settlements in the country, it was difficult to verify whether or not the country was indeed as rich as it was then presumed to have been. But in reality, the country was totally neglected by the Spaniards. They were only concerned with the success of the galleon trade.

Moreover, they were terrified of losing one of their valuable galleons to adventurers, privateers, pirates and enemies of Spain such as the English or the Dutch. It was well known throughout European circles that the Spanish galleons traveled annually from Manila to Mexico and vice versa, carrying cargoes of immense wealth. They also knew that the massive ships were often under threat of attack and seizure on the high seas.

Even though the Spaniards had closed off the Philippines to all European trade, a clandestine trade continued to exist as British and other European merchants arrived in Manila sailing aboard for example Muslim ships. These vessels with their Muslim flags were permitted to enter Manila Bay and conduct trade with the Spaniards, Chinese and Filipinos of the capital city. The British traded goods for Mexican silver which they, in turn, needed for their trade with the Chinese in Canton and Macao. Any Europeans discovered by the Spaniards aboard the vessels, while anchored at Manila Bay, were often explained away as being interpreters for the Muslim captains.

Manila and the port of Cavite were both as heavily fortified and guarded as was then possible even though there was a serious lack of manpower, cannons, weapons and ammunition. Thus, Spanish secrecy was assured, as the colonial government also feared that outsiders might learn of how poorly they maintained their fortifications and garrisons. In any case, the secrecy surrounding the true economic condition of the Philippines helped fuel the growing mystique concerning the actual wealth of the Spanish possession. Its true state of affairs remained hidden from view until the British invasion of 1762.

General Draper's Proposal

In his proposal, Draper provided various reasons why an expedition should be mounted against the Philippines. Given the fact that as Spain had become aligned to France, her possessions in the Americas and in Asia were clearly viewed as open for an attack by the British, as they had become legitimate targets of war.

"Manila is a proper object of the war from its known wealth and opulency, and if the expedition be properly timed, the Acapulco ships will have brought their treasures there, which will still add to the importance of the conquest and further detriment of the enemy." 4

Another reason for the invasion was the belief that Cavite could provide British ships with a fully functioning, highly equipped port for the repair of their own ships, as well as its shipbuilding facilities. Moreover, Draper suggested that capturing the Philippines could provide direct trade with China by exchanging Philippine commodities the Chinese had long been trading for in the islands in lieu of paying in silver.

Trade with China had increased significantly and the British were unable to provide Chinese merchants with the sort of goods they were interested in purchasing. Thus, whatever the British purchased from Chinese merchants had to be paid for in silver, which was the only acceptable method of payment. It was becoming increasingly difficult to find enough silver to pay for the many goods the British desired from China.

By establishing an East India Company post in the Philippines, a country with a tradition of trading with China for many centuries long before the arrival of the Spaniards in the sixteenth century, the British could tap into a market offering numerous natural resources for trade with the Chinese. Another positive point was the fact that they could also grow their own spices in the archipelago and trade these in European and American markets.

Additionally, Draper proposed that the expedition would be allowed to proceed, as it was possible that the Spaniards might blockade or attack the Company's vessels, which were then traveling from India to China. It was true that the Spaniards, from their port in Cavite, had at times mounted offensives against their enemies in the region including the Dutch in Java and in the Moluccas and the Chinese in Formosa. So his point was a valid concern.

Thus, Drapers' motives for the invasion could be viewed as being multi-faceted in scope and with the ability of eventually providing the East India Company with a host of new possibilities for further growth in profits. This was especially so given their expansionary plans in Asia. However, it was evident from the start that if they planned to seize and occupy the entire archipelago, their efforts to do so were quite anemic in scope. But this was obviously not their intention. Compared to other major campaigns carried out by the British government such as the massive offensive launched against Havana during the same time period, the fleet sent to the Philippines was too small to conquer little more than Manila and Cavite.

However, there was a secondary plan to conquer the island of Mindanao once Manila and Cavite had been seized and this was prepared by Lord Anson and the directors of the East India Company. The plan called for the retention of Mindanao, which was recognized as being an independent entity from Spain. Whilst the British could have seized the island and kept it as part of the terms and conditions of a peace treaty, they would have been presumably trying to receive Spain's cooperation for their anticipated presence in the archipelago if it came to that.

George Anson, First Lord of the Admiralty

Lord Anson expressed an interest in Draper's plan, as it entailed not having to incur any additional expense and eliminated the need to provide ships and soldiers from England to assist in an expedition. As the East India Company would provide their own vessels and troops for the military campaign, this was an inducement to extend the Admiralty's full support for the venture. But his approval of Draper's plan may have been based upon the fact that he too had captured a galleon in his younger days and had become exceedingly wealthy because of it. No doubt his adventurous campaigns in the Americas and in the South Seas also had some influence upon Draper's own enthusiasm for the expedition.

His experiences as a 43 year-old naval officer had taken him to the Philippines, where he became familiar with the archipelago and the Spaniards who controlled the territory. As the Captain of the British Royal Navy war vessel the *Centurion,* Anson's actions in the Americas and in the Pacific are worth noting.

Participating in the British offensive against the Spaniards in the Caribbean and in the Pacific, Anson sailed from England in 1740 with six war vessels and two store ships, as well as more than 1,900 men. He had been ordered by the Admiralty to create as much of a disturbance as was possible in any of the Spanish settlements he encountered in the West Indies and the South Pacific. His flagship, the *Centurion* was a fourth rate, 1000-ton vessel of sixty guns with thirty-two officers, 367 sailors and 122 marines.

Anson enlisted in the navy at the young age of fourteen and within four years had been elevated to the rank of acting lieutenant. At the age of twenty-four, he received the command of a sloop and by twenty-seven, he was deputy captain. Whilst serving as a subaltern for a time, he was able to gain valuable experience in the navy where he was established as one of England's most highly experienced naval commanders by the time he sailed to the Caribbean and the Pacific.

Sailing through South American and Mexican waters, he encountered Spanish vessels and was engaged in some conflict with these. However, he soon decided to sail to China and the port of Canton, where he anticipated repairing his two remaining ships, the *Centurion* and the *Gloucester*. He was also very determined to capture a galleon. His scheme entailed sailing from Canton to the Philippines where he planned to cruise around the islands and await the arrival of the Manila galleon, which was making its return journey from Mexico. He was aware of the enormous quantity of Mexican silver the galleon would be carrying to Manila, and it was this treasure Anson coveted.

However, disaster struck when he lost the *Gloucester* in a severe storm. He was left with the only remaining vessel his flagship and 350 men. By the time he reached China, most of his men were suffering from the effects of scurvy. The flagship limped into the harbor of Canton with two thirds of her crew – all the others had died on the journey to Asia. Once off the coast of the island of Tinian, his remaining crew regained their health and he sailed to the Portuguese colony of Macao, where he anchored for six months. While there, he had the flagship refitted and fresh provisions taken aboard. As far as anyone in Macao knew, Anson was preparing for the return journey to England. But in reality, he was still hoping to capture a galleon. By October 1742, he set sail for the Philippine island of Luzon.

As the Spaniards in Macao had also been convinced that Anson was planning to return to England once his ship was ready to sail, they were not overly concerned. They did not see the need to warn the governor of Manila of any supposed danger. Meanwhile, back in Manila, Governor Gaspar de la Torre, had already dispatched a galley, the *Pilar*, to pilot the incoming galleon through the hazardous San Bernardino Straits, a body of water located near the Philippine island of Samar. But before the *Pilar* could intercept the galleon the *Nuestra Senora de Covadonga*, Anson spotted the massive ship off the coast of Samar and gave chase, capturing her and the treasure she held on 19 June 1743.

Aboard the galleon was the highly trained Portuguese Captain, Geronimo de Monteiro. He was devastated by the loss of his ship. The galleon had briefly anchored off the island of Guam before proceeding to the Philippines, and there he was informed of Anson's presence in the region. But Monteiro was also under the impression that the English commander had every intention of sailing straight to England.

During a short but severe battle with the galleon, Anson lost one man and seventeen were wounded. The Spaniards had 644 people on board the vessel and of these sixty-four perished during the conflict. Though mortally wounded, Captain Monteiro was transferred to the *Centurion* where he was attended to by the British ship's surgeon. He was completely demoralized and embarrassed by the loss of his ship to Anson's smaller force, albeit, one that was highly trained in military tactics by Anson. Whilst waiting for the arrival of the galleon Anson had continuously drilled his men to the point that upon intercepting the galleon, they had become a formidable opponent.

Along with the captured prisoners, Anson towed the galleon to Canton where he arrived on 11 July 1743. Of the prize money taken from the galleon, as well as from the sale of that vessel, Anson had in his possession the sum of 130,000 Mexican silver dollars plus a quantity of silver ingots for a total in prize money amounting to approximately 10 million dollars. The silver sent from Mexico to Manila, was in payment for goods shipped the previous year by the Spaniards and Chinese investors in the galleon trade. The cargo shipped to the Americas had consisted of everything from silks to spices and other commodities. The loss of the galleon and silver came as a terrible blow to the investors and was obviously the cause of deep anger and despair in Manila.

On 15 December 1743, Anson set sail for England arriving there in June 1744. He had been away for three years and nine months, but when he returned to England the Admiralty gave him a frosty reception. However, they soon warmed towards him especially after seeing how the general public praised his accomplishments in the South Seas. He was elevated to the rank of Rear Admiral and later to the position of Vice Admiral. During this time he served as a member of the Admiralty where he introduced a number of reforms, which helped raise the standards of the British Royal Navy. After defeating the French fleet off Cape Finisterre in the Iberian Peninsula in 1747, he was raised to the peerage and named First Lord of the Admiralty. Thus, in January 1762, when it was decided to attack Havana and Manila, Anson was a highly influential man who remembered the days when he had captured one of the famed Spanish galleons.

William Dampier, Alexander Dalrymple and the Spice Trade

In addition to Lord Anson's adventures in the South Seas, there were two other Englishmen whose exploits in and around the archipelago may have influenced Draper's dream of seizing territory in the Philippines and capturing a galleon or two. These two individuals were the seventeenth century privateer, William Dampier and Draper's contemporary, Alexander Dalrymple, who was then employed by the East India Company in Madras. Draper had no doubt read of Dampier's exploits in the books he wrote, and which had sold well in England. As Dampier detailed his adventures in the

Orient and in particular the Philippines, the books helped to create a greater interest in the Asian region.

Moreover, it was Dampier's travels in Asia, which filled the minds of many a young man with the dream and a longing for a life of adventure on the high seas. Whilst exploring Mindanao, Dampier found many of the much sought after spices growing wild across the island. Spices such as nutmeg and cloves, then in great demand in Europe, had remained uncultivated by the natives out of a fear that the Dutch would seize the island for its spices if they knew that they could be grown there. Perhaps they were not growing as abundantly as they did in the Spice Islands to the south of Mindanao, but they were nonetheless growing on the island. This was an important bit of news for the directors of the East India Company, as they longed for their own sources for the spice trade.

"They have plenty of clove bark, of which I saw a shipload; and as for cloves, Raja Laut ... told me that if the English would settle there, they could order matters so in a little time, as to send a shipload of cloves from thence every year. I have been informed that they grow on the boughs of a tree about as big as a plumb-tree, but I never happened to see any of them. I have not seen the nutmeg trees anywhere; but the nutmegs this island produces are fair and large, yet they have no great store of them, being unwilling to propagate them or the cloves, for fear they should invite the Dutch to visit them, and bring them into subjection, as they have done the rest of the neighboring islands where they grow. For the Dutch, being seated among the Spice Islands, have monopolized all the trade into their own hands, and will not suffer any of the natives to dispose of it, but to themselves alone. Nay, they are so careful to preserve it in their own hands, that they will not suffer the spice to grow in the uninhabited islands, but send soldiers to cut the trees down." 5

At a time in history when spices were extremely important to European merchants, the need to obtain them often led to armed conflict amongst nations who fought to control the trade in Southeast Asia. Of all the islands in the Philippine archipelago, it was thought that only Mindanao appeared to have had the most suitable terrain necessary to grow spices. However, spices were also available on the northernmost island of Luzon. Nevertheless, if an East India Company post could be established in Mindanao at the end of the Seven Year's War, the Company would be able to have its own sources of spices. This would enable them to compete against the already lucrative trade conducted by the Dutch East India Company in the Moluccas. This in itself was an attractive proposition if it could be carried off and Draper's plan provided the opportunity to turn it into a reality.

Spices were so highly sought after as they served many purposes. For example nutmeg was used as a preservative and to counter the rancid conditions of rotting meat. It was also used in medicinal preparations for ailments such as dysentery, which was known as the *bloody flux*. To mask offensive odors, it was used in pomanders along with cinnamon, cloves and cardamom, as well as in many food recipes and hot drinks.

William Dampier, the English buccaneer, was born in the village of East Coker, Somerset in 1652. As an educated young man of seventeen, he sailed to France and Newfoundland. Years later, he served as sailor aboard a vessel traveling to Java, for a two-year absence from England. In 1674 he participated in conflicts with the Dutch and then traveled to Jamaica where he worked as a planter for one year. Meeting some adventurers in Mexico he was influenced by their exploits in the Caribbean. He returned to England in 1678 and began leading the life of a privateer.

By 1686, he traveled to Asia and to Guam, as well as the Philippines with his buccaneer friends. His ship cruised along the Mindanao coasts until 1687 and whilst there he decided to remain on the island for some time. He became quite accustomed to the habits of the natives even deciding to bathe every day, a practice which was viewed by the other English buccaneers as being a very strange habit to adopt. But by then, he was convinced that cleanliness kept one healthy and he felt better adopting the daily ritual. While back in England, he was once again instructed to return to Southeast Asia by the British government on a voyage of discovery in 1699. Other voyages to the region occurred in 1703-07 and 1708-11. He died in 1715 at the age of sixty-three.

The other Englishman who was to influence William Draper was Alexander Dalrymple. He traveled to Southeast Asia on behalf of the East India Company in Madras, where he was employed as a civil servant. His reports to the Company led to their growing interest in the region. Consequently, Dalrymple's exploits in and around the Sulu Islands where he was attempting to establish a trade post for the Company had factored greatly in the decision taken by the directors to support Draper's plan. The Company was aware of Dalrymple's mission and if he was successful, they could establish a settlement not only in the Sulu Islands, but also in Mindanao.

After the British had been ousted from their settlements in Indonesia by the Dutch during the seventeenth century, they longed to establish new trade centers in the region. Thus, the alignment of Spain and France during the Seven Year's War had suddenly provided them with the opportunity they had been hoping for. Understandably, the Company directors were also very pleased by Dalrymple's glowing reports describing the friendliness of the Muslims who seemed amenable to allowing the British to establish trade posts in their territories.

Dalrymple was born in 1737 in Edinburgh, Scotland. The seventh son of an aristocratic family of thirteen children, he had at first few career prospects at his disposal. Whilst a young man finding himself at loose ends at the age of sixteen, he joined the East India Company as a clerk. He rose rapidly through the ranks of the Company hierarchy as he exhibited a natural ability for trade and navigation. In 1757, at the age of twenty, the Company promoted him to the position of deputy secretary in Madras.

In 1759, whilst returning to the East India Company's headquarters in Madras, Dalrymple and Draper came into contact as they sailed aboard the Company ship the *Winchelsea*. Draper was then on sick leave and no doubt was enthralled with Dalrymple's descriptions of the archipelago and its abundant natural resources, as well as the political and military situation in existence in the neglected Spanish colony.

His mission was primarily centered on the Sulu Islands, the chain of smaller islands located to the south of Mindanao. During the years of 1759-62, he traveled aboard the Company ship the *Cuddore* visiting the islands of Sulu, Mindanao, Palawan and the capital city of Manila. In the Sulu Islands, he was engaged in sales and purchases for the Company. This was the first time that the British had made an attempt to establish trade with the Philippines on a formal and legal footing. Then in January 1761, he secretly arrived in Manila and met with the Sultan of Sulu Alimudin I, who was being held under house arrest by the Spanish colonial government. Despite this fact, Dalrymple succeeded in signing a treaty with the sultan. The document legally opened the door to the archipelago and British trade, as well as to the Company's obtaining the island of Balambangan as a trade post.

The East India Company directors may have also been interested in retaining Mindanao for its strategic location just north of the highly prized Dutch Spice Islands. One could presume that the Company envisioned a time when it might possibly return to the lucrative Spice Islands even though it had its share of run-ins with the Dutch in the Southeast Asian region. It is not at all inconceivable that some Company directors had thought it possible to one day actually seize the Spice Islands away from the Dutch and reestablish their presence there. As the British were already feeling quite invincible militarily by the mid-eighteenth century with their victories in North America and in India almost anything was possible.

While in the Philippines, Dalrymple may have also come into contact with an Englishman living in Manila during this same time period, Nicholas Norton Nicols. Although he was born in England, Nichols traveled to Spain from the Philippines to become a naturalized Spanish citizen in 1757. With his citizenship papers in his luggage, he was allowed to return to Manila where he soon converted to Catholicism. In 1761, he purchased land and established a cinnamon plantation in Caraga, Mindanao. It was Nicols' contention, that of all the islands in the archipelago, only Mindanao had the right environment to grow spices such as cinnamon, pepper and nutmeg. His enthusiasm for Mindanao as being an ideal site for an East India Company post, had probably been related to Draper and this too would have helped fuel his plans for the expedition.

Plan Approved to Seize Havana and Manila

Consequently, at the January 1762 meeting between the Admiralty and government officials in London, a consensus was reached that the Spanish possessions of Havana and Manila would be seized. Newcastle wrote of the meeting saying, *"We began with my Lord Anson's project of attacking Havana, and, after hearing the facility with which his lordship and Lord Ligonier apprehended there was in doing it, we all unanimously ordered the undertaking."* 6

Strategically important to Spain, the two possessions were both considered to be immensely wealthy settlements. A Spanish governor administered each settlement. In Havana, the governor was Don Juan de Prado, whilst in Manila, Archbishop Manuel Antonio Rojo, was filling in as the temporary Deputy Governor General for the Philippines until Mexico could appoint a new governor to the position.

Both settlements were provided with major seaport facilities for ships plying the Atlantic to the Caribbean and those sailing across the Pacific to the Philippines. They were heavily fortified with military strongholds in their respective regions. In the case of Havana, ships sailing to Spain from Mexico and other Spanish possessions in the Americas, routinely stopped at the Caribbean port before progressing across the Atlantic. The Havana harbor was continuously filled with a variety of sailing vessels anchored at the port to take on board provisions, water and cargo bound for Spain.

"Havana was the main hub for ships coming to New Spain (Mexico) *from Spain or returning to that country. It was there that all the ships gathered before setting sail together for Spain, each vessel carrying merchandise, people, ideas, etc., gathered from America and Asia and bound for Europe. Chinese silks and spices from the East Indies were shipped from the Philippines to Mexico, Cuba, Seville and Cadiz."* 7

For this reason, the Spanish maintained a considerable naval force in Havana to protect the port city. As the settlement had become so vitally important to Spain, an extensive network of mighty forts, numerous ships and armed forces had been established to defend it.

The Havana campaign was considered the primary target for the British offensive of 1762, as the Caribbean port city served as the center for communications and transportation between its settlements in the Americas and Spain. Consequently, the British decision to attack Havana was calculated to strike at what was then perceived as being the nucleus of Spain's network in the Americas. The main target in Havana was the *El Morro* citadel, which was the most heavily fortified with soldiers and arms.

Further attacks against French Louisiana or any other Spanish settlements in the region such as Florida or Veracruz, Mexico had been discussed at the January meeting, but it was decided to leave this decision to the discretion of the British commanders who were leading the offensive in the Caribbean. In any case, it was determined that once Havana fell if there remained a large enough force to launch additional strikes against French and Spanish possessions in the region that these would be attempted.

As for Manila, it was strategically important to Spain, as it served as a center of trade between China, the Philippines and Mexico. Goods purchased in China by the Spaniards and Chinese investors in Manila and bound for the Americas and Spain, were first brought to Manila where they were transferred to the galleons. One galleon sailed from the port of Cavite a year to Mexico and vice versa.

What is particularly interesting is the fact that the members of the Admiralty's Secret Committee meeting in January 1762, had clearly indicated that the seizure of Philippine territories was not an intimation that they had any plans to permanently colonize the entire archipelago. This was distinctly not a part of their overall plan for the Philippines or for Draper's expedition to the archipelago.

On the contrary, the official reason as indicated by George III in his formal instructions to the commanders of the campaigns against Havana and Manila stated that the two military expeditions had been launched in an effort to destroy or hamper Spain's commercial activities. The motives behind the Havana campaign, was an attempt to interfere with Spain's economy and to persuade her to abandon her ally France. In the case of Manila, the venture had a two-fold objective. Firstly, to harass the Spaniards by attacking her possessions in Asia and secondly, to retain Mindanao at the war's end on behalf of the East India Company's expansionary plans for the region.

The British clearly realized that Mindanao had managed to remain outside the sphere of Spanish influence in the archipelago. Hence, the Company directors in Madras were intrigued by the enthusiastic reports submitted by Dalrymple, where he described the courteous reception he had received from the Muslims wherever he traveled in the Philippines. The Muslims had an acrimonious relationship with the Spaniards who periodically tried to conquer their lands and convert them to Catholicism. For this reason, they welcomed the British who they realized were primarily interested in trade and did not appear to pose the same sort of threat they had encountered with the Spaniards.

The simmering animosities between the Spaniards and the Muslims of the Philippines was interpreted as being a situation the British could turn to their advantage. This was especially so if they were to eventually set up a trade post in Mindanao. These favorable reports provided the Company with a greater incentive to pursue their goals of retaining the island and establishing a settlement there. Consequently, Mindanao became the main objective of the expedition even though the East India Company would later reduce the amount of support it had originally intended to extend to the commanders of the Manila expedition.

Once a decision had been reached to attack the Spanish settlements, the members of the Secret Committee quickly began making preparations for the mobilization of the fleets. The two campaigns brought together a massive collaboration of military, naval and artillery used to mount one of the more fascinating missions conducted by the British government against the Spanish settlements of Manila and Havana. *"The capture of Havana was the largest, the most complex, and perhaps the most difficult campaign undertaken by the British in America during the Seven Years War."* [8]

Sixteen thousand men participated in the Havana campaign. They were recruited in England, North America and in the Caribbean for the venture. On the other hand, as there were already British Royal Navy ships and sailors, as well as military units in Madras, the Manila campaign became a joint effort with the East India Company's own private ships and troops.

The Havana campaign was commanded by Admiral George Pocock and General Lord Albemarle (George Keppel). Rear Admiral Samuel Cornish, commander of the naval forces and Brigadier General William Draper, in charge of the army, led the Manila expedition. However, while the British eventually invaded and captured both Havana and Manila, there were not enough soldiers in either place to launch further attacks against Spanish or French possessions. Too many of the British sailors and soldiers had contracted deadly tropical diseases and were either sick or dying. The unhealthy and unfamiliar tropical environments the men had been exposed to in the Caribbean and in Asia soon took its toll. In Manila, there were already too few men from the start of the expedition to its conclusion to consider conquering further territories outside of the capital and port cities. All they could do was to protect the territories they had seized, until further reinforcements and instructions arrived from Madras.

Chapter Two
Preparations for the Invasion Begin in India

"They are fully sensible it is a great national object, and it is clearly their opinion that a continued possession of this settlement will greatly extend the commercial interests of this kingdom; and the East India Company will cheerfully assist in carrying out this important scheme into execution so far as their abilities and the safety of their trade and settlements may allow." [1]

The East India Company

When George III, was informed by Prime Minister Bute of the government's decision to attack the Philippines, the king wrote to the directors of the East India Company in Madras requesting that they extend their utmost assistance to the commanders of the expedition. Similarly, the Admiralty instructed Rear Admiral Charles Steevens, Acting Commander in Chief of the British Fleet in the East Indies, to cooperate with General William Draper. But after the Commander's untimely death, Rear Admiral Samuel Cornish, who was already in India, replaced him.

Hence, it was Admiral Cornish who was to closely work with General Draper in the preparatory stages of the expedition. The rapport between the two commanders was remarkable and led to their working together quite pleasantly from the start. Working in unison and forming an ideal team, they began to immediately mobilize the ships and military forces required for the enterprise.

However, the obviously amicable relationship between the two men was overshadowed by some dark clouds looming across the horizon. And this became a difficulty, which almost ended the expedition before it even had a chance to begin. The East India Company in London submitted a petition to the king on 19 January 1762, requesting that he obtain on their behalf a trade settlement with Spain for the retention of Mindanao at the end of the war. Despite this fact, Draper discovered that there were some directors of the Company who were opposed to the expedition. Later in Asia, he learned why they were against the venture from going forward.

The East India Company

The British trade entity known as the East India Company had its beginnings on 31 December 1600, when Queen Elizabeth I granted a

Charter to a group of London based merchants. Innovative and enterprising, the merchants were eager to extend British trade to Asia. The Charter provided the Company with a number of trade privileges. These consisted of permission to set up trade posts or factories in Asian countries; governing powers over any territories the Company obtained; permission to formulate treaties with Asian rulers; and, it was allowed to establish military and naval forces to protect its own settlements and trade.

Following in the footsteps of the Dutch and Portuguese who were reaping financial successes through their trade companies established in the Asian region, the British merchants longed to penetrate into the lucrative markets of the Far East. *"The news coming out of Amsterdam was what made them lick their lips most greedily in anticipation, and they had determined to make the bulk of their fortunes in the same area the Dutch had been plundering so fantastically. They went forth initially in the naïve assumption that the Dutch would countenance rivals in the East Indies, found themselves fighting more battles than they had ever bargained for around Java and the Moluccas."* 2

With an interest in the commercial profits that a trade company of their own could furnish British merchants and investors, the members of the new company were initially not interested in military pursuits, but desired to quietly conduct their day-to-day business whilst expanding into new markets throughout Asia. But although their initial intentions were peaceful in nature they were soon involved in difficulties with the Dutch.

A decisive conflict erupted between the two European powers at the East India Company trade post of Amboyna (Moluccas Islands, Indonesia). Also known as the Spice Islands, the Dutch had taken the territories from the Portuguese in 1605. Nevertheless, they allowed the British to establish a Company post there, but in 1623 disaster struck. As part of the Dutch trade network, the two countries had previously signed a treaty to coexist peacefully. But the Dutch were still apprehensive by the presence of the British in the region, as they were viewed as competitors in the profitable spice trade. This was a trade they were unwilling to share with any European rivals.

This air of suspicion led to a horrific incident, which occurred when the Dutch massacred a number of British merchants. They had been falsely accused of planning a sinister plot to attack Dutch forts and to seize their lucrative spice trade. The flimsy evidence was obtained from prisoners who confessed under torture that they were aware of a plot against the Dutch. As a result of the grisly murder of the innocent Englishmen, the British retreated to India where they were to eventually achieve commercial supremacy. The Dutch, on the other hand, remained the ruling force in the

When Britain Ruled the Philippines 1762-1764

Spice Islands of the Moluccas and continued to control the spice trade from their settlements there.

With the onset of the Seven Years War, the animosities between the French and English spilled over into India where the two countries had established trade companies. Up until that point, both companies had existed peacefully following a policy of mutual coexistence whilst staying militarily neutral. But the Seven Year's War changed the relationship between the two companies. They became involved in one conflict after the other to determine which country would commercially dominate trade in India.

At the end of various conflicts with the French, the British East India Company had emerged victorious and was now placed in a position of commercial supremacy in India. Thrilled with their successes, the Company directors turned their attention to either invading the island of Mauritius, the French East India Company's main base in the Indian Ocean or the Spanish possession of the Philippines. Rear Admiral Samuel Cornish had been instrumental in the preparation of a feasibility study in 1761 concerning a possible attack of Mauritius, as it was thought at the time that the French might use it to launch further attacks against the British settlements in India. However, the plan was rejected and instead the Company decided to concentrate its efforts against the Philippines.

According to the instructions of George III sent to the commanders of the offensive, once the Spanish capital of the Philippines had been seized, the territory was to be retained until he had determined what was to be done with the archipelago. Until that time, Draper was to turn over the city of Manila and the conquered territories to the East India Company for their commercial use.

However, before the country could be turned over to the administration of the civil servants of the East India Company, the king requested that a number of inventories be prepared and sent to him. The inventories were to list all the Spanish artillery, ammunition and any other military equipment found in the Philippines. Additionally, to maintain civil order once the invasion had been completed, Draper was instructed to leave a garrison of soldiers in Manila equipped with a supply of weapons and provisions for their use. He was granted the authority to provide security and defense for Manila and any other conquered territories, as well as deciding on the fate of any captured prisoners.

The East India Company established a Secret Committee in Madras to determine the plausibility of an invasion. Still, the directors of the Company, who supported the expedition in the anticipation that Mindanao would become theirs, had been completely unaware of the true political situation existing between the Muslims of that island and the Spanish colonial government. Mindanao had been a Muslim enclave for centuries and although the Spaniards continuously tried to subjugate its inhabitants and bring it under the Spanish colonial system, it was never able to accomplish its objective. Instead, as the Spaniards had unsuccessfully tried to settle the entire island, they had become continuously engaged in a number of conflicts with the Muslims.

Consequently, if the original plan, as approved by the East India Company, called for the seizure of Mindanao, both the Company and the expedition's commanders were already off to a bad start. They would have, no doubt, had similar problems with the Muslims as those already experienced by the Spaniards. Mindanao was independent from Spanish rule and the Muslims were determined to keep it so.

Adding to their misinformation concerning the relationship between the Spaniards and the Mindanao Muslims, Draper and Cornish would arrive in the Philippines with too small a force to adequately penetrate other regions of the archipelago other than Manila and Cavite. However, it is possible that the real objective for the expedition was not so much as to seize the supposed Spanish island of Mindanao, which served as a good pretext for the invasion, but to gain as much wealth as possible by taking prizes during the entire episode.

Opposition to Draper's Plan

After Manila had been seized, Draper was instructed to immediately return to Madras with as many of his land forces as possible to assist in the defense of the Company's settlements located there. With the Company still recovering from the after effects of the Anglo-French wars, Draper still had to grapple with the few directors who were against his plan to invade the Philippines. The opposing directors stated that they were concerned for the safety of the Company's settlements. With so many ships and soldiers being reassigned for the expedition, they felt that this would leave the settlements in a completely vulnerable state and open to attack by the French or possibly by the Dutch.

The fear was that the Dutch, who were continuously cruising in and around Indian waters, might take advantage of the lesser defended British settlements to mount an attack against them. At the time, it was thought that the Dutch were preparing ships to sail to India.

The apprehensive Company directors were so concerned that they wrote a letter dated 14 January 1762 to the Earl of Egremont. In it they detailed their valid objections to the venture. The letter, signed by Laurance Sullivan, Chairman of the East India Company, Charles Cutts, Thomas Rous, John Boyd and Christopher Burrow, expressed their uneasiness for the Indian settlements, which would become vulnerable if the expedition was allowed to proceed to the Philippines. As a result, the Company was not prepared to approve the release of many of its ships and soldiers for the military campaign.

They also argued that the expense involved in sending an expedition to the Philippines would be so costly at a time when the Company could least afford it. Still recovering after the many conflicts with the French in India, the Company was financially strapped and could not bear any new expenditure. Another difficulty with the plan was the retention of territories seized in the Philippines. They suggested that any captured territories would surely have to be returned to Spain at the end of the war and as part of the terms of a treaty. During the interim, they would have to pay for the expense of maintaining a Company post in the captured land. This was an expense they could clearly not afford to undertake at the time. Moreover, the directors could not envision any clear-cut benefits for the Company in return for its participation in the expedition. In their letter to the Earl of Egremont, the directors wrote,

"Manila being an object of infinite importance to the Spanish nation, the Company can hardly flatter themselves with holding it when peace takes place – great sums must certainly be expended on the works and fortifications, and in garrison charges. The advantages are distant; trade must be created and new channels opened; for we can expect no intercourse with the South Seas, and before we are thus established, according to human reason, the Company must deliver it back again. These considerations, of such moment to a trading Company, obliges the Committee most earnestly to entreat, they may be secured in an equivalent for all disbursements should they be ordered to restore Manila to the Spaniards." 3

However, Draper later discovered the true motives behind the directors' objections to the Philippine expedition. In a letter to the Secretary of War dated 2 November 1762, after the capture of Manila, he described why the directors had been so uncooperative. He had learned that the civil servants in Madras were conducting a clandestine trade with Manila, traveling to the archipelago aboard Muslim ships to conduct trade in the country. At the time, it was the only way the British would enter the archipelago and the capital city, as foreigners were not welcomed there. The Philippines was one of the few places in Asia where the British could get the silver they needed to pay for the goods they purchased from the Chinese in Canton and Macao. Consequently, anything seen to interfere or disrupt this covert trade was viewed negatively and Draper's plan to invade the Philippines was perceived as being a direct threat to the Company's trade and profits. The directors made their objections known in an attempt to forestall the expedition from going ahead. In response Draper angrily wrote,

"The contingent of Sepoys which the governor and council at Madras promised to assist me with was 2000. They gave me only 600, the half-raw and new raised. It was not difficult to discern their motives for this shameful behaviour. They had sent a ship to Manila to trade clandestinely under Moorish colours, the cargo valued at 70,000 (pounds), most of it the property of the chief people of Madras and Bengal. They were afraid their ventures would suffer by the loss of Manila and took every method in their power to discourage the attempt. I must except Mr. Pigot (Governor of Madras) as a man of better and more generous principles. They prevailed upon Mr. Lawrence, to give a negative to the expedition under the pretence of an invasion expected from the French who have neither troops or a fleet of any consequence in India." [4]

But the directors, who were still in favor of the expedition going forward not to mention the fact that the king had already approved the venture as had Lord Anson and Prime Minister Bute, overruled their objections. In any case, from that moment onwards, the opposing directors decided to provide the commanders of the expedition with as little cooperation as possible including minimizing the number of ships and men they would release for the undertaking. This, in turn, meant that the enterprise was basically left to Draper and Cornish to organize and carry out. They had no choice but to lease additional vessels, as the Company would only provide a fewer number of their ships and men for the campaign. Infuriated by the lack of assistance or enthusiasm for the expedition, both Draper and Cornish contemplated reducing the Company's share of prizes from one-third to a lesser amount.

Even though the East India Company provided what little assistance it was prepared to offer Draper and Cornish, they made sure that the British government would reimburse them for any funds expended in the venture. As the Company's finances were already stretched to the limit, and there was clearly no foreseeable profits to be had through the invasion of the Philippines in the near future, they were most concerned that the government approve this measure before they participated, if only minimally, in the scheme.

In reply to the concerns for the financial side of the campaign, the Earl of Egremont assured the directors on 23 January 1762, that the British government would take under consideration the Company's expenses incurred through its participation in the expedition and occupation of territories in the Philippines. Even though a treaty was signed with Spain and the Company had yet to realize any financial benefits, he assured the directors that they would be reimbursed.

Manila and Cavite's Presumed Wealth

Despite opposition to the expedition, in the end it was Draper's arguments for the venture that had finally swayed the East India Company to provide the little assistance it was prepared to extend to the two commanders. Draper was still convinced that Manila was one of the wealthiest cities in Asia and worthy of an attack as a possession of Britain's enemy Spain. He also knew that an attack against Manila could lead to the capture of one of the treasure-laden galleons. And he was, no doubt, eager to try his best to follow in Lord Anson's footsteps, as the providential opportunity to seize one of the galleons was just too good to ignore.

Thus, and as far as Draper was concerned, the Philippine islands offered abundant natural resources to exploit, as well as treasure and booty to be had by plundering the seized territories and capturing Spanish ships. But again, the British were operating under a false set of perceptions. Manila had never been the enormously wealthy city they had been led to believe. In fact, the opposite was true as Le Gentil, a French scientist and traveler to the Philippines in 1779 pointed out when he stated that, *"Strictly speaking there is no trade in Manila, and consequently no merchant marine. The result is that the city has never been rich. I realize that this is a sort of paradox, for Manila has always enjoyed a great reputation in Europe; but up to the present time we have had only a very imperfect idea in Europe of the power, the wealth, and the trade of that city, which a few traders have exalted simply because they themselves had made money there, but without considering the intrinsic condition of affairs."* 5

While the commanders of the expedition and the East India Company were operating under the incorrect assumption that Manila was one of Asia's richest cities, Draper was correct in his assessment of Spain's inability to adequately govern the Philippine islands. As there were never more than a handful of Spaniards living in the country during the entire period of colonial rule, the only consistent and long-term Spanish presence in the archipelago was that of the influential religious institutions.

Moreover with the country's economy and natural resources still remaining untapped by the Spaniards, Le Gentil pointed out that the Philippines, if developed, could become an economic powerhouse. *"I observed that although the Spaniards derive no benefit whatever from these Islands, situated as they are close to China and to India, they might be made one of the most flourishing colonies in the world."* 6

Alexander Dalrymple pointed out the mismanagement of the Philippines by the Spaniards and lack of development when he stated, *"It may appear wonderful that so many islands so excellent in situation should yield so little for foreign commerce except provisions however that is not to be ascribed to the bareness of the country but solely to the indolence and bad government of the Spaniards ... were there a more equitable jurisdiction established, that the benefit attending the possession of these islands would be very considerable."* [7]

Although a governor general administered the Spanish colony from the capital city of Manila, it was the Spanish viceroy in Mexico City, who had the final jurisdiction over the entire archipelago except for Mindanao and the Sulu Islands. Appointed to that position by the Spanish king, the viceroy made all appointments to the Philippines for both the government offices and the military commanders.

Nevertheless, it was the Catholic Church and the other religious institutions operating in the Philippines, which to a greater extent than the government itself was to influence the hearts, minds and souls of the Filipino people. Consequently, Spanish colonial rule in the Philippines was a precarious undertaking at the best of times, having to contend with numerous conflicts within the country amongst the Filipino, Chinese and Muslim communities. The few Spaniards living in the archipelago found it almost impossible to endear themselves to the native population. They basically kept to themselves in government, militarily and socially, and this led to a further alienation with the inhabitants of the country.

With the imposition of a harsh feudal type system fostered upon the native population, under which, they were expected to pay heavy annual taxes to a resented government, Filipinos did not develop any warm feelings towards the Spaniards. In addition to the severe tax system probably one of the most dreaded schemes initiated by the Spaniards was the arbitrary recruitment of Filipinos, against their will, for various work projects such as the construction of buildings or to serve in the military. This often entailed removing Filipinos away from their loved ones for long periods of time, and this system of enforced labor became a source of much bitterness towards the Spaniards.

By September 1762, when the British sailed into Manila Bay, the Spanish rulers of the country had been in power for one hundred and ninety one years and during that time the civil and religious institutions had grown corrupt and complacent. The military situation was no better as the various fortifications spread across the country had suffered from years of neglect and decay.

The Colony's Weaknesses

It was not surprising that both Draper and the East India Company had become aware of Manila's weaknesses under the Spanish colonial government. It was then commonly known that the military garrisons in

Manila were composed of very few soldiers with at the most four hundred mainly Mexican recruits. While the Mexicans were considered competent enough to guard the walled city of Manila, they were not skilled in the military tactics needed to defend against a European force. In fact, many did not know how to fire a weapon. So it was with some bravado on the part of the British commanders who planned the strategy for the invasion, that they boasted if faced with a well-trained British force, the Spanish led soldiers would not amount to much of a challenge.

Complicating the situation was the fact that a number of the Mexican soldiers were either convicts or debtors exiled from Mexico or recruited by the Spanish authorities for duty in Manila under peculiar circumstances. One story of how these men were recruited in Mexico for service in Manila goes as follows, *"Tis reported that as soon as the galleon arrives a standard is planted in Mexico and who ever comes has 5 dollars advanced to him by the Royal Officers to try his fortune at the gaming table – if he comes a winner he pays back the same sum and is at liberty with his gains but if he loses he becomes a soldier for Manila."* 8

The Manila garrison was augmented by a larger number of Filipino soldiers mainly recruited from the province of Pampanga. The Pampangans were apparently some of the country's fiercest fighters and for this reason they had been preferred for recruitment into the Spanish military garrisons.

While the British discounted the strength of Spain's military forces in the archipelago, the Spaniards, on the other hand, were confident that their meager fortifications could withstand an attack by the Muslims of the southern islands or any other interloper from one of the Asian countries in the region. However, what they were totally unprepared for was an assault by a powerful European country such as Britain. Even though, in the past, they had survived several attacks by the Dutch in the seventeenth century, these had not been on a par with the British invasion of the eighteenth century. As the Deputy Governor-General of the Philippines in 1762, Archbishop Manuel Rojo stated in his journal, he had realized that Manila was not able to adequately defend itself against the British onslaught saying,

"Manila never expected to be attacked by European nations. It relied upon the distance and remoteness of its position with respect to Europe, and on the fact that nothing of the sort had ever happened, although the two crowns had often been at war. In such confidence, they had been satisfied with putting the place in a state of defense against the Moros (Muslims) *and neighboring nations who were little skilled in the art of war, the management of large artillery, muskets, and in the terrible artifice of throwing bombs, grenades, shells, etc. For in order that Manila might be defended against European nations, it would have needed four thousand*

well-drilled men and all the corresponding equipment, things which this city has lacked even to the present." 9

Rear Admiral Samuel Cornish and Mobilizing the British Forces in India

When discussions concerning the expedition had concluded in London, General Draper returned to India. He boarded the frigate the *Argo* then anchored at Portsmouth, which was to transport him to Madras. The ship was under the command of Captain King who was ordered by the Admiralty on 25 January 1762 to sail for India with Draper. After an uneventful journey, Draper arrived at the British settlement six months later in July. He began to immediately set about arranging meetings with George Pigot, the British Governor of Fort St. George (1755-1763), as well as Rear Admiral Samuel Cornish. Draper was also to meet with Major General Lawrence or the commander of the land forces in the East Indies to organize the upcoming expedition.

Consultations were held with these individuals to determine how many soldiers and ships would be needed to carry out the invasion. If it was deemed that an attack could be carried out, then Draper was to immediately prepare for the expedition. Working side-by-side with Rear Admiral Samuel Cornish, who provided Draper with his full support, the two men prepared the ships and military units for the venture.

Rear Admiral Cornish was then fifty years old and possibly thinking of how and when he would retire from the British Royal Navy. The Manila expedition could provide a nice nest egg on which to retire to England if the expedition could be carried off successfully and depending upon how many prizes they could take whilst in the Philippines. Capturing the Manila galleon would surely make them all rich.

Of the little that is known about Rear Admiral Cornish, there is an allusion to his origins as being quite humble. He first entered into the service of the East India Company's sea vessels where he was employed as a foremastman. When he was in his thirties, he enlisted in the British Royal Navy as a lieutenant and served aboard the frigate *Lichfield* in 1739. Later, as the captain of the *Guernsey*, he devastated a French privateer off Cape de Gatt in 1743. In 1759, he was commended for his part in the naval battle at Pondicherry, India, against the French. After Pondicherry, he was elevated to the status of Rear Admiral in 1759, and in 1762, he was given the command of the entire British Royal Navy in the Far East. The admiral was a man who made quick decisions when needed. He did not hesitate to appoint officers to positions when required even though he may not have been ordered to do so by the Admiralty. Thus, he quickly assessed a situation and took the appropriate action when it was necessary.

One of the issues discussed as Draper and Cornish began mobilizing the expeditionary fleet was the question of how prizes taken in the Philippines would be divided amongst the navy, military, the East India Company and the troops involved in the venture. As most civil servants of the East India Company, as well as individuals in the British navy and military were not paid very well, they knew that there was always the opportunity to become rich through the spoils of war. But it was important to ensure the loyalty of the soldiers and sailors involved in a military campaign and this could only be done at times with the promise of a share in prize money. It was commonly known amongst commanders and sailors that there was a great deal of money to be had by taking prizes. Many examples included the activities of the British ships in and around North America.

"Anson's 'lucky hit,' the first battle of Finisterre in 1747, gained prizes worth 300,000 pounds. His second in command, Rear Admiral Warren, made over 48,000 pounds in that year, and 125,000 pounds in that war. At the fall of Havana in 1762, the naval and military commanders in chief, Admiral Pocock and Lord Albemarle, received 122,697 pounds each. Albermarle's brother, Commodore Keppel, the naval second in command, received 24,539 pounds, and every one of forty-two captains gained 1,600 pounds." [10]

Still, the primary motives for the venture continued to outwardly remain commercial in nature. But there is no doubt that the members of the expedition, as well as the few East India Company directors who supported the endeavor, were very interested in any plunder, booty and prize money taken as a result of the invasion.

With so many young Englishmen searching for fame and fortune during the mid-1700s, it was undoubtedly considered worth taking the risk to life and limb to serve in the navy or military. Trying one's luck on the dangerous open seas or on the battlefield sometimes became the only option open to an adventurous young man. If they were lucky to survive, an expedition such as the one to the Philippines could provide the money to comfortably live back home. So it was important to determine how much of a share all participants would receive for their role in the campaign.

Within the short span of three weeks, all preparations had been quickly completed for the expedition. A squadron of fifteen barely seaworthy ships, most having seen battle in India, had been mobilized and these consisted of eight warships, three frigates, two East India Company Indiamen and two store ships. Draper was somewhat disconcerted that he had not been provided with a larger number of ships and soldiers, but he reckoned that with the two thousand men allotted for the military side of the enterprise, he could still capture the lesser defended cities of Manila and Cavite.

Of interest is the fact that Admiral Cornish's nephew, Samuel Pitchford, was serving as the captain of one of the ships in the expedition and this was the *America*. The ships, captains, military units, weaponry and men aboard the fifteen ships employed in the attack against the Philippines were composed of two divisions, East India Indiamen vessels and store ships. 11

1st Division Under Commodore Tiddeman

Grafton, Captain Hyde Parker, 68 Guns, 520 Men
Panther, Commander George Ourry, 60 guns, 420 men
Elizabeth, Commodore Tiddeman, Captain Isaac Curry, 64 guns, 420 men
America, Captain Samuel Pitchford, 60 guns, 420 men

2nd Division Under Rear Admiral Cornish

Norfolk (Flagship), Rear Admiral Samuel Cornish, Captain Richard Kempenfelt, 74 guns, 615 men
Weymouth, Captain Richard Collins, 60 guns, 420 men
Falmouth, Captain William Brereton, 50 guns, 350 men
Lenox, Captain Robert Jocelyn, 74 guns, 600 men

Frigates

Argo, Captain Richard King, 28 guns, 180 men
Seahorse, Captain Charles Cathcart Grant, 20 guns 160 men
Seaford, Captain John Peighin, 20 guns 160 men

East India Company Indiamen

Essex, Captain George Jackson
Osterly, Captain Frederic Vincent

Store Ships

Admiral Steevens, Captain William Sherwood
Southsea Castle, Captain William Newsome

Before setting out from Madras and in order to ensure the safety of the Company's settlements, a military force was to remain in India for its continued protection. It was agreed with Major General Lawrence and the

East India Company directors, that two battalions of Company soldiers, six thousand Indian Sepoys and some highlanders, would remain at Madras. As the ships, *Medway, York* and *Chatham*, were momentarily expected to arrive, they would remain at Madras to protect the Company's trade. In any case, the fleet was instructed to return to Madras as soon as it could once the expedition had successfully seized the Philippine territories by at least March 1763.

Moreover, at the request of Company directors, Admiral Cornish ordered the *Essex* and the *Falmouth* to remain at Madras. The two vessels were sailing to China where they were to deliver a payment in silver to the Chinese merchants there for goods the Company had already purchased, but were scheduled to return to the settlements in India. Both ships would later sail to the Philippines and join the fleet at Manila Bay. If the invasion proved successful, the two vessels would also transport the civil servants required to set-up the first British government of the Philippines.

By 1 August 1762, all preparations had been completed for the fleet's journey to the Philippines and Rear Admiral Samuel Cornish and Brigadier General William Draper were ready to set sail from India. They sailed aboard the admiral's flagship the *Norfolk,* accompanied by the other vessels in the fleet, the *Panther, America, Southsea Castle, Admiral Steevens, Seaford* and the *Osterly*.

Earlier in July 1762 Admiral Cornish had dispatched Commodore Tiddeman to Malacca with the *Elizabeth, Grafton, Lenox, Weymouth* and *Argo*. The ships were sent on ahead with many soldiers and supplies to await the remainder of the fleet. By sending the five ships ahead of the remaining fleet, it was Cornish's intention that the time entailed to take on water and fresh provisions would be lessened if the entire fleet had put in at the same time. He was just as eager as Draper to arrive in the Philippines as quickly as possible as both men realized that the Seven Year's War would soon be ending. If they did not act quickly, they would miss the opportunity to seize the Philippines and take valuable prizes.

Arriving in Malacca on 19 August 1762, Cornish was disappointed to find that Commodore Tiddeman had not yet arrived. Encountering calm winds, which slowed the movement of the ships, the five missing vessels eventually appeared in Malacca on 21 August. Due to this delay, as well as difficulties of taking on fresh water, the fleet did not sail to the Philippines until 27 August.

In addition to sending Commodore Tiddeman to Malacca, Cornish had earlier instructed Captain Grant of the *Seahorse*, to cruise along the Straits of Malacca. Grant sailed to Singapore and the China Sea, where he was ordered to intercept any vessels suspected of traveling to Manila and warning the Spaniards of the approaching fleet. Maintaining an element of surprise was strategically important to their plans of seizing Manila and Cavite, especially if the Spaniards could be kept ignorant of their plan to invade the archipelago.

The fleet sailed into Manila Bay on the evening of 24 September 1762 and anchored off the fortification of Cavite. Those Filipinos and Spaniards on shore who first spotted the sailing vessels were astonished to see the arrival of so many ships. They were unsure of the intentions of the newly arrived visitors, but by early morning on 25 September, they had no doubt realized that the Spanish colony was in mortal danger.

Chapter Three
Spain's Contentious Colony

> *"The first Governors of Manila did very little for the progress of Spanish arms and for the extension of her dominion over the archipelago, At first, they even found difficulty in maintaining their foothold there. Their neighbors looked upon them with suspicion and were by no means pleased to see foreigners so redoubtable in possession of such an advantageous position as the City of Manila."* [1]
>
> **Le Gentil**

During the centuries of colonial rule in the Philippines from its earliest beginnings in the sixteenth century to its loss of the colony in the nineteenth century, the Spanish government had been continuously entangled in a number of conflicts. Not only did they have to weather the many revolts initiated by the country's native population, but they endured uprisings by the Chinese migrants who settled in the country, as well as conflicts with the Muslims of Mindanao and the Sulu Islands. Moreover, they faced a number of attacks against their possession by forces located outside of the country. In one instance, the Chinese of Formosa (Taiwan), attempted to invade Manila. The Dutch also proved a continuous threat to the colony as they sailed from either Holland or their base in the Moluccas (Spice Islands), and in Java (Indonesia), to the Philippines where they had successfully blockaded Manila Bay several times during the seventeenth century.

However, the Spaniards were not always on the receiving end when it came to conflicts with their enemies in Asia. At times they became the aggressor and launched offensives against the enclaves of the Dutch in the Spice Islands, as well as orchestrating attacks against the Muslims of Mindanao in retaliation for their assaults against Spanish and Filipino settlements. Nevertheless, Spain's shaky hold of the archipelago proved to be not only a costlier enterprise than they had at first anticipated, but it would also become an exceedingly frustrating possession to govern. Still, Spain was able to achieve a certain level of success in turning the archipelago into another Spanish colony – similar to her possessions in the Americas even though the country was never considered to be as prosperous as her settlements in the New World.

The Spaniards had assimilated a large number of Filipinos and migrant Chinese into the Spanish realm mainly by converting as many individuals as they could to Catholicism. But this success did not extend to the entire territory of Mindanao and the Sulu Islands where Muslims had managed to resist all attempts to bring them under the rule of the colonial government including their conversion to the European religion. As the followers of Islam had consistently avoided conversion to Catholicism, this had become a source of continued irritation for the Spaniards. Consequently, whether through acts of friendship or through the use of military force, during the entire period of colonial rule the Spaniards would only have a minimal influence in the Muslim-held regions.

In addition to Muslim resistance, there were various pockets of indigenous tribal people who made their homes in the remote mountainous and jungle regions of the archipelago and they too resisted Spanish subjugation. Zealously clinging to their independence, they continued to practice their animistic beliefs and opposed conversion to Catholicism. Thus, they were able to avoid participating in a religion, which was used by the Spaniards to manipulate the native population for their own ends. This led to the fact that during much of the Spanish colonial period many of the indigenous people remained on the outer fringes of the administrative system.

What should be noted is that the Englishmen employed by the East India Company in Madras were apparently unaware of the true state of conditions in the Philippines. They had not realized how neglected the colony had become under the governance of the Spaniards, nor did they understand the powerful influence of the religious institutions upon the native population. They were also unaware of the incredible growth of corruption, immorality and dishonesty amongst the various governmental, military and religious institutions, which had been allowed to fester during the many centuries of Spanish rule.

The appalling state of the colony was due mainly to the fact that the Spaniards were concerned with only three major issues. Firstly, they were determined to maintain the governmental systems they had established, albeit in a very cynical almost uncaring manner. Secondly, they genuinely desired to convert as many of the country's natives as they could to Catholicism. Thirdly, they intended to continue the only worthwhile business in the country, the profitable galleon trade. There was almost no incentive to develop the archipelago's economy. With the passage of time, only the galleon trade dominated the thoughts of the Spanish and Chinese investors, and this eventually took precedence over religious matters.

As the Spanish government in Manila had never considered the economic development of the country as one of their primary concerns, the colony had gradually drifted into a state of decline. The galleons, on the other hand, became the main focus of attention in Manila. The Spanish and Chinese investors greedily pursued profits through the galleon trade with the conversion of natives to Catholicism taking a secondary role. This came about despite the fact that the Spanish monarchs in Europe had indicated this was the main reason for maintaining the islands in the first place. But the Spanish king dejectedly came to realize that the island colony would never become the profitable possession he had anticipated in the same manner as the more successful settlements in the Americas.

Although a rudimentary political network was established in the provinces, which was governed from Manila, the spread of Catholicism was the real glue that bound the Filipinos and converted Chinese, to the Spanish administration. There were Muslims who converted to Catholicism and became aligned to the Spanish government, but these individuals were in the minority. Catholicism was the only religion accepted by the Spaniards and its rapid spread and wide acceptance enabled the Spaniards to use it as a controlling factor in the archipelago.

By the mid-eighteenth century, the Spanish, Filipino and Chinese communities had learned to reluctantly coexist with each other even though animosities, misunderstandings, anger and resentment, bubbled below the surface of an environment of mutual tolerance. But no matter how many difficulties arose between the three groups, the slow-paced life of Manila was suddenly turned upside-down when the British fleet sailed into Manila Bay in September 1762.

The unexpected appearance of the British ships in Manila Bay was quite a surprise for the inhabitants of the capital city. While they had come to expect Dutch and Muslim conflicts with a sort of regularity, they had never expected a powerful European country such as England to launch an offensive against her settlement in Asia. With the suddenness of the offensive and its magnitude, the Spaniards were caught completely unprepared to mount an adequate defense of Manila. As the Spaniards scrambled to defend Manila's fortifications, they were still in a state of astonishment knowing that they had been unaware of the impending British attack.

The British offensive had become the first major threat to Spain's sovereignty in the Philippines. Dutch attempts to destroy Spain's control of her Asian possession paled in comparison to the British attack. But to understand why the Philippines was so strategically important to both Spain and Britain, it is necessary to review a short history of the country and how Spain came to possess the archipelago in the first place.

Prehispanic Period

Prior to the arrival of the Spaniards in the Philippines in the sixteenth century, many of the seven thousand islands in the archipelago were inhabited. Archaeological excavations have shed some light into identifying the earliest people to reside in the islands. Stone artifacts have been found dating from as far back as 50,000 to 500,000 years ago. While human fossils were not found in association with the artifacts, the data indicates that humans were already present in the archipelago. From 50,000 years onwards, information gathered from various excavations indicates that humans were living in caves such as the Tabon Cave on the island of Palawan, which has been dated to 24-23,000 BC.

By approximately 10,000 to 5,000 BC, artifacts indicate that an early Filipino people had already established a number of communities within the archipelago. These communities were small in size, but evidence points to the fact that the individuals living within these settlements used stone tools, ceramics and that they were hunters and gatherers using fire for cooking by 5,000 BC.

During the twentieth century as systematic archaeological excavations had begun, a number of theories arose as to the origins of the earliest Filipinos. One theory as to how the islands became populated was attributed to a migratory pattern, which eventually saw the gradual arrival of Malays, Indonesians and natives from Borneo. These individuals intermarried with the natives already living in the islands thus creating an indigenous population, which later became fused with the arrival of Spaniards, Chinese and Japanese. But the anthropologist, F. Landa Jocano, has largely discounted this theory and instead offers the *Core Population Theory.*

"It might be argued, on the basis of fossil evidence, that premodern humans represent the core population in the area around which genetic accretions were superimposed, as later groups of people trickled into the region, thus giving rise to new populations which we now recognize as contemporary Southeast Asians." [2]

In an effort to explain the origins of the Filipinos, Jocano states that the core population already living in the archipelago during the distant past was also found in Indonesia, Borneo, New Guinea and Australia. *"Fossil evidence suggest that the peoples in the region – Indonesians, Malays, Filipinos – are the results of both the long process of evolution and the later demographic events. They stand coequal as ethnic groups, without any one being the dominant group, racially or culturally."* [3]

While Jocano's theory attempts to describe the origins of the Filipinos through the Core Population Theory, there is no question that other populations, which arrived in the archipelago throughout the centuries, influenced the inhabitants already living in the islands. Muslims of Indonesia and Malaysia arrived in the Sulu Islands and then spread to Mindanao and further north to the Visayans. The Muslims of Borneo sailed directly to the island of Luzon settling in Manila. Chinese, Japanese,

Portuguese, Armenians, Dutch, Indians, Americans, French and the English, each arrived in the country and left their imprint upon the islands and their inhabitants. Some of these visitors to the Philippines whether on friendly trade missions or through wars, stayed in the islands eventually leading to a society that is so blended together that it now obscures the true origins of the Filipino people.

By the time the Spaniards arrived in the Philippines during the sixteenth century, the Filipinos, on the whole, enjoyed a lifestyle of relative freedom and tranquillity. Each inhabited island operated as a self-contained, independent entity. A thriving culture flourished and grew with inter-island trade. Merchants from China, Siam, Indochina, India, Indonesia, Borneo and the occasional Portuguese and Dutch vessels arrived yearly to conduct trade with the Filipinos.

Commerce was conducted with the foreigners on a limited, unscheduled basis although most trade vessels arrived at the end of the monsoon season. Historically, and as mentioned in ancient Chinese texts, the archipelago was well known throughout Southeast Asia long before the arrival of the Spaniards – having a culture of its own and regularly trading with the neighboring countries in the region. But as far as the Spaniards were concerned, the islands and their inhabitants were there for the taking to exploit and profit economically.

When the Spaniards arrived in the Philippines, to their surprise they found that there were a number of villages in the islands. A chief, or headman, known as a *datu* governed each island. It was to this chief that the early Filipinos turned to for leadership in their communities. On the whole, the islanders lived relatively harmonious and peaceful lives. However, from time to time inter-island conflicts arose and then armed natives brandishing spears and bows and arrows interrupted the tranquillity.

While the majority of the natives followed a religious belief in animism, through the archipelago's close proximity to Muslim Borneo, Islam first began spreading into the Sulu Islands, Mindanao and later to the Muslim-held territories in the Visayans and in Luzon. The Spaniards discovered that in several of the islands the chief was also a Muslim sultan or rajah. Rajahs ruled in the city of Manila, as well as on the islands of Cebu, Panay and Leyte. The Spaniards referred to the *Muslims* as *Moors* or *Moros*, using the same name they had used in Spain when referring to the Muslims they had fought and expelled from their own country in the fifteenth century.

Arrival of the Spaniards

The relationship between the Spaniards and the Filipinos was not an easy one. One could say that things began going downhill with the arrival of the first Spaniards in the islands in 1521, and life was never the same after that momentous occasion. The peaceful traditions of the Filipinos, established over the centuries, were dramatically shattered with the appearance of the Spaniards.

The first Spanish expedition to travel to the Philippines was commanded, not by a Spaniard, but by a Portuguese explorer, Ferdinand Magellan. After having failed to win the support of his own king in Portugal for the expedition he envisioned taking to the Far East, he turned to the Spanish king, Charles V, for funding. Magellan was able to convince the Spanish king, that he could find a shorter, faster and more convenient route to Asia and to the lucrative Spice Islands. This was an objective that had alluded Christopher Columbus in 1492. Convinced that he had found the route to the East Indies, Columbus referred to all the native people he encountered in the New World as *Indians* or *Indios*. The term was used from then onwards by all Spaniards for any indigenous inhabitants they came into contact with in the Americas or in the Philippines, and only the Muslims were referred to differently as Moros.

With the financing provided by Charles V, Magellan set sail with a small fleet of five ships from the Spanish port of Seville in 1519. Traveling across the Atlantic, the ships were manned by 265 men. They arrived in Brazil where the South American seacoasts were explored before venturing through the hazardous channel later named after Magellan (Straits of Magellan) connecting the Atlantic and Pacific Oceans.

Intrigue, murder and mutiny plagued the expedition. By the time they reached the Pacific, the small fleet was reduced to 140 men and three vessels, the *Concepcion*, *Trinidad* and *Victoria*. One of the original vessels of the fleet, which sailed from Spain, the *Santiago,* was destroyed in a squall off South America. Another vessel, the *San Antonio,* filled to the brim with the expedition's provisions for the long journey, suffered a mutiny. Many of the ship's crew had been convinced that Magellan was a madman and that he was leading them to their deaths by sailing through the treacherous straits. After successfully taking control of the ship, the mutineers returned to Seville.

Traveling aboard Magellan's flagship was a young Italian man of noble birth, Antonio Pigafetta. When Pigafetta learned of the Magellan's proposed expedition to the East Indies, he began lobbying any influential persons he could find to assist in his plans to join the venture. He yearned to participate in what he reckoned would be an exciting adventure to the Far East. As a former diplomat with the Italian Embassy in Seville, he faithfully kept a journal in which he detailed the highlights of the voyage to the Americas and then to Asia and the Philippines.

Magellan agreed to hire the young man as one of his personal assistants. Pigafetta reported directly to Magellan with duties assigned at the commander's discretion. As a member of the nobility, no doubt his assignments were not at all strenuous, and apparently he had enough leisure time to devote to his journal.

The narrative is a fascinating first hand account of the lives of the individuals who tempted fate by traveling across the perilous Pacific Ocean to reach the East Indies. At the time, an expedition such as the one undertaken by Magellan was probably considered one of the most dangerous endeavors one could risk taking. No one knew what lay across the vast expanses of ocean or even if one risked falling off the edge of the world as little was know about the geography of the planet. Thus, the participants in the expedition valiantly faced overwhelming circumstances in an effort to endure the journey. They were often faced with life and death situations. At one point, as they crossed the Pacific, with no land in sight and little food remaining, they were forced to eat whatever was available in order to survive. The daily meals consisted of a nauseous menu of rats, biscuits infested with worms and boiled leather.

"We were three months and twenty days without getting any kind of fresh food. We ate biscuits, which was no longer biscuits, but powder of biscuits swarming with worms, for they had eaten the good. It stank strongly of the urine of rats. We drank yellow water that had been putrid for many days. We also ate some ox hides that covered the top of the main yard to prevent the yard from chafing the shrouds, and which had become exceedingly hard because of the sun, rain, and wind. We left them in the sea for four or five days, and then placed them for a few moments on top of the embers, and so ate them; and often we ate sawdust from boards. Rats were sold for one-half ducado apiece, and even then we could not get them." [4]

Despite the unsavory diet, and after a journey of ninety-eight days, the fleet reached the Philippine island of Samar on 17 March 1521. By this time, a number of the officers and sailors were either sick or dying from the debilitating effects of scurvy. *"The gums of both the lower and upper teeth of some of our men swelled, so that they could not eat under any circumstances and therefore died. Nineteen men died from that sickness."* [5]

Magellan's first priority was to find shelter for the sick men and a source of fresh foods to restore them to good health. A small uninhabited island was found and the sick were taken ashore to recuperate. Soon after, friendly Filipinos arrived in canoes and offered assistance by providing Magellan and the sick men with fresh foods. In return for their kindness, Magellan gave them small items of, *"red caps, mirrors, combs, bells, ivory ... and other things. When they saw the captain's courtesy, they presented fish, a jar of palm wine, which they call uraca, figs more than one palmo long* (bananas), *and others which were smaller and more delicate, and two coconuts."* 6

After a much-needed rest, the expedition was once again on its way. Arriving at the island of Limasawa, Magellan met with the island's chief, Rajah Colambu, who was completely covered in tattoos. Accompanying the chief was his brother, Rajah Siagu. The Spaniards were surprised to see that the two rajahs were splendidly attired in cotton garments decorated with silk embroidery and wearing head coverings also made of the expensive material. The heavily perfumed Rajah Siagu wore dazzling gold earrings in his ears and carried heavy gold encrusted weapons in wooden scabbards. To mark his distinguished position in the community, three dots of gold inlays had been set into each of his glinting teeth.

The Filipinos had established their communities along any available body of water - the seacoasts, riverbanks, and mountain streams or along the shores of inland lakes. Not only did these bodies of water provide a source of nutrition with abundant seafood, but they were also a convenient means of transportation by boats and canoes. From their strategic locations along the waterways, Filipinos conducted trade and bartering with Chinese merchants who arrived aboard their heavily laden trade junks from China.

The Filipino settlements were known as *barangays*, which was also the same word used for boats. Presumably the term for a settlement originates from the assumption that at some point in the history of the archipelago, the earliest people of the country arrived in boats and settled along the country's waterways and coastlines. The boats were captained by a chief, who later became the village leader once communities were established on solid ground.

The populations of the villages ranged in size from fifty to several thousand inhabitants. Villagers were usually members of several extended families with one chief who held the responsibility of maintaining order and settling disputes within the community.

Rajah Colambu politely welcomed Magellan and his men into his home, which was a much larger structure than the other houses in the village, but similar in design. It was raised high above the ground and constructed using a combination of wood and bamboo poles with a thatched roof of palm fronds. The rooms were light and airy and had a spacious area serving as a communal meeting place, which was decorated with floor mats. Here, the family's daily activities took place and visitors were entertained. Magellan and the rajah shared a meal served on Chinese porcelain plates of cooked rice and roast pork flavored with ginger and accompanied by palm wine.

After exhausting all the provisions he and his men were able to consume at Limasawa, Magellan set sail for the island of Cebu. During the short voyage to Cebu, Magellan came upon several Chinese trade junks with their large cotton sails. It was the first time Magellan had become aware of an existing trade in the region. It was also while at Cebu, that he came into contact with a Muslim merchant who traveled to the Philippines from Thailand for the express purpose of trading goods with the natives.

Magellan arrived in Cebu on 7 April 1521 and proceeded to scare the local natives of that island by firing artillery from the ship. Although the salute was meant as a gesture of friendship, the islanders were, of course, terrified, as they had never seen or heard anything like it before.

As soon as he was ashore, Magellan met with the local headman, Rajah Humabon who was able to provision the expedition with the additional supplies he requested. After staying with the friendly inhabitants for some time, he eventually managed to convert the rajah and his followers to Catholicism. He declared the rajah a Christian and vassal of the king of Spain. No doubt, the rajah was unaware of the ramifications of his actions in accepting the European religion, but as a Muslim, he too worshipped a sky god in the same manner as the Christian visitors, and so it was easy to accept what they offered.

Eventually warm and friendly ties were established with the rajah and his followers. Magellan desiring to show his gratitude, as well as to demonstrate the soldiers' Spanish military techniques, boldly offered to crush any of Rajah Humabon's enemies. The Spaniards thought that they were invincible against natives whose only weapons were roughly made spears and lances made of bamboo. Humabon was grateful for Magellan's generous offer and sent the Portuguese commander and his soldiers to the neighboring island of Mactan, where he had an ongoing feud with chief, Rajah Lapulapu. During the confrontation with the Filipinos of Mactan, Magellan was stabbed in the only exposed part of his body, his legs, and mortally wounded on 27 April 1521.

After Magellan's death, the friendly relationship between the remaining Spaniards and the natives of Cebu quickly vanished. In fact, the Spaniards fearing for their lives decided to leave the island or face death at the hands of the Filipinos. Taking command of the expedition and replacing Magellan, was Duarte Barbosa who was later replaced by Juan Sebastian Elcano.

As the commanders of the expedition were intent on circumnavigating the globe, they sailed to the Philippine island of Bohol where they set fire to their vessel the *Concepcion*. They did this in order to consolidate their provisions and take that vessel's smaller crew onto the one remaining ship. They eventually made their way to the larger islands of Palawan, Mindanao, Borneo and the Moluccas before sailing home.

As captain of the last remaining ship in the expedition the *Victoria*, Sebastian Elcano successfully managed to return to Spain on 6 September 1522, with only eighteen men of the original crew of 265. But although

Magellan has become a legend and known as the first circumnavigator of the world, in reality he obviously never returned to Spain but perished in the Philippines. The men who actually returned to Spain after Magellan's death never received the recognition they deserved as the first Spanish circumnavigators of the globe.

Four Additional Expeditions Mounted

Spain mounted four additional expeditions to the Philippines between the years of 1525 and 1542. Two of the expeditions sailed from Spain while the other two were organized in Mexico. Friar Garcia Jofre de Loaysa, and Juan Sebastian Elcano, captain and chief navigator jointly commanded the first expedition. For his invaluable experiences in the Southeast Asian region and the Magellan expedition, Elcano had been selected to command the voyage. The two men sailed in July 1525 from La Coruna, a city in the northern part of Spain, which was then known for its profitable trade in spices. The fleet consisted of seven ships and 450 men. The objective of this particular expedition was to search for the Spice Islands and to make every attempt possible to wrest the spice trade away from the Portuguese who were then controlling the region. The commanders were also instructed to rescue any stranded Spaniards still remaining in the archipelago from the Magellan expedition.

During the course of the expedition, three ships were lost when rounding the Straits of Magellan. To make matters worse, Commander Loaysa died on 30 July 1526 while the fleet sailed across the Pacific. The command of the remaining vessels passed to Captain Elcano, then to Alonso de Salazar, but both men died during the journey. Finally, Martin Iniquez Carquizano took command of the expedition, arriving in Mindanao and eventually reaching the Spice Islands.

While in Mindanao, they were able to conduct some trade with the Muslims and explored the islands to the north. Later, they sailed to the island of Tidore in the Moluccas, where Captain Iniquez Carquizano died of poisoning. While Hernando de la Torre succeeded him, the remaining Spaniards of the expedition were marooned in the islands.

The second expedition under the command of Sebastian Cabot, son of the Venetian explorer John Cabot and employed by the Spanish government, set sail to rescue the survivors of the Loaysa expedition. The expedition consisted of four ships and 250 men. Traveling to South America, the fleet failed to reach the Straits of Magellan. After the failure of this rescue mission, the Spanish government decided that all future voyages to the Southern Seas of Asia would leave from the West Coast of Mexico to avoid the danger of sailing through the Straits of Magellan.

Alvaro de Saavedra Ceron undertook the command of the third expedition. Sailing from the port of Zihuantanejo, Mexico in October 1527, he had received additional instructions from Hernan Cortez, the conqueror of Mexico, to locate plants and spices which could be grown in the Americas. The expedition of three ships and 110 men arrived at the island of Yap in the South Pacific and took possession of the territory on behalf of the Spanish Crown. The ships then sailed to Mindanao where three survivors of the previous expeditions were rescued. Continuing on their voyage, they sailed to the Moluccas and Tidore where they stayed for a time and rescued survivors of the Loaysa expedition. Saavedra attempted to sail back to Spain twice, but was unsuccessful. He died in 1529. The remaining survivors of the expedition with the assistance of the Portuguese returned to Spain in 1535.

On 1 November 1542, Spain mounted the fourth expedition to the archipelago, which was under the command of Ruiz Lopez de Villalobos. The expedition, which sailed from the Mexican port of Juan Gallego (Navidad), consisted of six ships and 370 men. They reached the islands of the Philippines in early 1543. When Villalobos anchored off the island of Leyte, he named it *Las Phelipinas* after Philip II of Spain. From that point onwards, the archipelago was known by that appellation, but it was changed slightly by the Americans after the Spanish-American War in 1898 to the *Philippines*.

The Villalobos fleet sailed to Mindanao and the Moluccas. While there, it was engaged in conflict with the Portuguese who were angered by the presence of the Spaniards in their jealously guarded possession of the Spice Islands. With the death of Villalobos at Amboyna, the fourth Spanish expedition had ended in failure.

The Spaniards waited more than twenty years before attempting another expedition to the Philippines in 1565, but when they did, they chose Miguel Legazpi to command the venture. During the journey, Legazpi proclaimed the Philippines as a possession of Spain.

Philippines Becomes A Spanish Colony

On 22 April 1529, the ruling monarch of Spain, Charles V, made a decision he came to regret. He had regrettably sold the profitable Spice Islands of the Moluccas to Portugal for 350,000 gold escudos. The transaction was finalized in the Treaty of Zaragoza, which stated that Spain had relinquished her claims to the Portuguese Spice Islands.

After Magellan's expedition to the Philippine archipelago and the Moluccas in 1521, a dispute arose between Spain and Portugal over which country actually had jurisdiction over the territories of Southeast Asia and in particular the Spice Islands. Two meetings were held by officials of both countries to finally settle the dispute. The first meeting took place at Victoria, Spain in February 1524 and the second occurred at Badajoz from 11 April to 31 May 1524. An agreement was reached on 22 April, culminating with the enactment of the Treaty of Zaragoza. Not only did Spain sell her rights to the Moluccas, but also new lines of demarcation had been established setting western limits to Spain's empire.

The only positive outcome of the treaty was the gold Spain received, which helped offset the expenses of the previous expeditions to the Philippines. In any case, with the signing of the Treaty of Zaragoza, Spain withdrew for a time from further expeditions and any plans to expand her colonial empire to the East.

Spain altered her decision to launch new expeditions to the region after realizing that the Orient offered vast wealth through its lucrative spice trade. Demand for spices had been on the increase in Europe and this led to the Spanish king announcing that he was once again interested in the exploration of the East and the lands where spices could be grown. He planned to do this while attempting to avoid the Portuguese held territories of the Moluccas. This was Spain's idea of pursuing a roundabout way of adhering to the terms of the treaty with Portugal, while trying to find their own sources for a spice trade they could control.

Portugal had been aware of the Philippine archipelago as early as 1512. An expedition under the command of the Portuguese, Antonio de Abreu, sailed from Malacca on 11 November 1511 on an exploratory mission to the Moluccas reaching the islands in 1512. On the return journey, the fleet encountered a severe storm and the survivors were marooned on a small island in the southern most region of the Philippines. When rescued by pirates, they were taken to Mindanao.

Consequently, while the Portuguese knew of the existence of the archipelago, they did not consider the islands as profitable as the Moluccas. They had been under the impression that environmentally, the Philippines did not possess the right conditions for the cultivation of large quantities of spices. And as it was spices they were most interested in selling to European markets especially if they could have a source of their own to exploit, the Philippine island chain held little interest for them. As a result, they ignored the Philippines and left it untouched, but in turn, the archipelago became of great interest to the Spaniards who were still determined to have a settlement of their own in Southeast Asia.

The Spaniards, who intended to grow their own spices for the trade, began preparations for a new expedition, which would provide them with the colony they yearned to establish in the region. Long ago, it had been Philip II of Spain's contention that the Philippines lay outside the demarcation line established in the papal bull of 1493. When it was issued by Pope Alexander VI, it had essentially divided the world into two sections – one section for the exploration and discovery of Spain and the other for the same purpose, for Portugal. Both countries would be free to reign in the territories designated as theirs. But this applied only to those lands still undiscovered by the two countries. On 6 October 1493 the papal bull was amended to include the lands discovered in the East Indies, indicating that Spain could lay claim to any countries discovered if her expeditions sailed westward.

Portugal objected to the conditions stipulated in the papal bull. They had realized that the Spaniards planned to encroach beyond the demarcation line established between the two countries. This issue was addressed at discussions held at Tordesillas with a compromise reached in 1494.

Another papal bull issued in June 1497 by Pope Alexander VI indicated that both Catholic countries would have as their primary mission, when discovering and exploring new lands, the objective of spreading the Catholic religion to those countries. The acceptance and conversion of the natives encountered in the new lands could only be conducted if the natives showed a willingness and a desire to accept Catholicism.

To justify their claims to the Philippines, the Spaniards reckoned that the archipelago was located in an area, which had been designated as solely theirs to explore and colonize according to the terms of the papal bull. Utilizing this rationale, another expedition was mounted by the Spaniards in an effort to finally colonize the archipelago. However, there were other motives for launching a new expedition.

In the sixteenth century, Luis Velasco, the Spanish viceroy in Mexico, was informed by Andres de Urdaneta, that it was possible to easily sail from Mexico to the region of the Spice Islands if one had the navigational skills to do so. Urdaneta, a former mercenary who joined an Augustian religious order in Mexico when he retired, had also been a member of the Loaysa expedition to the Philippines.

The Mexican Viceroy, Velasco, was intrigued by Urdaneta's comments and immediately convened a meeting of his naval officials where the cleric was asked to repeat his claims. Establishing a quick and convenient route to Southeast Asia from Mexico was at that time considered of immense importance to the Spanish government. But although the Spaniards were interested in colonizing the Philippines, Urdaneta was personally convinced that the islands came under the realm of the Portuguese, and that any attempt to colonize them would be counter to the treaties established with Portugal. However, as he was mainly interested in his own agenda of rescuing the survivors of previous expeditions who had been marooned in the archipelago, he decided to go along with the campaign to organize a new expedition to the Philippines.

Urdaneta was one of the few men in the Legazpi expedition to have actually survived the rigors of the journey to the South Seas and lived to tell of its difficulties and dangers. Although he was by this time an elderly priest and daunted by the task of undertaking another voyage, his loyalty to the throne remained unquestioned. Thus, he agreed to travel as the chaplain and pilot for the expedition.

Velasco informed the Spanish king, Philip II (1556-1598), of Urdaneta's proposal. The king enthusiastically endorsed the plan giving it his full support, instructing the commander that his main task was to find an easier route from Mexico to the Philippines. Consequently, the king signed an official order for the preparation of the expedition to the Philippines on 24 September 1559.

The commander of the fleet was Miguel Legazpi, a career lawyer with a military background. When approached to lead the expedition, he was employed as a secretary to the Spanish government in Mexico City. Little did he know that he would eventually have to supplement the expedition's growing expenses from his own private funds. In the instructions sent to Legazpi by the Royal Audiencia, the Spanish governing body in Mexico, he was ordered to fulfill several objectives. He was to sail to the Philippines, but while doing so, to stay clear of the Portuguese held Moluccas. Once in the Philippines, he was to take possession of the islands in the archipelago in the name of the Spanish Crown. He was to establish friendly ties with the natives of the conquered territories, as well as to learn as much as possible about their culture and customs and then report back to Spain with his findings. He was to set up a Spanish settlement, find spices to send back to Spain, and last but not least, his pilot Urdaneta, was to return to Mexico with a new travel route from the Americas to Asia and vice versa.

Legazpi's fleet initially consisted of four ships, the *San Pedro, San Pablo, San Juan*, and the *San Lucas*, and 400 Spaniards and Mexicans. Sailing from the Mexican port of Navidad on 21 November 1564, one of the vessels returned to port shortly after departing with the expedition. Consequently, the expedition was reduced to three ships and 350 men. The fleet reached the island of Guam on 22 January 1565, which was promptly seized on behalf of the Spanish Crown. From there, the expedition sailed to the Philippine island of Samar, which was taken on 13 February 1565. The fleet anchored off the island of Mindanao, and then sailed to several islands in the Visayan region of the Philippines, finally stopping at the island of Cebu.

Having captured Cebu by force and destroying many of the homes of islanders, a truce was signed with the Filipinos on 4 June 1565. Legazpi had established the first Spanish settlement in the archipelago. At the time, he wrote to the Mexican viceroy detailing his impressions of the Philippines and describing the land as having great potential for future exploitation.

A number of missionaries had accompanied the Legazpi expedition and they began the process of converting Filipinos to Catholicism. However, while many Filipinos including the chief had adopted the new religion, the relationship between the Spaniards and the islanders could hardly be described as being amicable.

The situation on Cebu was becoming hostile. Filipinos were growing weary of the Spaniards' continuous demands for additional provisions, as well as their unruly behavior. The fleet was rapidly exhausting all food supplies available to them on the island, and it was becoming increasingly difficult to obtain sufficient provisions to satisfy the voracious appetites of the Spanish soldiers.

To maintain a sense of order and to continue in control of his soldiers, Legazpi felt compelled to send Urdaneta back to the Mexican viceroy for food supplies and assistance, as well as to request additional instructions for the expedition. Urdaneta returned to Mexico aboard the *San Pedro*, which was captained by Legazpi's grandson, Felipe Salcedo. Taking advantage of the westerly winds found in that region, the *San Pedro* reached the coast of California on 3 August 1565, arriving in Mexico in early October. By locating a better route to the Americas, the Philippines was thereafter able to more conveniently remain in contact with Mexico and Spain without violating the Tordesillas Treaty.

In the meantime, as Legazpi waited for supplies and assistance to arrive from Mexico, he moved to the island of Panay, where he established a second Spanish settlement in 1569. The move was necessary as he was in dire need of fresh provisions, and Panay was said to have a large supply of food and in particular rice. Here indeed, Legazpi found the provisions he needed for his voracious soldiers, but the settlement also provided the missionaries with a number of new souls to convert to Catholicism. From Panay he explored other islands in the region where additional settlements were established. The area, known today as the Visayas, was the home of a people referred to as the *Pintados*, or *painted people* as they covered their bodies in intricately executed tattoos.

At the island of Panay, the Spaniards were soon exhausting the food supplies they found there and were already in the process of creating the same sort of havoc as they had at Cebu. It was while he was in Panay, that Legazpi decided to create a Spanish settlement in Manila, or occupy it, if need be, by force.

Assistance finally arrived from the Mexican viceroy along with instructions from Philip II indicating that the islands were to be pacified and settled by the Spaniards. From that point onwards, very little assistance arrived in the archipelago from Mexico. It was very difficult to find individuals who were willing to travel to the archipelago to work in government or military positions unless forced to do so. Nevertheless, Philip II appointed Legazpi to the position of first governor of the Philippine islands in August 1569.

As governor, Legazpi was given the authority to take possession of any of the islands in the archipelago whose natives expressed a desire to become a part of Spain. That same year, a fleet of three ships arrived from Mexico with fifty married couples destined to live at the Cebu settlement. The settlement in Cebu was initially recognized as the capital of the Philippines, but Manila later replaced it once it was seized by the Spaniards from the Muslims who controlled the area.

The City of Manila

Legazpi first became of aware of Manila through discussions he held with Muslim merchants who arrived in Cebu whilst on a trade mission. They described what was then known as the city of *Maynilad,* which was the name the Muslims had given to it. The Muslims who settled in Manila had traveled directly from Borneo to Luzon in the mid-fifteenth century. Once there, they established a colony where the present day Manila now stands.

Known as a rich outpost, it had been regularly engaged in trade with merchants from China, Siam and Borneo, as well as with other foreigners who sailed to Manila Bay. The Muslim city was also described as possessing an abundant array of food products and an excellent naturally created harbor. As provisions were once again dwindling on Panay, where Legazpi's men were rapidly depleting supplies faster than they could be replenished, a new source was clearly needed. If Legazpi was going to maintain order and discipline amongst his soldiers, he obviously needed to make sure they were well fed, so finding another source of provisions became one of his primary concerns.

While the Muslim merchants were willing to provide the Spaniards with trade goods and provisions they had purchased in Luzon, Legazpi was curious to learn more about Manila. With this objective in mind, he wrote to the Muslim rajah who was then ruling the city. The letter was delivered to the rajah by the same Muslim merchants he spoke with earlier and who were about to depart from Cebu for the island of Luzon and hence, Manila. In his letter, Legazpi had requested that the rajah grant him permission to send one of his emissaries to the city. Legazpi waited for a reply, which failed to arrive. Growing impatient, he decided to send one of his commanders,

Martin Goiti, to Manila with a fleet of vessels and 120 Spaniards and 600 Filipinos to open negotiations for a Spanish settlement in Manila.

As Goiti's fleet sailed into Manila Bay, passing by the small island of Corregidor at its entrance, he noticed that there were four Chinese trade vessels anchored in the harbor. Along the shore, he could also see that the Muslims had erected a wooden fort with earthworks. Surrounding the walled citadel were a number of villages and tilled farms with houses constructed of cane and palm fronds. The inhabitants of the city and suburbs consisted of Muslims, Filipinos, Chinese and Japanese who were all going about their daily business (the few Japanese living in the city were religious migrants who fled Japan after they were persecuted for their Christian beliefs during the sixteenth century). As Goiti sailed closer to the seafront, he noted the number of soldiers and artillery visible along the walls of the fortified city.

Once his ships had anchored in Manila Bay, Goiti discovered that he had stumbled into a dispute between the Muslims of Manila and the Chinese merchants aboard their ships. It was then the practice that when trade ships arrived at Manila, the merchants had to remain aboard their vessels and were not allowed to come ashore. They were expected to conduct all trade with the city whilst staying aboard their vessels. However, with the arrival of the Spaniards, the Chinese merchants appealed to them for assistance in their dispute with the Muslims.

As a token of friendship, the captains of the four Chinese vessels presented Goiti with a number of gifts including silks, brandy, rice, ornaments and live chickens. In return, Goiti invited them to come aboard his flagship. Once there, the Chinese expressed their dismay with the Muslims who had forcefully taken the helms of their vessels and would not allow them to regain control of their own ships. Moreover, they argued that the Muslims were refusing to pay for goods they had already purchased.

The Spanish captain sympathized with their dilemma, but as his own mission to Manila was a supposedly peaceful one, he had no desire to become embroiled in difficulties with the Muslims. He dismissed the Chinese as cordially as he could without offending them, and as soon as they had left his ship, he sent an envoy to Rajah Sulayman, the chief of Manila, requesting that they meet. The envoy returned to the flagship with a message that the Muslims had consented to meeting the Spaniards along the seashore at an appointed time. The Spaniards landed on the beach and were instead greeted by an entourage, which was so impressive that the Spaniards had at first assumed that they were indeed meeting the rajah. However to their disappointment, the splendidly attired individual who arrived to greet them turned out to be the rajah's uncle.

When Rajah Sulayman finally appeared, he seemed so arrogant even though he expressed a desire for friendly relations with the Spaniards. He emphasized the fact that the Muslims were clearly a very different sort of people from the natives the Spaniards had conquered at Cebu, and stressed that they would not tolerate any offensives or threats made against them.

Initially, the Muslims were under the impression that the Spaniards were sincere in their desire to establish friendly ties with them, but the cordial relationship soon began to unravel. When they had been audaciously asked to submit to the will of the Spanish king, a fierce battle erupted and ended with the Spaniards seizing Manila on 24 May 1570. During the conflict, Rajah Sulayman and the other Muslims of Manila managed to flee across the Pasig River to villages located there.

Goiti remained in Manila for a time, but eventually returned to Panay to report to Legazpi. With his departure from the city, the Muslims returned to Manila confident that they had seen the last of the Spaniards. But after listening to Goiti's glowing report of Manila, its fine harbor and abundant provisions, Legazpi decided to lead a larger expedition to the city. He had already decided to establish a Spanish settlement in the Muslim enclave.

On 20 April 1571, Legazpi sailed from Panay with a fleet of twenty-seven vessels, 200 Spaniards and 1,500 Filipinos. Before arriving in Manila, the fleet anchored off of the island of Mindoro where they stayed for fifteen days. Even though a Muslim sultan from Borneo had ruled the residents of Mindoro, they showed an eagerness to form an alliance with the Spaniards.

The Spaniards arrived at the port city of Cavite, Manila Bay, in May 1571, where they awaited the arrival of their remaining vessels. Meanwhile in Manila, the two rajahs of the adjacent town of Tondo, Rajahs Lakandula and Matanda, were aware of the arrival of the Spanish ships and were already discussing the methods they would employ to negotiate with the Spaniards. The two rajahs were convinced that the best course to take was to establish peaceful ties with the Spaniards, but Rajah Sulayman, remembering the conflict he had already encountered with Goiti, was against this plan and sought revenge for the earlier attack.

In the city, panic ensued when the news of the arrival of the Spanish fleet began spreading. The city's residents started burning their houses and many fled to the safety of the village of Tondo across the Pasig River to avoid the Spanish soldiers. However, Legazpi managed to convince the rajahs that he had only the best intentions in mind and spoke of his desire to establish amicable ties with the people of Manila. To show he meant well, he established a small camp across the river and away from the city. By May 19, Rajah Sulayman's suspicions were allayed and he felt certain that the Spaniards meant no harm. In a gesture of friendship, he provided them with a parcel of land near the Pasig River close to where they had been given permission to establish a settlement.

From the confines of the small settlement, Legazpi began sending emissaries to the other areas lying beyond Manila's boundaries in a bid to establish friendly ties with the natives located in those regions. But the envoys were not successful and instead came face to face with one hostile group after the other.

The Muslims of Macabebe, Pampanga, were still enraged with their fellow countrymen in Manila for giving in so easily to the Spaniards. The Pampangans had convinced the rajah of Tondo to join them in an armed combat against the Spaniards. Eventually Rajah Sulayman decided to join them. The Spaniards became aware of the plot against them and sent messages to the Muslims still insisting that they were interested in the establishment of friendly ties and not war. But the Muslims refused to believe Legazpi, and this led to confrontations between the two groups. During one skirmish, Rajah Sulayman was killed. The Spaniards were victorious and now firmly in control of Manila.

Legazpi moved his camp to the Muslim fort where he officially proclaimed the city as the capital of the Spanish possession of the Philippines on 24 June 1571. He then began the process of designing an urban plan for the city according to the time-honored patterns already established by the Spaniards in the Americas. Construction began by replacing the simpler walls of the Muslim fort with sturdier wooden walls (these would later be replaced by massive stone blocks by the beginning of the seventeenth century). Additionally, the earthworks surrounding the fort were improved to better defend the city and to separate it from the villages located outside its perimeter.

The architectural plans for the city provided spaces for the future construction of buildings such as those allocated for government use, churches, monasteries, hospitals, schools, a military fort and one hundred and fifty houses for the Spaniards who were expected to live there. A central square or *plaza major* was to form the focal point of the city around which all of the most important buildings including the *Ayuntamiento* (the seat of government for the colony), a cathedral and the governor's residence would be located. The city's streets were designed to follow a pattern known as the *cuadricula,* a grid system consisting of a number of city blocks from which straight perpendicular streets radiated from the central square.

The Muslim name for the city, *Maynilad* was retained, but the spelling was slightly altered to that of *Manila.* However, the territory of Spanish Philippines was known to the Spaniards as *New Castille.* It became an integral part of the Spanish Empire and continued to report to the Spanish viceroy in Mexico City. Eventually the Spanish king approved the title of *Distinguished and Ever Loyal* for Manila, which was confirmed by royal decree as the capital of the Spanish Philippines.

Political Dynamics of Manila

The earliest governor's of the Philippines accomplished very little while they were in control of the colonial government. Moreover, they found it was extremely difficult to rule the entire archipelago. In addition to being regularly in conflict with the Muslims, disgruntled Filipinos and Chinese residing in the colony, a number of revolts were mounted against the Spaniards. The revolts erupted for a multitude of reasons usually involving what was then perceived as being the oppressive dictates of the Spanish regime such as the imposition of a harsh tax system and a coerced labor force. During one revolt in 1583, Manila and its wooden walls and buildings were set afire and quickly destroyed.

The governor's role in the colony had evolved into a position, which could only be described as dictatorial. While the governor was still acting on behalf of the Spanish king and Mexican viceroy by carrying out the wishes of both men in the archipelago, he resembled a lord of the manor in his own fiefdom. Governors ruled the country as they saw fit, which led to their becoming corrupt and abusing their position of authority in the archipelago.

The viceroy's office in Mexico (*Nueva Espana*), was established in 1535. It served on behalf of the Spanish king in the American colonies. His authority extended to the various possessions across the New World, and he made appointments to governmental offices as deemed necessary. Consequently, the Philippines, from as early as the sixteenth century, came under the authority of the *virreinato* in Mexico. The man chosen to govern the archipelago from the capital city of Manila had, in turn, jurisdiction over the entire country and its provinces.

"The Spanish Crown organized a set of institutions for the administration and government of its territories in the New World. The 'virreinato' of New Spain and Peru headed the organization of territories in the New World that were under the control of the Spanish Crown up until the eighteenth century when the 'virreinato' of New Granada and Rio de la Plata were created. The virreinato were divided into regional demarcations known as governments. Each government was responsible for a territory with a specific number of towns or villages, which were grouped together and controlled by magistracies. From the point of view of administration of justice, the territory was divided into 'Audiencias' and in accordance with military bureaucracy into 'captaincies,' which were located in the principal regional governments." [7]

No doubt one of the main difficulties in curtailing the governor's inappropriate behavior was the inability to provide a day-to-day surveillance of his activities in the colony. Due to the vast distances between Manila and

Mexico City it was almost impossible to know what the governor was doing in the archipelago. Official documents and decrees took forever to arrive in the country. For example, a letter sent from Manila to Mexico or Spain via a galleon could take as long as year to reach its final destination. A return reply could take even longer or perhaps as much as three years to arrive back to the original sender.

A governor usually served a term of three years and earned an annual salary of approximately 13,000 Mexican silver dollars. If the governor died while in office, the Archbishop of Manila temporarily replaced him until Mexico could appoint a successor. However, this system was altered after the British invasion of 1762, when the practice of routinely sending a deputy governor to Manila became the norm. This eliminated the need for the Archbishop to fill in as a governor when required, as he was viewed as not being sufficiently qualified to assume the post of governor.

For many Spaniards involved in the political arena of Mexico City, the opportunity to become the governor of the Philippines was viewed as a chance to amass a fortune. Few individuals were willing to allow the opportunity to pass them by. When referring to the corruption he witnessed in Manila in 1767, Le Gentil wrote in his journal, that the governor of the colony expected to be paid in gold for any small favors he extended to petitioners.

"Once in 1767, having had occasion to call on the governor, hardly had he finished his inquiries concerning my health when he hastened to show me a pint bottle of French make, covered with gold plate. He showed it to me, saying that it was a present which someone had given him that very day" [8]

At the end of a governor's term of office, it was almost impossible to avoid not being subjected to an investigation or the *residencia*. Even if the governor was one of the rare and exceptional individuals who was honest and tried his best to improve the lives of the country's inhabitants, unless he died, he could not under any circumstances avoid being investigated at the end of his term as governor.

During the period of the residencia, the former governor had no choice but to remain in Manila for up to a year while the investigation was conducted. Rarely did a governor escape the residencia, as the history of the colony demonstrates. Most governors were accused of corruption or worse even though at the time of the investigation he professed his innocence of all wrongdoing. *"During this time they were exposed to complaints from those whom they may have regarded as their most faithful supporters. During the whole period of the residencia anyone is allowed to carry complaints and accusations to the new governor, who takes them down in writing and is required to send them to the Spanish court."* [9]

The governor's duties included the approval and selection of minor appointments to the clergy below the rank of bishop, as well as subordinate civil servants such as the provincial governors, mayors and judges. He could dismiss any individual he took a dislike to for whatever reason whether his objections were sound or concocted. Furthermore, it was not uncommon for his friends and relatives to receive key appointments in the government. The governor was also considered the commanding officer of the Manila galleon, a position, which brought much power, strength and additional opportunities to amass further wealth.

The *Royal Audiencia,* established in 1584, served as the colony's legislative arm, as well as assisting to curb the governor's insatiable appetite for power. This branch of government was the only entity in Manila, which could observe the governor's actions and keep his activities in check. It consisted of the president, four judges or *oidores,* an attorney general and his deputy, a clerk, solicitor, usher, chaplain, disbursing officer, four Filipino door guards, lawyers for prisoners, a spokesperson for the poor, a warden for the prison and his lieutenant and four bailiffs. Just how effective the Royal Audiencia was in curbing the governor's conduct remains unclear as he also presided over this august body as its president.

There were often conflicts between the governor and members of the Royal Audiencia, but as it was instrumental in preventing the governor from becoming completely despotic, it was of vital importance to the overall running of the colony. It was also absolutely necessary to maintain the institution in order to help safeguard both Spaniards and Filipinos from the governor's abusive actions. Furthermore, the Royal Audiencia protected the positions of those officials appointed to Manila by the Mexican government. But despite its protective veneer, there were times when some government officials preferred not having a Royal Audiencia as it monitored the governor's movements much too closely for them.

In addition to the Royal Audiencia another important institution was the *Royal Treasury*. Managed by a factor, an accountant and a treasurer, the Royal Treasury housed the funds used by the government to manage the colony. The treasury funds could have been considerable if the Spaniards had taken a greater interest in developing the country's economy and natural resources. But as this was not the case and instead maintaining the galleon trade and converting Filipinos to Catholicism became their primary concerns, the funds in the Royal Treasury were never adequate to run the colony. Consequently, the colony came to depend upon the yearly subsidy received from Mexico to cover its huge expenses. Funds in the treasury consisted of taxes or tributes collected from Filipinos and Chinese. The prosperous Chinese merchants were the most heavily taxed, although to the impoverished Filipinos, any sort of tax was a burden difficult to bear at the best of times.

However, while the Spaniards were satisfied with their success in transforming the archipelago into another colony, there were still problem areas to address. One of the difficulties emanated from within the Spanish community itself. Several friars voiced an opposition to Spain's continued involvement in the Philippines, and expressed a hope that the Spaniards would eventually leave the islands. Their complaint was based upon the abusive practices of the Spaniards, which impacted upon the lives of Filipinos under the protection of the church.

Another area of concern was the fact that the colony did not have a well-established military presence in the country to defend it against outside forces. They also lacked a police force to maintain order in the colony, and they needed to establish policies to regulate trade with the Spanish colonies in the Americas and with Asian countries. The Manila government worried that both China and Japan posed a threat to their continued retention of the archipelago. At one point, the Spaniards mulled over the idea of sending missionaries to the two Asian countries in an attempt to convert the Chinese and the Japanese to Christianity. They also considered sending an invasion force to conquer the two countries, but these plans were purely speculative and never acted upon.

To address the difficulties faced by the colonial government the Spanish king, Philip II was consulted. But as he was preoccupied with the Spanish Armada sent to confront the British in 1588, he decided to retain the islands even though several of his courtiers advised the withdrawal of all Spaniards from the Philippines. The king was equally against sending any expeditions to China or to any other territories in Asia to either convert or conquer at that time. He was in favor of developing regulations for trade with the Americas. However, the primary issue he addressed was to select a future governor of the archipelago who would make a vast difference in how the colony was administered. The individual selected was Gomez Perez Dasmarinas. He served as governor of the islands from 1590 to 1593. In the space of three years, he was able to effectively organize a military force to defend the country. Moreover, he was credited with the construction of a formidable defensive stone wall and moat surrounding the city of Manila.

During the remaining years of the sixteenth century, the Manila Spaniards continued to strengthen their position in the colony. By continuously replacing the governors, as well as providing a steady stream of governmental officials and clergy for the various religious institutions spread throughout the islands, the Spaniards slowly assimilated a larger number of the country's inhabitants into the Spanish realm.

One of the more interesting measures established by the Spanish government came about after what was then perceived to be the growing numbers of Chinese in the city. Even though the much-needed Chinese community provided a number of services, as it consisted of very prosperous merchants and skilled artisans, the Spaniards felt insecure with the increasing number of Chinese migrants in the colony.

By 1581, the Spaniards set aside a special section of the city, located just outside Manila's walls, exclusively for the Chinese. In this area which became known as the *Parian,* the Chinese were forced to live and have their businesses. To monitor all activities within the Chinese community, soldiers were positioned atop the fortified walls of Manila with guns pointed directly towards the Parian to quell any uprising. As there was a fear that the Chinese would revolt against the colonial government, the Spaniards were apprehensive by the continued growth of the Chinese population. It was becoming far larger than the number of Spaniards in the entire country, and it was a cause of great anxiety as the Chinese were considered a threat to their very existence in the archipelago.

Governor Dasmarinas began adding further improvements to the city such as a military garrison for Manila's defense. An engineer, Leonardo Iturriano, was in charge of the massive undertaking, which was paid for by a tax on exports. A number of other buildings were constructed at the same time to house military supplies, arsenals and at the port of Cavite to aid in the building and repair of sea vessels.

By 1591, there were 667,612 Christian Filipinos in the archipelago under the direct influence of 140 missionaries of the Augustinian, Franciscan, Dominican orders. The country had been divided by the Spanish government into twelve provinces with each one headed by an *alcalde* or mayor appointed to that position by the governor in Manila.

Chapter Four
The Endless Cycle of Conflicts

"Manila never thought that it would be attacked by European nations. It supported the security in which it existed on the distance and remoteness of its position, in relation with Europe, and on the fact that such an example had never happened, although the two crowns had often been at war. In such confidence, they had been satisfied with putting the place in a state of defense against the Moros and neighboring nations who were little skilled in the art of war." 1

Governor, Archbishop Rojo

As the seventeenth century commenced, the Spanish colonial government of the Philippines was already in possession of Luzon, the Visayans, and had established a small settlement in Mindanao. Defensive fortifications had been erected in all three regions, largely serving to protect the Spanish and Filipino settlements from Muslim pirates who regularly raided the communities.

In Manila, the number of Spanish homes grew from 150 in the sixteenth century to more than 600. Massive stone walls had replaced the old wooden walls of the city. The governor continued to report to the viceroy in Mexico, and the government and church were able to consolidate their control of the colony through the conversion of large numbers of Filipinos and migrant Chinese residents to Catholicism. But the Spaniards still found it difficult to bring the Muslims of Mindanao under the rule of Spain. Even though expeditions sailed to the Muslim held territories in an attempt to pacify the natives, conflicts soon arose between the two groups.

The Muslims and the Spaniards

During the fifteenth century, Muslims had begun arriving in the archipelago from Borneo and Indonesia. Once settled in the country, they established sultanates from which they ruled the inhabitants they came into contact with in the areas they populated. Their missionaries soon began to busily convert the natives from their religious practices of animism to Islam. Eventually, they spread northward to the Visayas from their settlements in Mindanao.

Consequently, Islam spread from Malaysia into Indonesia, then to Borneo and eventually to Mindanao and the Sulu Islands. But the practice of

Islam was not completely widespread throughout the entire archipelago even though the sultans, rajahs and missionaries did have some success in converting the natives they met and the chiefs of the villages they influenced to the Muslim religion. In the villages they ruled in, the Muslims established a number of mosques and religious schools to help convert the inhabitants to Islam.

Thus, by the sixteenth century, Muslim sultans and rajahs were in control of the island of Mindanao, several of the Visayan Islands and Manila. The major portion, however, of the archipelago still remained under the rule of the more traditional non-Muslim Filipino village chieftains. This was a system, which had been in existence long before the arrival of the Muslims, Spaniards or the British.

In Mindanao, the largest island in the Philippine archipelago, the Spaniards were only able to establish a small settlement in the region of Zamboanga. They were never successful in conquering the entire island. According to Le Gentil, the Spaniards of Manila informed him in 1767, that the region of Zamboanga, was considered an extremely unhealthy place where many diseases flourished. At one point the Spaniards had to abandon their settlement in Zamboanga for this reason alone. Between the heat of the swampy terrain and the mosquitoes, he considered this Mindanao's best defense against a sweeping Spanish invasion.

The Spaniards returned to the settlement at a later date, despite the fact that there were so few benefits to be had by retaining the post. According to Le Gentil, it was just too costly to maintain. *"The post of Zamboanga is of no value whatever to the king. It is of no benefit to anyone, except to the governor general of Manila who has the right of appointment to the offices in that district and who, as I shall have occasion to show ...always expects to be paid for his favors."* 2 The Spaniards eventually turned the settlement into a horrific penal colony. Prisoners in Manila dreaded being sent there. But if one had the funds to bribe key officials, it was possible to gain one's freedom or avoid being transported to Mindanao.

Except for the area of Zamboanga, where the Spaniards managed to convert some of the natives to Catholicism, the rest of Mindanao was still largely Muslim. *"There are very few Christians in the island of Mindanao. If any at all are to be found, it is in Zamboanga where the Spaniards still have a fort, for in the town of Mindanao, which is the capital of the province where the Sultan resides, there are at present no Christians at all – all the inhabitants of that place are Mohammedans."* 3

However, the Spanish king still considered it important to maintain a fort in Zamboanga as it served as a barrier between the Spaniards and the Muslims. But despite the presence of the small fort, Muslims continued to raid Spanish and Filipino settlements. The governor in Manila received appeals from the besieged Spaniards and Filipinos for additional military assistance, which never materialized.

While the governor tried to assist in any way he could, more often than not, the settlers were left to fend for themselves. Filipinos appealed to parish priests for protection from the marauding Muslims as they felt that the taxes they paid to the government entitled them to some sort of protection. They threatened to abandon the towns and flee to the hills, if the Spanish government did not protect them. But the government lacked the funds to establish or maintain a military force wherever the Muslims attacked, and instead they asked the Filipinos to stop bothering the governor.

But probably the most problematic issue the native population faced was the fact that the Spaniards were not really concerned with the plight of the Filipinos, migrant Chinese or Muslims. The Spaniards living in the country had never developed a feeling of belonging to or being a part of the archipelago. They saw themselves as transients residing in a foreign country and were completely alienated from the rest of the population. As long as the galleon trade continued and was successful, all other matters were of little importance to them.

Eventually the government went so far as to suggest that communities construct their own small forts to defend their villages. But the small fortifications constructed by the Filipinos received almost no support or military assistance from the government. The parish priests had no choice but to pay the salaries of the workers involved in the construction of the smaller fortifications, as well as providing for their defense out of their own meager funds. Inevitably, political infighting erupted over the issue of who was in control of the smaller fortifications – the priests or the provincial mayors. In the end, they were abandoned.

The Muslims who raided the Filipino settlements had only one objective in mind, and this was to kidnap Filipinos for their thriving slave trade. The Visayan Islands became the main focus of operation for the raids, as they supplied the Muslims with a steady stream of potential slaves for the illicit trade. The slaves, in turn, were sold in Borneo and Malaysia, as well as to buyers in other Southeast Asian countries.

In order to facilitate the process of assimilation into the colonial system, the Spaniards began learning the languages and dialects of the Muslims. But their attempts to study the Muslim languages was interrupted by the arrival of a Chinese fleet from Formosa. Manila was threatened and the Spanish military forces in Zamboanga had to abandon their fort in Mindanao in order to help defend the capital city. As soon as the Spaniards evacuated the fort, the Muslims set it afire and carried off whatever weapons and cannons they could find. The few clerics still remaining at the fort were immediately expelled.

From that time onwards, the Muslims prevented the re-establishment of a stronger Spanish presence in Mindanao. Although faced with Muslim opposition, the Spaniards did manage to return to Zamboanga. They once again established a fort for as far as they were concerned, they were not prepared to abandon all hope of conquering the entire island and converting its inhabitants to Catholicism.

The Muslims fought against the Spaniards' every attempt to infiltrate their stronghold in Mindanao. Consequently, to the Spaniards, the Muslims posed a serious threat to their security. The earliest conflicts between the Manila Spaniards and the Mindanao Muslims occurred in 1570, when the Filipinos of Aklan and Ibahay petitioned Legazpi for assistance. As marauding Muslims ransacked their villages, Legazpi was asked to defend their homes.

In a bid to establish a peaceful coexistence with the Muslims, the Spaniards sent an expedition to Mindanao to persuade the Muslim leaders to accept Spanish colonial rule and convert to Catholicism. But by April 20, 1596, after a fierce battle with the Muslims, Captain Esteban Figueroa in command of the Spanish expedition was killed. His only success was to establish a very small fort in the area known as Tampacan, Mindanao. With this defeat, the Spaniards decided to mount a larger and more aggressive campaign to force Mindanao into submission. The command of the mission was turned over to Juan Ronquillo, as he was at the Mindanao fort with his soldiers during the earlier Figueroa expedition. They too, had been fighting the Muslims and although they were victorious, they were recalled to Manila, leaving Mindanao still outside Spanish jurisdiction.

While some Spaniards were growing weary with the militant Muslims, others were suggesting a total abandonment of any further attempts to pacify Mindanao. Nevertheless, another expedition was sent to Mindanao in March 1609 under the command of Captain Juan Xuarez Gallinato. This expedition was successful to the extent that it was able to secure a peace treaty with the Muslim leaders, but it lasted two short years. The Muslims, on the other hand, continued raiding Spanish and Filipino settlements.

During the thirty-year period of Muslim raids approximately twenty thousand individuals had been captured. Despite this, a Royal Decree was issued on February 16, 1636, once again calling for the pacification of Mindanao. The Royal Decree was an attempt to protect the Christian Filipinos who inhabited the islands then under attack by the Muslims.

Consequently, an expedition sailed from Manila to Mindanao in another attempt to subdue the Muslims. Under the command of Captain Nicholas Gonzalez, the expedition became enmeshed in a conflict with the Muslims, which was successfully put down by the Spaniards. Governor Hurtado de Corcuera, upon hearing Gonzalez's good news, sailed from Manila with a fleet of eleven ships on February 2, 1637. With seven companies consisting of 760 Spanish soldiers and two companies of Filipinos, the Muslim stronghold of Lamitan was attacked and 2,000 of Sultan Kudarat's men were defeated. While the sultan managed to escape, another Spanish force was sent to the island of Jolo, which was also captured. The Spanish successes brought the Muslims to the peace table.

A peace treaty was signed with the Manila government and the Sultan of Mindanao, Kudarat, on June 24, 1645. Under the conditions of the treaty, the sultan ceded certain territories in Mindanao to the Spaniards, as well as permitting Catholic missionaries the freedom to set up missions and preach on the island. However, the few Spanish garrisons established on the island of Jolo, had to be abandoned as the soldiers were needed back in Manila to assist in fighting the Dutch who were posing a threat to the capital.

Another treaty was signed with the Sultan of Jolo, Bungsu, in April 1646, which also allowed the entrance to that island of Catholic missionaries. But while the island came under the protection of the colonial government, the Spaniards were not permitted to rule there. This particular treaty was worthless as no sooner was it signed than the Muslims of Jolo began attacking Spanish settlements in the Visayan Islands.

In 1662, the small citadel the Spaniards had fought so hard to establish in Mindanao, had to be abandoned. After so much blood was spilled in their continuous attempts to pacify the Muslims, by the mid-seventeenth century, the Spaniards had accomplished very little. A new danger was suddenly confronting Manila, and this time, it came from the Chinese of Formosa.

A letter arrived in Manila from a Chinese warlord, Kue Sing, demanding that the Spanish government submit to his rule and become a tributary of Formosa. The Manila Spaniards were absolutely astounded by Kue Sing's audacity and even wondered if this was some sort of joke. Nevertheless, the outrageous demand created havoc in Manila as Governor Manrique Lara rushed to reinforce the city's garrisons and defenses. The governor instructed the Spaniards at the Zamboanga fort to immediately evacuate the citadel and return to Manila to assist in the defense of the capital against a possible invasion by Kue Sing.

As a number of Filipinos living around the fort area had converted to Catholicism, church clerics worried that the abandonment of the fort would soon return the area to Muslim control. The sultan of Jolo already had his eye on the area and was just waiting for the Spaniards to pull out so that he could take the settlement.

With the death of Kue Sing in January 1663, peace was restored through the signing of a treaty between Formosa and Manila. After Formosa was no longer considered a threat, Spain issued a Royal Decree in 1666, calling for the restoration of the Zamboangan fort in Mindanao.

Shirley Fish

As the tense relationship between the Muslims and Spaniards eased during the early part of the 1700s, Spaniards enjoyed a relatively peaceful time during which they turned their attention to individual agendas. The Sultan of Jolo had ceded the island of Palawan to the Spaniards in a gesture of friendship. The Spanish king sent letters to the sultans of Mindanao and Jolo formally requesting a peace treaty with the Muslims, but his letters were virtually ignored.

Then to the surprise of the Spaniards in Manila, a peace treaty was offered by the sultan of Jolo, which was signed only to be broken a year later when attacks against the small Spanish settlement in Mindanao occurred. However, with the arrival of the militarily trained governor, Field Marshal Don Fernando Valdes Tamon in August 1729, a number of improvements were made to the Manila garrison and a renewed campaign was launched against Mindanao and Jolo.

The only successes Valdes Tamon was able to accomplish through his expeditions was to set up commercial ties with Mindanao, and this was a first for the Spaniards who had for centuries been in conflict with the Muslims. In Manila, on the other hand, Valdes made a brave attempt to tackle the rampant corruption, which had grown unabated and out of control in both the government and in the military. He also made an effort to strengthen the twelve military garrisons maintained by the Spaniards and located throughout the archipelago.

A peace treaty, orchestrated by Valdes, was finally signed between the sultan of Jolo on February 1, 1737, but this again was short-lived as Muslims continued raiding Spanish settlements. The Spaniards found that they had no choice but to increase their military presence by enhancing their fortifications and garrisons especially in the Visayan Islands which were prone to marauding Muslim pirates.

By 1762, when the British invasion forces arrived in the archipelago, the relationship between the Mindanao Muslims and the Spaniards remained in limbo. While the Muslims had at times offered to establish peaceful ties with the Spaniards, the well-intended gesture was just as easily rescinded with renewed attacks launched against Spanish and Filipino settlements. The situation between the two camps remained the same, with Spaniards achieving few inroads into Muslim held territories.

The Dutch Threat to the Philippines

While continuing in their attempt to subjugate the Muslims, the Spaniards were confronted by their other adversary - the Dutch. They were more afraid of the Dutch than the Muslim pirates. The Dutch were perceived as being a greater threat to the colony and its galleon trade. The galleons were constantly at risk of being captured by the Dutch. Whenever the Dutch posed a threat to Spanish settlements, it was the galleons that the Spaniards of Manila were most concerned about protecting. Consequently, they would hastily make improvements to their fortifications and recruit larger numbers of Filipino soldiers at the slightest hint of an impending attack by the Dutch.

The Dutch were quite familiar with the Spanish held possessions to the north of the Spice Islands and frequently traded with the Muslims of Mindanao and the Sulu Islands. Of particular interest was Jolo, which was considered to possess a healthy environment and was a valuable source of pearls and amber. To the Dutch, who traveled regularly to the island for its pearls, it was known as the *Island of Pearls*.

According to the British sixteenth century adventurer, William Dampier, the Muslims of Mindanao feared the Dutch, hated the Spaniards and preferred the company and trade of Englishmen. *"They are now most afraid of the Dutch, being sensible how they have enslaved many of the neighboring islands. For that reason they have for a long time desired the English to settle among them and have offered them any convenient place to build a fort in, as the general himself told us, giving this reason, that they do not find the English so encroaching as the Dutch or Spanish. The Dutch are no less jealous of their admitting the English, for they are sensible what detriment it would be to them if the English should settle here."* 4

The Spaniards had valid reasons for their anxiety, as Holland was the only European power to mount a number of direct offensives against their colony in the Philippines during the seventeenth century. The Dutch, who were viewed as Protestant heretics by the Spaniards, were always suspected of having ulterior motives in Asia. They had, on one particular occasion, sent as many as fifty ships to attack the Spanish colony. But the feeling was mutual, as the Dutch were equally apprehensive and distrustful of the Spanish presence in the South Seas. The Spanish colony was located much too close to their own settlements in the Moluccas, and this fact, made them very uneasy. Thus, the Dutch jealously guarded their moneymaking possession whilst repulsing any encroachments into the region or the trade they had come to dominate.

The widely held perception then prevalent in European circles was that the Philippines had become one of Spain's most powerful and wealthiest possessions, but nothing was further from the truth. The Spanish possession was not all it appeared to be, as it was continuously operating at a deficit. Moreover, as the colony was so inefficiently managed with rampant corruption the norm, no other trade of any major significance existed in the archipelago. Except for what could be gained through the highly profitable galleon trade, the Spaniards made no effort to turn the rest of the archipelago into a money-making enterprise. However, the Dutch remained completely unaware of all this, as the Spaniards also kept their activities in the Philippines a closely guarded secret. This was particularly true when it came to determining the sailing schedule for the galleons, as the Spaniards were terrified of losing one of the vessels to their enemies.

In their settlements in the Moluccas and in Java, the Dutch were equally suspicious about the Spaniards. They viewed the Spanish held Philippine islands as a direct threat to their own colonies and control of the spice trade. The attacks launched against the archipelago constituted a bold attempt to oust the Spaniards from the Philippines, as well as to carry out their threat to destroy the galleon trade. Hence, during the years of 1600, 1606, 1609/10, 1614, 1616, 1617, 1626, 1628, 1646 and 1647, the Dutch engaged the Spaniards in a series of conflicts. But to their chagrin, they were never able to successfully topple the Spanish regime or to interfere with the number of galleons sailing from the Philippines to Mexico each year and vice versa.

In addition to the provocative assaults launched against the Spaniards, the Dutch made an attempt to turn the natives of the archipelago against the colonial government. They did this by trying to convince those Filipinos they encountered, particularly in Mindanao, that they would be better off under their protection. They urged Filipinos to expel the colonial government claiming that unlike the Spaniards, they would be treated fairly. Moreover, the highly resented tax system imposed upon them would be eliminated.

The first Dutch offensive against Manila took place in December 1600. The Dutch, who were attempting to establish trade centers in Asia, were especially interested in expanding their role in the spice trade. For this reason, they had dispatched a number of expeditions to the region to explore the area and to trade with the natives. The Flemish, Oliver Van Noort, a retired seaman and tavern owner in Rotterdam, commanded the first mission.

Van Noort sailed from Holland aboard his flagship the *Maurice*, captained by Lambert Wiezman, an Englishman. With a fleet of four ships and 248 men, Van Noort and Wiezman crossed the Atlantic to South America and then rounded the Straits of Magellan in 1597. Aboard the ships was a cargo consisting of a variety of goods to trade with the people he encountered in the South Seas. Their objective was to establish friendly ties with the natives of the lands they visited, as well as to set up a trade settlement. He was also instructed not to become involved in any conflicts unless it was a matter of self-defense.

Whilst sailing along the west coast of South America, Van Noort came into conflict with the Spaniards. He had attacked Valparaiso. By this time, Van Noort sailed with only two remaining ships as the other vessels were lost when he rounded the Straits of Magellan. Nevertheless, the two vessels sailed across the Pacific to the islands of the Ladrones and then reached the Philippines in 1600. Van Noort searched for the galleon the *Santo Tomas*, which was returning from Mexico with the silver in payment of cargo sent to Acapulco the previous year. When he failed to capture the galleon, he plundered various settlements in the Visayas. He then sailed to Manila, where he seized several Chinese junks and other valuables.

Governor Francisco Tello sent one of his most trusted and capable government officials, Dr. Antonio Morga to confront the Dutch ships in Manila Bay. At the time, Dr. Morga was the vice-governor of the colony and a judge with the Royal Audiencia. Inexperienced in military matters, he had recruited as many soldiers and sailors as possible and quickly equipped two ships the *San Diego* (formerly known as the trade ship the *San Antonio)* and the *San Bartolome*, to battle with the Dutch intruders.

On 14 December 1600, Morga, aboard his flagship the *San Diego*, engaged the Dutch in a six-hour battle. As the badly damaged *San Diego* sank, Morga and the rest of his crew swam to the shore. Despite the sinking of the ship, the Spaniards were able to capture one of the Dutch vessels, which was taken to Manila. The ship's crew of twenty-five men were later executed by the Spaniards as enemies of Spain. Van Noort managed to escape making his way to Borneo.

The Spaniards decided to launch an attack against the Dutch in 1606. Under the command of Governor Pedro Acuna, a fleet of ships and more than 3,000 Spaniards and Filipinos, sailed to the Dutch Moluccas. Their objective was to capture the Moluccas and put an end to the threat the Dutch continued to pose for the Spanish colony. A ferocious battle erupted at Ternate, which led the leaders of Tidore, Batachina, Lalabua and Cangaje to concede to Spanish rule. After successfully ousting the Dutch from their settlement in Tidore, the Spaniards returned to Manila with the Sultan of Ternate who was captured and later imprisoned.

In another confrontation, which may have been launched in retaliation against the Spaniards for their attack of the Dutch settlements in the Moluccas, Manila was threatened anew in 1610. The Dutch East India Company organized a fleet of thirteen ships. Commanding the vessels were Admiral Francois de Wittert and Pieter Willemsz. When they sailed into Manila Bay on 25 April 1610, they were reduced to five ships and only Admiral Francois de Wittert was in command. A six-hour battled erupted with the Spaniards during which Wittert was killed and all but one of his ships was destroyed. In addition to capturing 250 Dutch prisoners, the Spaniards seized fifty artillery pieces and other valuables worth at least $500,000.

The Dutch attacked Manila once again in 1614. This time, they blockaded Manila Bay, disrupting all trade with the colony for several weeks. The Spaniards organized a preemptive blow against the Dutch in 1616. Governor Juan de Silva of the Philippines, still fearful of further attacks by the Dutch in the future, decided to send an expedition to the Dutch settlements in Java. His objective was to strike a blow against the Dutch, which would hamper their activities in the entire region of Southeast Asia and cripple their chances of attacking the Spanish settlement.

An agreement was reached with the Portuguese at their settlement in Goa in India, as they had offered to assist the Spaniards in the joint action against their mutual enemy the Dutch. The Spanish fleet consisted of sixteen vessels, which included a 2000-ton galleon and three hundred bronze cannons. The ships were manned by more than 5,000 soldiers, most of whom were Filipinos. The vessels sailed first to Malacca, but by then it was clear that their plan to attack the Dutch was about to fall apart. When they arrived in Malacca, the Portuguese were no where to be seen. To make matters worse, Governor Juan de Silva died of a fever whilst at Malacca on 19 April 1616. The plan was finally abandoned and the Spaniards dejectedly returned to Manila.

Unbeknownst to the Spaniards whilst they were still in Malacca, another Dutch fleet was on its way to the Philippines. Under the command of Admiral Joris van Speilbergen, the fleet of ten ships sailed directly from Holland to South America and then to Acapulco where the commander hoped to intercept the Spanish galleon, but the vessel was not in port at the time. Still, he cruised along the Spanish coast of Mexico for several months causing much anxiety amongst the Spaniards who worriedly watched the ships from land. The Spaniards had been under the impression that the Dutch were searching for a suitable base from which they could attack the galleon.

After taking on fresh provisions, Speilbergen headed towards the East Indies. He had been instructed to sail the fleet through the San Bernardino Straits in the Philippines, and search for the returning Acapulco galleon. While there, he attacked the island of Iloilo on 29 September 1616, but was repelled by a combination of Spanish and Filipino forces. Speilbergen then sailed to Manila Bay where he perhaps had thoughts of attacking the capital city. The Spaniards upon spotting the Dutch vessel in the Bay had begun to prepare to defend the city. But suddenly the ship sailed away from Manila Bay to the relief of the Spaniards. They were unaware that the Dutch captain, Speilbergen, had decided to sail to the Moluccas.

In April 1617, the Dutch, under the command once again of Speilbergen, returned to Manila and came into conflict with the Spaniards off the small island of Corregidor located at the entrance to Manila Bay. The Spaniards sent their galleons and other vessels to confront the enemy when a two-day battle ensued. Ultimately, two of the Spanish ships were seized while three of the Dutch vessels were destroyed including their flagship the *Sun of Holland*. What remained of Speilbergen's fleet limped back to their base in the Moluccas.

When the new governor, Juan Nino de Tabora, arrived in Manila in June 1626, he brought to the country a number of military officers and soldiers, as well as the considerable funds from Mexico for the financial assistance of the colony. Tabora was given a hearty welcome by the Spanish residents of Manila who were grateful for the economic and military assistance he delivered to the colony. By then, the economic condition of the colony was in such a serious predicament that the government's yearly income of $150,000 proved completely inadequate to cover its expenses of $550,000.

Governor Tabora was soon confronted with the stark reality of managing the colony with insufficient funds. At one point, he grumbled that he would resign his post as governor if Mexico did not increase its financial assistance to the Philippines. He claimed that he was not prepared to accept responsibility for the colony if it collapsed due to a lack of funding. Meanwhile, officials in Spain were once again advising the king to abandon the financially strapped islands, as there were few benefits to be had by maintaining the colony. Some advisers even suggested exchanging the Philippines for the Portuguese colony of Brazil, but Philip IV refused as had Philip II. Both monarchs felt that Spain had an obligation and moral duty to convert as many Filipinos as possible to Catholicism no matter what the circumstances were in the archipelago.

Despite the fact that the Philippines was financially strapped, Governor Tabora decided to send an expedition to attack the Dutch settlement in Formosa in 1628. Given the enormous expenses such a venture entailed at a time when the colony could least afford to do so, it was a risky move to launch an attack of the Dutch settlements. Nevertheless, Tabora stubbornly sent the fleet of eight galleons to oust the Dutch from Formosa. Sailing into a raging storm, the Spanish fleet met with disaster, and was prevented from reaching its destination. Another Spanish fleet was prepared and sent to Malacca in Malaysia and to Thailand, where the Spaniards in an act of revenge, attacked various Dutch settlements. Hostilities between the Dutch and Spaniards continued to simmer leading to further conflicts in 1646 and 1647.

By 1674, almost the entire archipelago of the Philippines was under Spanish jurisdiction. The Spaniards had added the Pacific islands of the Marianas and Guam to their realm. All three regions were of the utmost importance to Spain as missionary centers from which they had anticipated spreading Catholicism to other Asian countries and in particular to China.

The military defenses of the country by the latter part of the seventeenth century consisted of twenty-four companies of Spanish infantry, which were assisted by 390 Filipino companies of soldiers. The Spanish companies were primarily composed of Mexicans or American born Spaniards from the various colonies in the New World. These individuals were oftentimes forced to serve in the Philippines. In many cases, they were also prisoners sentenced to serve out their time in the archipelago as a form of punishment. As a result of the Mexican policy of shipping criminals to the islands, many of the soldiers in the Manila garrison were of the worst sort adding to the abuses encountered by the local population.

With the onset of the eighteenth century, the colony had degenerated into one of complacency and corruption. Spaniards dreamed of possessing vast wealth and obtaining it in the shortest period of time. Getting rich became the object of everyone's attention, and this pursuit led to numerous abuses and corrupt practices in both the government, military and in the religious institutions.

Relationship with Foreign Settlers in the Philippines

The Chinese of both Manila and Canton predominantly controlled the galleon trade even though Spaniards often invested in the trade. Consequently, it was the Chinese entrepreneurs who became exceedingly wealthy as they shipped the majority of the goods to the Americas each year.

The Chinese began traveling to the Philippines to trade with the natives in the early part of the thirteenth century. Chinese historical documents indicate that merchants arriving in the archipelago found that there were numerous villages and thousands of people living along the riverbanks of the islands of the archipelago. Trade with the natives was conducted aboard the Chinese vessels where bartering took place and an exchange of goods. Dr. Antonio Morga (1600) provided a description of the types of merchandise brought to the Manila by the Chinese to sell in the colony as well as for the galleon trade.

"The goods they generally bring to sell to the Spaniards are raw silk in bundles of fine silk, medium quality silk, fine loose white silk of various colors in small skeins, velvet, plain and elaborated with various designs, colors and quantities, other fabrics with ground of gold, with gilt edges; fabrics and gold and silver brocades on silk of various colors and designs; skeins of gold and silver on woven threads on cotton and silk but the gold and silver threads are tinsel like, also damask, satin, taffeta, gorboran, glossy silk stuff and other cloths and fabrics of all colors, some finer and better than others; linen handkerchiefs, white cotton blankets of different kinds for all purposes; musk, benzoin, ivory, various curio beds, pavilions, bed covers, hangings, embroidered on velvet ... table covers, pillows, rugs,

harness ornaments, glass beads, pearls, rubies, sapphires, hollow stone crystal beads, copper kettles and glasses, nails, iron kettles and sheets, soldering tin, lead, saltpeter and gunpowder, wheat flour, orange preserves, peaches, viper roots, pears, nutmeg, ginger and other Chinese fruits, ham and bacon and other dried beef, live chickens, capons, fruits, chestnuts, almonds, pears ...sewing thread of all kinds, needles, spectacles, gilt and jasper decorated boxes, desks, beds, tables, chairs and benches, buffaloes, geese, horses, mules, donkeys, caged birds ... toys and trinkets highly esteemed by the Spaniards by the thousand and at cheap prices, aside from bric-a-brac of all kinds ...and other countless curios which if listed would make an endless job and would require a considerable amount of paper." 5

The Chinese did not begin to settle in the country until the arrival of the Spaniards in the sixteenth century. During those early decades of colonial rule, the Spaniards welcomed the Chinese migrants as they recognized their natural ability in both in business and as artisans. The Spaniards paid in silver for the goods they purchased from the Chinese, as it was the preferred type of payment. Silver was then highly prized and the Spaniards had access to vast quantities of the precious metal as they shipped it to Manila from the mines in their colonies in the Americas.

Nevertheless, an uneasy relationship appeared to bedevil the Chinese and Spaniards throughout the entire colonial period. On the whole, the Chinese who migrated to the Philippines and who were only allowed to settle in Manila immigrated to the country due to the adverse economic conditions they experienced in China. They settled in Manila where they realized that there were far greater economic opportunities available to them than in their homeland.

The troubled relationship between the Spaniards and Chinese eventually led to the outbreak of a number of conflicts. The Chinese fought back against what they perceived as being the oppressive policies of the Spanish colonial government. In response to one revolt, which occurred in 1755, the Spaniards decided to expel the Chinese from Manila. This practice of mass expulsions of Chinese whenever they revolted became the norm, but oftentimes the threat was never carried out as the Spaniards came to depend upon the services and businesses provided by the Chinese community.

As the Chinese began to increasingly control the city's economy, the Spaniards also feared the growth of their numbers in the archipelago. Although restricted to their neighborhood of the Parian, there were more Chinese in the city than there were Spaniards in the entire country. This provoked fears of an uprising against the Spaniards who viewed their position in the country as being terribly vulnerable. But as the Chinese shopkeepers and craftsmen became an indispensable part of life for the Spaniards and Filipinos, the government was reluctant to rid the colony of their presence for any length of time. In the Parian one could find the numerous shops and restaurants frequented by the city's inhabitants. One could buy everything from chopsticks to noodles and the finest silks then available. Restaurants were especially popular and frequented by both the Spaniards and Filipinos who grew fond of Chinese cuisine.

According to Governor Manuel de Leon in 1671, the Chinese of Manila traveled outside their allocated area of the Parian to the other provinces of the Philippines to conduct trade with the Filipinos located there. Some Chinese also settled in the suburban areas of the city and turned to a life of agriculture. Nevertheless, all were required to pay taxes if they intended to stay in the country.

When the Spaniards, led by Legazpi, first arrived in the country, and came into contact with Chinese trade vessels, they asked the Chinese merchants who they were. They replied that they were *siang li*. This was the Chinese word for a traveling merchant, but the Spaniards thought that it was the name of their home country. From that moment onwards, they referred to the Chinese as *Sangleyes*. The Spaniards never bothered to correct their mistake and throughout the continuation of the Spanish regime, they referred to the Chinese as *Sangleyes*. Similarly, the Spaniards referred to Filipinos as *Indians* or *Indios*. This was a continuation of a practice they had established in the Americas when Columbus thought that he had arrived in the East Indies in 1492, and that the people he encountered there were, in fact, Indians.

Whilst the Spaniards tried to maintain an amicable relationship with the Chinese of the Parian, they were still distrustful. They still remembered their surprise when under attack by the Chinese pirate Lim Ah Hong. He had sailed from China to the Philippines arriving in Manila Bay on November 29, 1574. When he arrived in the archipelago with a fleet of 62 war vessels, he had every intention of settling in Manila. With an army consisting of more than 4,000 men, he posed one of the first direct challenges to the fledgling Spanish colony. Also traveling aboard the vessels were 1,500 women and a number of skilled craftsmen.

The Chinese arrived with every conceivable item needed to set up numerous households and farm the land. Six hundred Chinese landed just outside the city's walls where a battle took place. Marshal Martin de Goiti led the Spaniards confronting the Chinese. With the assistance of Filipinos, the Spaniards were able to defeat the Chinese soldiers. Lim and his remaining fleet retreated to another region of the Philippines, only to be met with Spanish and Filipino forces who destroyed his ships. Eventually, he returned to China, but from then on, he was considered an outcast in his own country. He fled to Thailand, where he was equally unwanted and lived the life of an exile moving from country to country in search of a home.

Even though the Lim Ah Hong incident added to the tense atmosphere of distrust towards the residents of the Parian, the Spaniards realized that they had become too dependent on the Chinese for the economic survival of the colony. After all, it was the Chinese the Spaniards turned to for their skilled labor and industry.

Attempts were made to control the growing Chinese population by imposing heavier taxes on the residents of the Parian. This factor and other grievances against the Spanish colonial government led to a number of rebellions by the Chinese residents of the Parian in 1603, 1639, 1662, 1686 and 1762, during the time of the British occupation of Manila.

Compared to the very few Spaniards and Mexicans living in the country where the highest number reached 4,000 by the turn of the century in 1900, the Spaniards were clearly intimidated by the size of the growing Chinese community. The relationship with the Chinese settlers was a continuous source of uneasiness for the Spanish government and the military.

In addition to the Chinese, there were other foreigners living in the Philippines. Although few in number, they had decided to remain in the colony. The other significant group of foreigners in the colony were the Japanese who arrived in the Philippines during the seventeenth century. They settled in small communities in the outskirts of Manila after having fled from Japan, where they had been persecuted for being Christians. As such, the Spaniards welcomed them to the colony and they were allowed to peacefully coexist with the native inhabitants of the colony.

However, at one point they too turned against the Spanish government following similar revolts launched against the regime by the migrant Chinese. But the Spaniards easily subdued the Japanese revolts. By the mid-seventeenth century, there were few Japanese still living in the settlements they had originally inhabited outside of Manila. Other than the Japanese there was a handful of Europeans who managed to live in Manila or its surrounding towns. These included French, Portuguese and Swedes, who served as pilots on the galleons.

Chapter Five
Spanish Manila

"Manila is inhabited by but few people ... for what are eight or nine hundred inhabitants at most, at the end of two hundred years of possession? If new residents did not come in each year, either from Spain or from Mexico, the population would not be capable of offsetting mortality. The same thing is true with respect to the friars, for as the population is sparse in the Philippines it can supply but few people for the convents. The Philippines, then, are maintained at the expense of Spain ... this colony can but be a heavy burden upon Spain because of the constant drain of its subjects and the expense it involves, especially on account of the priests." [1]

Le Gentil

In Europe, the secretive Spanish colony and its alleged spectacular wealth had become the stuff of legends. Its capital city, in particular, was viewed as being a mighty Spanish stronghold – invincible and solidly fortified. It was reputed to be Spain's powerful bastion in Asia. But nothing could have been further from the truth.

Under the mismanagement of the Spanish colonial government, the country was never able to realize its full economic potential. Instead, the colony became one of Spain's most neglected possessions - fueled by corruption and sustained solely through its prosperous Manila-Acapulco galleon trade. Moreover, except for this trade, there was no other commercial undertaking equal to its success in the colony.

One of the major problems faced by Spain in its Asian colony was the fact that so few Spaniards could be convinced to travel to the archipelago, and once there to actually stay in the country for any length of time. Consequently, throughout the entire Spanish colonial period, the number of Spaniards residing in the Philippines ranged from as low as 400 individuals to as high as 4,000. With so few Spaniards in the archipelago, it was difficult for the colonial government to fully exert its influence throughout the archipelago. While the majority of Spaniards lived and worked in and around Manila and Cavite, only a small number could be found in the other islands where they were employed by the government, military or the various religious institutions operating in the colony.

The main obstacle to relocating to the Philippines was clearly due to the fear of not knowing if they could survive the journey. Another concern was whether or not once in the colony if they could endure the hardships they would surely face in the archipelago. Their only incentive for accepting a position in the Philippines was the reputed opportunity a stint in the colony provided to amass a fortune. By investing in the galleon trade or by getting involved in the corrupt practices of the government, military or the religious institutions, a Spaniard found that he could accumulate enough funds to eventually return home to the Americas or Spain and establish a business, purchase an estate or simply retire.

But despite the opportunities to become wealthy, few Spaniards had any inclination to travel to the colony or to reside there as long-term residents. If they managed to survive the initial and very hazardous journey from Spain to Mexico, they were loath to risk another journey across yet another ocean to the archipelago. Consequently, the majority of Spaniards and individuals born in the Americas of Spanish descent who ventured to the Philippines for the long haul were primarily members of the various religious orders established in the country.

Under the *Laws of the Indies*, Spaniards were compelled to sign a contract for a fixed period of eight years of employment in the Philippines. When contracted for an appointment, it was not uncommon for some individuals to find excuses to avoid traveling to the colony. At times these same individuals hid away in Mexico and did everything they could to evade the government or church officials who were searching for them. In order to postpone the journey to Asia, they resorted to stalling the officials they reported to and in some cases, they even went so far as to abandon the clergy rather than going to their new assignments. At times, the Mexican government had no choice but to use physical force in order to get appointees to the galleon that was sailing to the Philippines.

But what were they afraid of? If the traveler was lucky enough to survive the perilous voyage, once in the Philippines he was subjected to the debilitating hot and humid climate, which had an adverse effect on individuals who were more accustomed to temperate climes. Additionally, a host of tropical diseases awaited the traveler, including the dreaded *bloody flux* or dysentery. This malady killed many a visitor to the islands. Consequently, many would be appointees to positions in the colony tried every means possible to avoid journeying to the country. While in Manila, Le Gentil may have slightly exaggerated when describing the climate of the country, but he was correct in his assessment of how over-whelming the heat can become.

"It is so hot in Manila that one cannot apply oneself intensely. The constant and profuse perspiration produces an almost continuous lassitude

and depression, and the mind suffers from it. In that suffocating country all one does, so to speak, is to vegetate. Intense study and too close application generally produces insanity." 2

Spain found it increasingly difficult to recruit Spaniards for the Philippines. It was already difficult having to find Spaniards for the colonies in the Americas. They had to supply government employees, officers and soldiers for their navies and army, and had to be continuously on the search for members of the various religious institutions spread out in the American settlements and in the Philippines. Once the positions in the American colonies were filled, it was then necessary to find individuals who could be appointed to Manila – and these were often scarce.

Nevertheless, the Spanish government in Mexico continued to make every effort to recruit as many Spaniards as it could for service in Manila. But except for the clergy, there continued to be very few Spaniards living in the Philippines if compared to the larger Filipino, Chinese, Muslim and indigenous populations of the archipelago. Most Spaniards, who actually arrived in the Philippines, saw themselves as brief visitors and likened their sojourn in the country to that of a short stay in a hotel. One Spaniard described the experience of living in the Philippines to that of a traveler who never quite unpacks all his bags, as he has no intention of staying there.

"The Castillas (Spaniards) are fond of counting patiently the number of days that remain before their return to Spain. This is not their 'patria' (homeland). This is simply a station at which a traveler gets off from a train with his baggage, as it were, to await patiently the departure of another train which will take him to his home. Naturally, as this, is considered only as a way station towards a better place, one tries to take advantage of his spare time therein as much as possible, hence the feverish activity, confusion ... and if after some years in this country, there is need for a good time in Spain, there is a premium for the money brought thereto." 3

There was no view towards settling in permanently, as had been the case in the Americas where Spaniards in the millions made their homes and established new lives. But in the Philippines, they faced the reality of knowing that they had no choice but to endure a number of hardships in order to further their careers or derive any monetary profit by completing their contact in the archipelago.

With approximately 1,200 Spaniards living in the Philippines by the beginning of the seventeenth century, the Mexican government tried its best to increase the Spanish population of the colony. In many instances, the Spaniards who arrived in the colony were the least desirable and basically consisted of individuals the Mexican government sought to expel from its American colonies. These included carpetbaggers, the chronically unemployable, vagabonds, who without any education or of good character, could be appointed to high government positions or serve in the military as officers in the Philippines.

As a last resort, the Mexican government began emptying its prisons and sent convicts to the colony to serve as officers and soldiers. When appointed to positions in the Manila garrison, these criminals became the country's worse nightmare, as they became the most abusive towards the Filipinos. Prisoners were offered a pardon if they agreed to go to the Philippines, as well as a yearly salary of $125. In 1677, Mexico sent a galleon the *Concepcion,* which sailed from Acapulco with a number of criminals aboard, to the Philippines. Once there, they were expected to work as soldiers at the various fortifications of the colony.

But not all of the Spaniards were criminals or of ill repute. Some were highly educated individuals following careers in the government, military or in the religious institutions and thus, found themselves in the archipelago for one reason or the other.

The Spaniards employed in the archipelago came from various regions in Spain and included Basques, Gallegos and Andalusians. However, once they were settled in the capital, each group tended to form small cliques with little social interaction with their fellow countrymen. Unless a newly arrived individual was from one of the same regions in Spain as those individuals already in the colony, he often found himself isolated from the others. The only sense of unity and loyalty amongst the Spaniards was relegated to the individuals born in their own hometowns or provinces in Spain.

Across the country, the Spaniards created a replica of the world they had left behind in Spain and in the Americas. By the time they settled in the islands during the sixteenth century, they had brought with them years of experiences garnered in their New World colonies. The cities and towns of their homelands became the models for those they established throughout the archipelago.

Life in Eighteenth Century Manila

The city of Manila was divided into two sections: *Intramuros* – the city within the walls and *Extramuros*, everything else beyond the city's gates. While the city became the exclusive domain of the Spaniards, some individuals chose to live in the various Filipino villages surrounding the capital. The designs for Manila originated in Spain where a central square formed the focal point of a town. Surrounding the central square were the city's most important buildings and these included structures such as the *Ayuntamiento* (Royal Audencia) the legislative arm of the government, the *Aduana* (customs building), the *Palacio de Gobierno* (governor's palace), the *Cabildo* (town hall), and the main cathedral. Beyond the central square were the houses of the Spaniards, churches, monasteries, nunneries, hospitals and schools including two universities. At the northernmost section of the city, flanked by Manila Bay on one side and the Pasig River on the other, was the city's military citadel, Fort Santiago.

The earliest structures built by the Spaniards in the city during the sixteenth century had been constructed of similar materials used by the natives for their houses - bamboo and nipa woods. They were later replaced by a combination of wood and stone. Sturdily built two-storied structures were constructed using thick volcanic stone blocks for the ground floor. The upper floors were constructed of wood covered in plaster and were surrounded by overhanging balconies and numerous windows. Windowpanes were made of translucent *capiz* seashells allowing a defused light to filter into the rooms. In the main entry way into the house was a courtyard, stables and storage areas where the family's carriages and horses were kept.

As the Philippines is located along Asia's *Ring of Fire,* a region studded with a number of highly active volcanoes, as well as being annually pelted by tropical typhoons (hurricanes), the country is often plagued by a number of natural disasters. As a result, the houses in Manila were constructed to withstand the aftereffects of earthquakes and severe tropical storms. Thick posts supported the beamed roof and were joined to the walls using pegs. Structures were built to allow the buildings to slightly sway if there were earth tremors without causing it to collapse.

The grandest house in Manila was the governor's palace. But although palatial, it provided the governor and his family with little privacy. He had to share the structure with various governmental offices. During the early nineteenth century Zuniga said that the governor's palace formed a perfect square and was positioned in such a way as to face Manila Bay. He said that the palace, *"presents one with very entertaining sights, besides delighting him (*the governor*) with fresh and healthful breezes. The front of the house gives a good view of the whole plaza. It is a very big edifice, not only does it have enough room for the Governor (even if he is married and has a big family), it also could house the Secretariat of the government in the first floor ... it likewise houses the court jail, the office of the Royal Accountant, and the Supreme Court which has stayed in the palace until these last few years when the King purchased a place for the Court and all the offices under it."* [4]

By the mid-eighteenth century, there were three groups of Spaniards living in Manila. The first were the wealthier Spaniards and their servants usually connected to the colonial government. The second group was composed of the members of the various religious orders. The third group consisted of officers and soldiers in the military garrison of Fort Santiago.

As there were so few Spaniards living in the city, the majority of the houses remained empty, abandoned or in various states of deterioration. And due to the fact that so few Spanish families lived for long periods of time in the colony, there was no sense of continuity. This too added to the city's decline. There was no desire to maintain the city or to make any improvements for the future generations of Spaniards who would live there. This lack of interest also meant that little was added to the country's infrastructure.

Nevertheless, those Spaniards living in the colony made an effort to maintain a European lifestyle. Family quarters were generally located on the upper floors of the houses. There, windows in the living quarters overlooked the streets below and when opened they allowed cool breezes to circulate throughout the rooms, thus helping to dispel the city's sweltering heat. A typical house consisted of a living and dining room, bedrooms, kitchen, bathroom and servants quarters. Homes were sparsely furnished, but succeeded in creating a European ambiance with paintings, mirrors, crystal chandeliers, writing desks, carpets and other European furnishings, which made the homes quite comfortable.

The daily activities of the Spaniards began early in the day before the tropical heat intensified towards noon. Rising in the cooler hours of the morning, most Spaniards began their day with a breakfast of their preferred beverage, a cup of hot chocolate and some bread. The city gates, which had been shut throughout the night, were reopened. They were also closed during the siesta hours of from noon until three in the afternoon, when all activities in the city stopped and Spaniards rested after lunch. They had adopted a practice of closing the city's gates as a preventative measure in case of a possible Chinese rebellion. In the past the city's gates had remained opened throughout the day. But at one point, the Chinese took advantage of the resting Spaniards to launch a revolt against the colonial government. Thus, as a precautionary measure, the Spaniards from then onwards made sure that the city's gates were closed whilst they rested during the afternoons.

Still, in an attempt to follow European fashions, even though they were uncomfortably hot in Manila's heat and humidity, a few Spaniards dressed in the latest fashions. Men in particular tried much harder to dress in European apparel even though Spanish ladies of Manila soon decided to dress more comfortably rather than fashionably choosing instead easy flowing dresses and shawls. But these simpler dresses were embellished in the time-honored Spanish manner with gold necklaces, crucifixes and other religious medallions.

"The ladies display dresses ... a chemise with tightfitting long sleeves reaching down to the fist (with a cotton shawl like those worn by country women in Spain), cotton skirt, and hose; cork soled shoes complete their dress. At times, they add a jacket of fine cotton. There are occasions when they dress 'a la Europea,' but it is rather rare for them to desire to appear even in gala affairs wearing a long, wide gown, which is the reigning fashion of the times. They fix their hair very simply but gather the tresses and tie them in an attractive manner, affixing a big, golden clip on the crown of the hair. Earrings, necklaces, and rings are usually diamond-covered; in addition, they wear rosaries or chains of gold to which is attached a keepsake surrounded by diamonds. These jewels sometimes cost as much as 30,000 dollars." [5]

As the Spaniards went about their everyday activities, it is interesting to note how the Chinese migrants of the city viewed them. One individual in particular was not that impressed with the Spaniards. He described them as, "*The barbarians inhabiting Luzon are of tall stature and have high noses, pupils like cats' eyes, a mouth like that of a hawk, and their clothing is much adorned.*" [6]

During the day, Manila was a bustling city filled with much activity as street vendors touted their goods and sold them to Spanish ladies. Horse drawn English carriages with liveried coachmen nosily plied the streets. They drove the members of the wealthier families around Manila, as well as taking Spanish gentlemen or members of the clergy to their government offices, to the church or their homes.

Spanish Manila came to a screeching halt at noon each day as family members gathered in their houses for the mid-day meal. A typical lunch, served from noon to one in the afternoon, consisted of soup followed by a meat stew of pork or beef, green vegetables, as well as poultry and seafood dishes and sometimes washed down with *sangria* (wine mixed with lemon juice). But usually very little wine was consumed with meals as it had a tendency to intoxicate one so easily in the tropical heat. For dessert, fruits were served as well as preserves followed by hot chocolate or coffee. On special occasions a roast suckling pig was prepared. After meals, both men and women enjoyed relaxing and smoking cigars or taking a nap. In the evenings it was a common practice to entertain and socialize. Cups of hot chocolate or an alcoholic beverage was enjoyed before the evening meal, which was served at ten or eleven that night.

There was a multitude of food items available in Manila and its environs, which the Spaniards readily took advantage of and purchased even though Le Gentil found them very expensive. Nevertheless, the various ingredients were prepared in a medley of recipes such as dried fish with beans preserved in oil or fried fish or fish stew.

"Food in Manila is very dear; and except the fish, it is not very good. Cattle are not fattened there, but are killed just as they happen to be. The meat is ordinarily tough and tastes as though one were chewing a mouthful of straw. Poultry would do very well if properly cared for, but as the climate is very damp it would perhaps be difficult to produce poultry as good as it is in France. For this same reason pheasants cannot be grown here and sheep are not successfully raised. The ducks there are excellent. The commonest kind is the duck which was introduced from Mexico, a large variety known in Mauritius and in the island of Bourbon under the name of 'Manila duck.' These birds do well in the Philippines and are excellent. Pork is very cheap and so a great deal of it is eaten in Manila. Pork is put into every kind of sauce." 7

In addition to the pleasure of drinking cups of hot chocolate during the day, Spaniards drank copious quantities of water. This practice, in turn, led to their suffering from a number of intestinal maladies which were often very difficult to cure. Just as an individual was cured of one disorder, he began drinking water, which once again led to the repetition of the whole vicious cycle. The Spaniards had other maladies, but only the intestinal disorders posed a major threat to their survival, as they were so difficult to cure and usually overwhelmed the individual leading to his death.

As Spaniards found the tropical climate so severely debilitating, they began taking their vacations during the hottest months of the year from April to June. April was also the start of the rainy season, which brought intense heat and high humidity. It was not unusual for temperatures to rise to a scorching 35 or 38 Celsius. The city was then deserted as Spaniards fled to higher ground and the cooler climates of the mountains in the interior of the country or to their houses along the riverbanks. They returned to Manila in early June when temperatures dropped to more tolerable levels.

For entertainment, Spaniards enjoyed social gatherings in the evenings. Larger events included dances, balls, and masquerade parties, theatrical performances, festivals and fiestas. One traveler to the archipelago was a bit dismayed with Manila and complained that there was little to do socially in the city. He said that most of the individuals he met were not in the least interesting. His observations of life in Manila helps shed some light on the lives of the Spaniards during the eighteenth century.

"The diversions of Manila are few. Society is on a dull and distant footing. The young ladies sing and play on the piano. The women are generally seated on one side and the men on the other. The women have rather high voices, and sing from the throat. They all smoke; the cigars for the women are about five or six inches long and thick as a good-sized finger ... I attended several balls, among others that given by Mr. De Alava, commander of the naval station. The governor, his lady, and all the people

of distinction in the city were invited. The archbishop and the vicar general were there, but kept themselves in an apartment adjoining that in which the ball was held. Country-dances, minuets, and even the fandango were danced, but very decorously. Boleros were sung, after the Spanish manner, some of the airs seem to me very pleasing." 8

Occasionally, bullfights were held in the city, which provided the Spaniards with much entertainment even though Le Gentil felt the practice was quite brutal. *"I was unable, without showing horror and even a sort of pity, to see the tragic end of the ox pursued by these butchers (on horseback). They repeatedly wounded him and seemed to derive pleasure from this brutal exercise."* 9

Numerous festivals and fiestas took place throughout the year celebrating the feast day of saints. In one instance, during the two-day festival of Saint Andrew, the city of Manila was closed for business. Catholics were immersed in the preparations for the festivities, as there was much ritual attached to the manner in which the day was celebrated.

"On the eve of Saint Andrew's Day the city officials, accompanied by the citizens, without any exception, go on horseback, at four o'clock in the afternoon, to the house of the alderman in charge of the festival for that year. From this place they go to the City Hall where the alderman received the royal standard (they call it pendon). From the City Hall the cortege, after riding through the streets of the city, goes to the Cathedral; the ensign places the pendon on the right side of the altar. Vespers are sung, after which the pendon is returned with the same ceremony to the City Hall. The alderman is escorted to his house, where all sorts of refreshments have been prepared and the people dance for the greater part of the night." 10

Ultimately, the lifestyle of the Spaniards in Manila was one of comfort and cool detachment from the plight of the other inhabitants of the country. This lassitude probably had much to do with the tropical climate, but clearly Spaniards were not that interested or concerned with the daily lives of the natives of the country other than paying attention to their own needs and survival in the colony.

Consequently, other than being employed in the government, religious institutions or in military pursuits, it was rare to find a Spaniard involved in any type of manual labor. This was left to the Filipinos and Chinese to tackle. They were usually forced to provide their backbreaking labor for the Spanish government's many projects such as building fortifications and shipbuilding at Cavite. If a Spaniard was not successful as an investor in the galleon trade, he often turned to a life of corruption. By skimming funds wherever possible, exacting larger taxes from Filipinos and the Chinese and by accepting gifts in the form of cash or goods, he could amass a fortune whilst in the Philippines or return home a pauper.

The Relationship Between the Spaniards and the Filipinos

Unlike their colonies in the Americas, where enormous numbers of Spaniards settled permanently, the Spaniards who arrived in the archipelago had never developed a sense of belonging to the Philippines. There was no sense of loyalty, devotion or affinity for the land or its people. Without having established this sort of bond, there was a lack of goodwill and friendship between the conquerors and the conquered. The Spaniards kept to themselves and had little social interaction with the Filipinos. This led to an air of mutual distrust between the two groups with the Spaniards remaining largely apart from the rest of the population, as they lived their lives behind the security of the city's fortified stone walls.

Needless to say, the Spaniards, who were biased in their views of the native population and completely intolerant of their needs and welfare, fostered the enforced separation. They were prejudiced and although some might have had intimate relationships with the local women, they usually returned to Spain or Mexico where they found Spanish women to marry. But despite this fact, a large number of *mestizos* (Spanish-Filipinos or Spanish-Chinese) were born and a new class of people arose in the islands. These individuals, in turn, developed their own prejudices against the indigenous people of the land. The mestizos, in time, became the recipients of greater privileges than their indigenous brethren in the hinterland of the country. These, mostly tribal folk, remained on the whole little influenced by outside forces. They lived in remote regions of the archipelago such as the mountainous terrain of Luzon. With the passage of time, mestizos were given positions in the government, albeit, at a lower rank than the Spaniards who continued to dominate politics, religion and the armed forces.

One Spaniard, who was painfully aware of the abuses suffered by the natives, voiced his regrets for that treatment and described the relationship between the Spaniards and the Filipinos in a memorial sent to Spain in 1586.

"The Spaniards have always managed the State for themselves, and separately from the natives of the land – disdaining to give them a share in any matter of honor or profit, but remaining always foreigners and aliens, and even objects of dread, to the natives. For when some of the Spaniards die, or return to Spain, others come anew, who are always strangers to the people of the country and regard the natives as barbarians. From this have resulted two serious evils, and the beginning of many others. First – the Spaniards are always few in numbers, and have but little experience or knowledge of the country; they have little affection for it, and few ties or interests therein. It is always their intention to return to the mother country, and to procure their own enrichment – whether it be by fair means or foul,

or even by destroying and consuming, in their eagerness to attain that end – not troubling themselves whether the country be ruled rightly or wrongly, whether it be ruined or improved. The second evil is that, to the Spaniards, the commonality of the Indians (Filipinos) is something new and strange, and the latter area always regarded as menials and slaves, and objects for the insolence of those who come into possession of them. Accordingly, they are always scorned, despised, overworked, exhausted, and even dying – as is actually seen to be the case." 11

During the sixteenth century, the Spaniards who first arrived in the archipelago had been rewarded for their participation in settling the country. They received large parcels of land to do with as they pleased. The Filipinos living on the land were also considered theirs to command. Prior to the arrival of the Spaniards, the concept of land ownership amongst Filipinos was unheard of. The land they lived on, tilled and where they grew their rice and raised livestock, did not belong to anyone in particular. Instead, the land was administered by the Filipino chiefs or Muslim rajahs in their respective villages and allotted to members of the communities to build their houses and have farms. The concept of land ownership arrived with the Spaniards and this led to anger and resentment amongst Filipinos. Large tracks of land were suddenly turned over to the Spaniards despite the fact that generations of Filipinos had been living there.

The colonial government created a land distribution system known as the *encomienda*, which was used in the Philippines in 1571 and ended in the late seventeenth century. While it was basically a system employed in other Spanish colonies in the Americas, it was in essence a method whereby the landowner and government could receive tributes or taxes. It was also viewed as a controversial and feeble attempt by the Spanish government to develop the country's agriculture. Land was to be cultivated by the Spanish landowners with the enforced labor of the Filipinos. In return for the labor and produce received from Filipinos living on the land, the Spaniards were presumably responsible for their welfare, defense and conversion. The Filipinos continued to farm the land and were expected to share with the Spanish landlord whatever crops they grew and domesticated animals they raised.

In order to spare the Filipinos from the difficulties of the day-to-day exposure to their landlords, the Spaniards were not expected to actually live on his land. According to the *Laws of the Indies 1562-1646,* Spaniards were not allowed to reside in Filipino villages as they were considered unruly and were known to oppress the natives. If faced with the presence of Spaniards living within their midst, it was not uncommon for Filipinos to pack up their belongings and head for the hills to avoid the Europeans. Consequently, instead of returning to his property, the Spanish *encomendero* (landowner), returned once a year to collect taxes in cash or in kind from the individuals living on his land.

However, while Spanish landowners were technically not allowed to live on the land they owned, Spanish presence in the islands was predominately provided by the numerous ecclesiastical orders. Members of the clergy were responsible for the establishment of an extensive network of churches throughout the archipelago. Independently operating in their own little fiefdoms, the clerics welded much power over the lives of the Filipinos. As they interacted with the natives in the communities under their jurisdiction, the people became familiar with them and accepted their presence, albeit at times reluctantly. However, in the main they were able to receive, to a certain degree, the respect and loyalty of the Christians they had converted.

Through the introduction of the tax/tribute system, all Filipinos and Chinese were expected to pay taxes to the government by providing a share of the crops they grew, domesticated animals, cash, as well as supplying a number of other goods such as cotton and textiles. The Spaniards used the funds collected each year to run the government even though expenses far exceeded the total amount of taxes collected annually. The colony had no choice but to turn to the viceroy's office in Mexico City for an annual subsidy of 250,000 silver dollars. This sum was sent out each year on one of the galleons to help defray the expanding costs of maintaining the colony and its increasing expenditures.

As an administrative region under the jurisdiction of *Nueva Espana* (Mexico), the Philippines was never considered as promising a commercial enterprise as Spain's colonies in the Americas. Even though it was located closer to the Spice Islands, it was not a large producer of spices, which could have turned the country into a worthwhile proposition. Moreover, unlike the other Spanish possessions such as Peru and Mexico, which were able to produce abundant supplies of gold and silver for export to Spain, the Philippines had little to offer the Spaniards in that respect.

Hence, for the Spaniards, the archipelago's only real attraction was the profitable Manila-Acapulco galleon trade. As galleons sailed back and forth across the Pacific carrying huge cargoes of valuable goods worth millions, and returned to Manila with silver, the investors impatiently awaited the safe return of the yearly galleon. It was the galleon trade, which became the main inducement for the retention of the Philippines. Although it can be argued that the other motive for retaining the archipelago was the religious zeal of the Spaniards who endeavored to spread Catholicism, the reality of the situation was that the economic incentives were of far greater importance to the Spaniards of Manila than saving souls.

"The Spaniard in Manila spends everything he makes without giving a thought to the distant future. He only thinks of the galleon which is on the way to Acapulco and which will bring back to him the means with which to pull through the year. Thus his ambition lags from galleon to galleon and goes no further. He sees that it is impossible for him to raise himself above his state. He thinks nothing about cultivating the soil or engaging in trade of any kind. The galleon suffices for his present means and with this he rests content. But if the vessel fails to return, which has happened more than once, he dies in misery or vegetates in poverty." 12

Manila had become so completely dependent upon the galleon trade as a source of revenue. Without the development of any other trade of any significance, which would have provided additional revenues for the colony, the governing officials came to depend on the Mexican subsidy. The *Real Situado* was desperately needed especially if a galleon failed to arrive when expected, if lost at sea or captured by the English, the Dutch or pirates. The income from taxes was never sufficient to completely cover the government's yearly expenses. The fact that corruption was also rampant in the *encomienda* system, meant that the Mexican subsidy became an absolute necessity to the continued retention of the colony. Taxes were used to pay the salaries of employees in the government, military, and church as well as paying for the expenditures of the hospitals, schools and other social projects.

Had the Spaniards placed a greater emphasis on developing the country's economy, they might have been able to reap the enormous benefits the archipelago offered, but instead they focused on the galleon trade and its continued success. As pointed out by Le Gentil, if the Spaniards had been able to develop the country in a similar manner to that of the Dutch in Batavia and in the Moluccas, the Philippines could have become a source of immense wealth for Spain.

There was only one way to reverse the spiraling decline of the colony and that was to open the Philippines to foreign trade. Unfortunately, the Spaniards were reluctant to pursue this course of action. Not only did they feel threatened by the European powers operating in the region - the Dutch, Portuguese and the British, they were equally distrustful of the Asian countries then surrounding the archipelago - China, Formosa, Siam, Malaya and Japan.

Prior to 1762 and the British invasion of Manila, the Spanish colonial government continued to enforce a policy of closing the Philippines to European traders. The only nations allowed to trade in Manila were Asian countries and in particular China. Even though the relationship between the Spaniards and Chinese was often tense especially as so many had migrated to Manila to engage in trade as well as the opportunities afforded by the Spaniards for a better life, China remained the country's main trade partner.

Free trade would be implemented twenty-one years later after the British evacuated the Philippines in 1764 and returned to their settlements in India. At that time, the Spaniards realized that in order to attain any sort of commercial success in the region it was imperative that they establish their own version of a British or Dutch East India Company. Eventually, the Royal Company of the Philippines was established in 1787 to compete with the British, French and Dutch trade companies. For the first time, European merchant vessels were permitted to anchor in Manila Bay and the Spaniards purchased the goods they brought to the colony.

The Galleon Trade

The Manila galleons formed a part of a larger network of trade vessels sailing, originally from Seville and then later from the port of Cadiz in 1717. They sailed from Spain to the Caribbean and their main port of Havana. The vessels anchored for a time at Havana, before proceeding to Veracruz, Mexico. In Veracruz, the ship's cargo was unloaded and transferred to the other Spanish colonies in the Americas, as well as to the Far East. Merchandise was taken along a land route from Veracruz to Mexico City and then to Acapulco or other ports along the West Coast of Mexico, where it was loaded onto the Manila galleon.

At first, the galleons sailed from Spain without any accompanying vessels during the early sixteenth century, but this was changed in 1526 when the Spanish government ordered that all galleons bound for the Americas had to travel in a fleet. The returning fleets always stopped off in Havana before sailing on to Spain.

"Until free trading with the Indies was introduced at the end of the eighteenth century, Havana held a monopoly over the exit from America of Spanish vessels bound for the Peninsula. Its bay was the anchorage for all the fleets arriving from Veracruz, Cartagena and all the ports on the Caribbean coasts before they set out together on the return trip." [13]

Only two galleons plied the Pacific each year. They were filled to capacity with cargoes of valuable silks, spices, porcelains and a multitude of goods from China, India, and the Moluccas. A royal decree issued by Philip II in 1593, stated that the galleons would be allowed to carry a cargo of 300-800 tons each. A third galleon remained in reserve at the port of Acapulco.

When the 30-meter length galleon returned to Manila, it usually carried a large quantity of silver dollars in payment of goods received the year before, as well as the annual subsidy for Manila. Some of the goods sent from Mexico to Manila included precious metals, weapons, books, documents, scientific instruments, wines and other Spanish food items, as well as Spanish produced furnishings, clothing, and household goods. The galleons also brought a number of passengers such as government officials, clerics and soldiers for the Spanish settlement.

But the galleons did not always arrive in Manila or Acapulco as scheduled. There were times when they disappeared due to the effects of severe weather or when captured by privateers, pirates or by the navies of countries such as England. For example, the *Santa Ana*, was seized in 1582, the *Encarnacion*, in 1709, the *Covadonga* in 1743, and the British forces while invading Manila, captured the *Santissima Trinidad* in 1762.

Sailing aboard the galleons was a risky business for both the officers and sailors. But no matter how many difficulties they faced during the precarious journey, it appears that for many, this was the only type of work they knew how to do. For this reason, they would repeatedly join a ship's crew to work, experience adventure, take advantage of the opportunity to take prizes, or if unlucky to undergo the danger of possibly being shipwrecked or attacked by an enemy.

"Notwithstanding the dreadful sufferings in this prodigious voyage, yet the desire of gain prevails with many to venture through it four, six, some ten times. The very sailors, though they forswear the voyage when out at sea, yet when they come to Acapulco, for the lucre of two hundred and seventy five pieces of eight the king allows them for their return, never remember past sufferings, like women after their labor. The whole pay is three hundred and fifty pieces of eight, but they have only seventy-five paid them at Cavite when they are bound for America; for if they had half, very few would return to the Philippine islands for the rest." 14

When a galleon was lost at sea due to the weather or was captured, it was not uncommon for some investors' back in Manila to become totally penniless. Financially ruined, they often faced a further disgrace of not being able to afford living in Manila or moving in the same social circles they had previously frequented. They often had no choice but to reside in one of the Filipino villages located outside the city walls, and to find some other method of supporting themselves or return to Mexico and Spain a destitute and disgraced person.

The irony is that Manila profited very little from the galleon trade. Clearly the galleons carried an astonishing array of goods and merchandise, but the silver received in payment for these items ultimately went back into the hands of the Chinese merchants of Manila and Canton and the few Spaniards who could afford to invest in the venture. Revenues received were not generally used to improve or develop the colony's economy or infrastructure.

The galleons were built in the naval dockyards at Cavite. The best quality woods available in the Philippines were used for the construction of the vessels. Teak was preferred, as it was insect-proof. But even though much time and effort went into building a galleon, and it was an expensive undertaking, the ship often sat idle for many months. Returning ships from Mexico also faced the same destiny. They would be left to the mercy of the elements - neglected and slowly eroding under the hot tropical sun or the effects of torrential rains. After a year's absence in Mexico the returning galleon was stripped and left abandoned from July to February. Little attention was paid to its upkeep until it was needed once again. Then there would be a mad scramble to bring the vessel back to its seaworthy condition as Filipino and Chinese dockyard workers began preparing the ship for her next voyage.

While the Spaniards and Chinese controlled the majority of the businesses in Manila including the galleon trade, it was the Filipinos who provided most of the backbreaking labor in their construction. In addition, they became seamen employed on the many Spanish vessels, as well as farming the land and growing the majority of the foods consumed in the colony. One member of the clergy who seemed sympathetic to the plight of Filipinos was Father Juan Jose Delgado. His comments clearly indicated how important Filipino laborers had become to the overall running of the colony.

"Who are the seamen who sail the galleons to Acapulco and other ports, and sail them back again? The Spaniards, perhaps? Ask the navigators, the marine officers, the boatswains, and they will tell you that this great and inestimable service is performed by Filipinos. Again, who are they that cultivate the lands and supply us with what we eat? Do the Spaniards, perchance, dig, or reap, or plant, any where in these islands? Of course not, for they no sooner land at Manila than they are all gentlemen. It is the Filipinos who plough the soil, who sow the rice, who weed the fields, who watch over the growing grain, who reap it, who thresh it under their feet, and who provide not only in Manila but everyone else in the Philippine islands with what they eat, and there is no one who can deny this." [15]

The galleons came under the administration of a guild and a manager who was referred to as the *General of the Sea*. This individual was usually a merchant and not an experienced naval officer. As the head of the guild, he was responsible for the selection of officers and seamen for the galleons. In addition to the manager, the second most influential person involved in the galleon operation was the captain. He was especially instrumental in the planning stages of each voyage. But as the captaincy position was purchased from the governor, this too became riddled with corruption and turned into another source of revenue for the head of state. Other members of a galleon's crew included a number of officers, as well as three or four pilots, two boatswains, royal quartermasters in charge of armaments, two surgeons, a scrivener, chaplain, auditor, shipwright, diver, steward and sailors.

Cargo was loaded onto the galleon according to a set of precise regulations. Loading took place based upon units of cargo known as *piezas* or pieces. Individuals allowed to ship cargo were allocated *boletas* or tickets, which provided the individual with a *permiso* or permission to load their cargo onto the galleon. Cargo was shipped in an assortment of crates, bales, packages, containers and barrels such as those used for fresh water. Each individual piece of cargo was allotted its own particular space on the ship to ensure an equal distribution of the weight taken aboard as well as the safety of the galleon.

When all preparations had been completed, the galleon set sail for Mexico after being blessed by the priests of Manila who offered prayers for her safe journey. The prayers continued until word was received in Manila that the galleon had left the archipelago and had begun its journey across the Pacific. As she sailed past the many islands of the Philippines, the galleon often anchored to take on additional cargo and provisions of fresh water and fruits for the long voyage. The galleon traveled in a northerly direction where she picked up the trade winds and was carried east towards the Californian coast and then south to Mexico and Acapulco.

Usually the galleon was scheduled to depart from Manila in July or at the latest the beginning of August at the start of the monsoon season. The galleon arrived in Mexico by December or January. Arriving in Acapulco, the galleon was greeted with much joy and celebrations. It became one of the city's happiest events, as the Spaniards of Mexico rejoiced in the galleon's safe arrival.

The galleon trade came to an abrupt halt when Mexico received its independence from Spain in 1813. The Manila galleon was no longer welcomed in Acapulco and the Spaniards had no choice but to find an alternative route for their Asian trade. The dismal situation meant that the Chinese and Spanish investors were suddenly faced with an economic disaster, as it was only the galleon trade which sustained their livelihoods. Moreover, as no attention had been paid throughout the many years of colonial rule to the country's economic development or exploitation of its natural resources, the colony became of less value than ever to Spain.

Chapter Six
Manila's Neglected Military Defenses

"The garrison of this place consisted of the royal regiment, which has been composed, since its creation, of twenty companies of one hundred men apiece, under the command of captains, lieutenants and ensigns. These companies have never been full, and have never amounted to fifteen hundred men. When the enemy arrived, this regiment was diminished to such an extent both by the mortality and desertion of some men, and by the different detachments which were for the galleons and for other posts, that there were not more than five hundred and fifty-six soldiers. There were only eighty cannoners, and those even were native Indians, who were but little skilled in the management of artillery. At the arrival of the enemy, four militia companies were formed, of sixty men each, and called commercial troops." 1

Archbishop Manuel Rojo

Governor and Field Marshal, Don Fernando Valdes Tamon (1729-1739), was in the process of preparing four detailed reports concerning the state of Spain's military defenses in its Asian possession. The request had arrived in Manila from Spain's ruling monarch, Philip V. Within the reports, Valdes Tamon provided one of the most informative descriptions of the colony's military fortifications, garrisons, galleons, soldiers, salaries, food allowances, weaponry and ammunition.

Of particular interest was the fact that as a military man, he was the best-qualified individual in Manila to evaluate the colony's defensive strengths and weaknesses. The conditions in existence then, as summarized in his reports had not changed much over the years leading up to the British invasion. The Spaniards had accomplished little during the intervening years and made few improvements to the country's military defenses. Consequently, his reports provide one of the most comprehensive descriptions of the colony's military defenses or lack thereof, during the eighteenth century

When Valdes Tamon received the king's request, he had been filled with a sense of apprehension. He dreaded having to report back to the king that the colony's defenses were not as strong as was then perceived at the Spanish Court. In fact, when Valdes Tamon arrived in Manila on 14 August 1729, he was extremely disappointed to discover that the colony's military fortifications were in an appalling state. Due to the serious effects of the tropical sun, heat, humidity and heavy rains, many of the fortifications had been steadily eroding throughout the years. Moreover, he found an inadequate number of soldiers manning the various garrisons. They lacked cannons, hand weapons and sufficient ammunition to tolerably defend the various military posts scattered across the archipelago.

The king's request had arrived in Manila in 1736. It was in response to an earlier and very disturbing incident involving the Dutch who were then operating from their settlements in Batavia, Java and in the Moluccas.

In 1735, the Spaniards of Manila captured a Dutch vessel as it cruised off the island of Mindanao. Presumed to be supplying the Muslims with weapons, which might have been used against them, the Spaniards felt justified in seizing the ship and sailing the vessel to Cavite. However, when the Dutch in Batavia realized that their ship had been seized, they immediately dispatched three vessels to the Philippines where they set up a blockade of Manila Bay. They intended to intercept and capture the Manila-Acapulco galleon, which was about to sail for Mexico. They also planned to capture the incoming galleon, which they knew was expected to pass through the archipelago's San Bernardino Straits as it sailed towards Cavite. But the Dutch were unaware that the galleon had run aground off the Bay of Calantas, and that the silver carried aboard the vessel had been removed by the Spaniards before the ship's location could be tracked.

Considering the weakened condition of colony's military defenses, Valdes Tamon was embarrassed by the incident and found he was in a quandary as to how to best handle the situation. Under the circumstances, he came to the conclusion that it was prudent to return the seized Dutch ship and pay some sort of compensation rather than risk exposing the galleons to further danger. But by giving in so easily, the Dutch interpreted this as a sign of weakness. After writing to the governor of Batavia regarding the matter and explaining his decision to return the vessel, the Dutch retreated from Manila Bay.

If anything, the incident had clearly indicated how great a threat the Dutch continued to pose for the Spanish possession. It was, therefore, crucial to reevaluate the colony's military capabilities and to implement whatever improvements were deemed necessary and with as little expense as possible. Given the fact that Valdes Tamon was considered one of the most eminently distinguished and highly trained military officers in Spain, there was no questioning his decision to improve the colony's defenses.

At the end of Valdes Tamons' term of office, there were several governors who also attempted to reinforce the city's military defenses with very little actually being accomplished. Acting Governor Juan de Arechederra (1745-1749), an intellectual and member of the clergy, voiced an insightful concern regarding the possibility of a future British attack long before it actually happened. When the Spaniards lost the returning galleon, the *Covadonga* in 1743, to the same Lord Anson who later approved the British invasion of 1762, the colonial government had been thrown into a panic. To ensure that the city's fortifications, weapons, and ammunitions were adequately maintained to at least defend against a foreign attack, Arechederra ordered improvements wherever necessary.

Francisco Jose Ovando replaced Arechederra in 1749 and served as governor until 1752. As a military man, Governor Ovando made an effort to improve the country's fortifications and increase the number of soldiers serving in the garrisons. In November 1752, another military man became the governor of the Philippines, Field Marshal Pedro Manuel de Arandia. He too was instrumental in re-organizing the army, as well as increasing the salaries of soldiers and improving discipline amongst the military personnel. When Arandia died in office in June 1759, a Spaniard born in the Philippines, Miguel Lino De Ezpeleta temporarily took over the reigns of power. As a member of the clergy, Ezpeleta served as deputy governor until Mexico could appoint a new governor to the post.

With the arrival in Manila of Archbishop Manuel Rojo on 14 July 1759, Ezpeleta surrendered the post to the archbishop who was lawfully deemed the next in line of succession if the governor's position was vacant. Archbishop Rojo administered the colony only in the interim period until a replacement governor was sent to the colony. Consequently, as a cleric with no military experience, he had the misfortune of having to lead the defense of Manila against the first successfully executed European invasion of the country.

Spain's Network of Military Fortifications

The fortifications found in the Philippines formed a part of a larger network of military installations established by Spain in its American and Asian colonies. In response to foreign aggression against their possessions by European powers, as well as numerous conflicts with pirates and adventurers, the Spanish government began erecting a network of military fortifications in the fifteenth century to thwart attacks upon its overseas possessions.

The architectural design employed in the construction of the fortified cities and ports followed an established pattern known as the *Spanish Buttressed Fortification*. Under the plan, those cities and ports, which were considered strategically important to the defense and security of the Spanish realm became the most heavily fortified. Both Manila and Havana fell into this category.

"The strategic reasons for capturing Havana are obvious, for the city was the center of Spanish power in the Caribbean. It was the strongest place in the West Indies, had a good harbor which was the site of the best naval base in the Caribbean, served as a rendezvous for homeward bound flotas, commanded the communications between Spain and her American mainland colonies, and was reputedly rich in booty. The loss of Havana would seriously weaken Spanish power in America." [2]

A successfully carried out offensive against both possessions meant that Britain would be able to strike a crucial blow to Spain's governance and influence in both her American and Asian possessions. As Havana was targeted along with Manila, it is interesting to note how the Caribbean settlement differed from its counterpart in the South Seas.

Founded by the Spaniards in 1515, the heavily fortified city of Havana was built in a similar fashion to that of Manila although on a much larger scale. In addition to both being fortified cities, the two had been established on protected bays and served as major seaports for Spanish ships sailing across the Atlantic and the Pacific Oceans. But there are a few differences between the two fortifications. Unlike Manila, which had a citadel, *Fort Santiago*, built within the city, Havana was defended by four heavily defended forts. These included the *Castillo de la Fuerza*, and the *Castillo de San Salvador de la Punta*. The largest and most important was the *El Morro Fortress*, which was located on a promontory at the entrance to Havana Bay and across from the city itself. A smaller fort was located within the city. All of the forts were heavily fortified and defended by many soldiers and artillery.

"The landward defenses of El Morro were formidable. The fortress had heavy walls situated behind an enormous ditch cut out of solid stone. Because the ground around El Morro was rocky, it was impossible to dig trenches and parallels. There was no earth with which to fill sandbags, nor was there any fresh water in the region around El Morro. The major weaknesses in the defenses of El Morro was the heavily wooded heights of La Cabana, which were not fortified and lay to the southeast of the fortifications along the eastern side of the harbor entrance. Guns mounted on La Cabana could bombard the city, part of the harbor, and El Morro." [3]

The city itself was located along the western shore of Havana Bay. It became Spain's most strategically placed port city in its American colonies. Vessels routinely sailing to Spain from the Americas stopped over at the Caribbean settlement before crossing the ocean. During normal conditions, when not engaged in war, but in the tamer activities of trade, the bay was large enough to accommodate many ships. It was not unusual to see, on any given day of the week, ships of varying sizes and types all anchored in Havana Bay. They were all waiting their turn to depart from the settlement to Europe or to other ports in the Americas. Whilst taking on water, provisions and cargo for the long journey across the Atlantic to Spain, officers and sailors from every nationality mingled in the city's bustling public places.

By the eighteenth century Havana had become one of the most fortified and militarily protected cities in the Spanish Empire. *"The harbor was, for size and draught of ships then used, of greater relative capacity even than it is today, and entered only by a narrow and curved channel. The maps show the advantageous location of the forts guarding the entrance. Given enough trained men, adequate guns, ammunition, and food, the advantages of position were such as to afford confidence to its defenders."* 4

Along the city's western flank, which faced the land, a heavy stone curtained wall was erected. Set within the walls were ten bastions and surrounding the entire area was a moat as the western portion of the city was its most vulnerable side. Within the city was the governor's palace and other important governmental structures, as well as the homes of the Spaniards lining the city's numerous streets.

But unlike Manila, which had only a small number of soldiers at the Fort Santiago garrison and at Cavite's Fort Felipe, Havana was manned by approximately 6,000 troops. Moreover, the Spaniards had an extensive number of marines aboard at least twelve vessels then anchored at Havana Bay when the British attacked the city in the summer of 1762.

Both cities had naval yards, but Havana's facility was not as large or extensive as the port in Cavite. At Cavite the fully operational naval yard was equipped to build and repair every sort of sailing vessel including the galleons. The establishment of a shipbuilding yard had become an essential component of military architecture and this entailed finding the right location to build the capital and the main port serving the colony.

Another necessary component in the design of a fortified city depended upon the military requirements of a particular area and the lay of the land. These two considerations were incorporated into the overall design of a fortification. By placing a military structure close to a body of water such as Manila or Havana Bay, a city's fortification could take advantage of the bay as part of its defensive system. For example the El Morro Fortress in Havana was surrounded on three sides by the protective bay, whilst in Manila, the city and Fort Santiago were surrounded by Manila Bay and the Pasig River with the exposed southern portion separated from it and the land by a canal. It was the side facing the water, which was less easy for an enemy to attack or to mount a breach of the fortification. Thus, the most heavily fortified side of a fort or city was the side facing the land.

The city's curtained wall was interspersed with large and mid-sized bastions, towers, parapets, main and secondary gates, and a moat surrounded a fortified city. Within the fortified city, a secondary structure consisted of a military citadel. The citadel was surrounded by its own stone walls with towers, bastions, gates and in many cases another moat. Equipped with its requisite number of officers, soldiers, barracks, canons, weaponry, and ammunition, the citadel also served as a final sanctuary for the city's residents if the colony came under attack.

The first governors to be appointed to the colonies in the Americas and in Asia by Spain were instrumental in designing the earliest fortifications. By the eighteenth century this formula changed as Spain introduced a *Corp of Military Engineers*. The establishment of this institution ushered in a new phase in the construction of military fortifications whereby trained individuals made it a practice of utilizing the most advanced construction techniques then known for the newer methods of fortification designs. However, in Manila and Cavite, few changes using the newer techniques had been employed even then. The Philippines had remained a backwater for the Spanish government in Madrid and as such, it was considered a territory of low priority. This led to fewer funds being allocated to the colony for its military defenses.

The Eighteenth Century Spanish Fortifications in the Philippines

The reports submitted to the king by Governor Valdes Tamon provided an analysis of each of the Spanish military fortifications found in the Philippines. Extensively detailed, they included ground plans, measurements, and the construction materials used in the building of each fortification. The names of the provincial capitals were provided, as well as the villages, which were located near to the citadels and the distance to Manila from the various locations. The number of soldiers posted to each individual military fort, weaponry, ammunition, and other supplies were carefully listed. By 1762, the Spaniards had constructed twenty-seven fortifications scattered across the archipelago. A few were in relatively good shape, but most were neglected and rapidly decaying.

The total number of cannons in the fortifications amounted to approximately 242 bronze and 494 iron cannons with 240,700 cannon balls, as well as 2,750 firearms, and 3,000 arrobas (a Spanish liquid measure) of gunpowder. There were 2,673 soldiers serving in the various garrisons across the country. Of this total, there were 1,684 soldiers based in Manila and 326 at Fort San Felipe in Cavite. Soldiers were paid a monthly wage and a rice allocation. Salaries were deducted from the Mexican subsidy.

The governor also provided information on the annual taxes the Spanish Manila government collected from the Filipino villages. By the 1738, there were 468 villages under Spanish protection. They contributed approximately

$134,999 annually in taxes. Of this sum, it was allegedly claimed that $93,822 was returned for use in the villages. In actuality, the taxes collected were returned to the owners of the land and the clerics for the given areas taxed. Little, if anything, was actually allocated to provide a better life for the native people. Consequently, the total amount of taxes received by the Royal Treasury of Manila each year amounted to little more than $41,177 signifying the colony's absolute dependence upon the financial assistance received every year from Mexico.

In the final reports submitted to the king in 1739, Valdes Tamon provided a brief overview of the cathedral cities of Manila, Cebu, Nueva Caceres (Naga), and Nueva Segovia (Vigan). Moreover, a history of each location, as well as on the government, employees, salaries, charity donations, church, missions, clergy, schools, hospitals, and housing subsidized by the government, and the estates owned by the Spaniards, was incorporated into the report.

The rationale used to determine where a fortification was to be constructed depended upon a number of prerequisites. These included the necessity of defending a particular location against attacks by Muslims or by Asian countries in the Far East. Other fortifications were required to protect the colony and quell unrest amongst the natives of a given area. The colonial defenses in the Philippines when Valdes Tamon prepared his reports included the following structures.

Playahonda Garrison, Luzon, was originally constructed to maintain peace with the Filipinos living in the area who had not been brought under Spanish rule. It was designed using masonry in a plain, square design. The garrison was equipped with four cannons and thirty-five cannon balls.

Fortress of San Francisco, Cagayan in Nueva Segovia, Vigan, was constructed in a square design with four bastions and was heavily fortified with soldiers and arms.

Fortress of Santiago de Yutagud, Cagayan. This fortress was used by the Spaniards to defend against the indigenous tribal people, the Igorots. It was badly equipped with just two iron cannons, twenty-five cannon balls and manned by eighteen soldiers (half of which were Filipino Pampangans). It was constructed as a simple palisade fort.

Fortress of San Jose de Cabucingan, had no cannons and was manned by twelve men. It was primarily constructed to defend against Filipinos who were not under colonial rule. It was damaged by earthquakes and was eventually demolished.

Fortress of San Pablo also known as Fort of Tuao, was a square, stonework construction with two small square bastions, no cannons, and manned by eleven men, seven of whom were Filipino Pampangan soldiers.

Shirley Fish

Fortress of San Jose de Capinatan, in Cagayan Province. Twelve soldiers manned the fortress. It was a square, palisade construction of functional but simple design.

Fortress of Santa Isabel was located in the village of Taytay, on the island of Paragua (Palawan), in the province of Calamianes. Facing the sea on one side, it was an irregularly shaped fort of stone masonry blocks. It had two main bastions, San Miguel and San Toribio, and a two-tiered stockade with an embankment. Its main function was to guard against Muslim attacks in the southern regions of the archipelago and for this reason it was more solidly built and manned by eighty-nine soldiers.

Fortress of Cuyo, in the province of Calamianes was located on island of Calamianes and built of stone, square shaped with three bastions. This fortress also served to defend against Muslim attacks. It was maintained and provisioned by the Filipinos as the government provided very little towards its upkeep.

Fortress of Linapacan, Calamianes was built by the sea and one needed a ladder to enter the structure. It was high atop a rocky coast and was used to defend against Muslim raids. It received no support from the government. Within the fort was a fresh water spring and quarters for Filipinos who sought protection when their villages were under attack by the Muslims and natives from Borneo.

Fortress of San Juan Bautista, island of Lutaya, province of Calamianes was a squarely constructed fort with four bastions. It was used to defend against pirates arriving in the archipelago from the Camucon Islands and Borneo, as well as Muslim attacks from within the country. It was supplied with enough provisions for a short period of time in order to serve as a last refuge when Filipinos were under attack. The Spanish landowner was responsible for its upkeep and expenses with the help of local friars of the Augustinian order.

Fortress of Culion in the province of Calamianes was a square stonework construction with bastions. Again, as with so many fortresses, it received little financial assistance from the Spanish government. Local Filipinos and Augustinian friars maintained and provided provisions for the fort.

Fortress of Capis was located in the province of Panay. Built with a triangular stockade, it backed onto a church. Its palisade was seriously deteriorated and exposed to attacks, but there had been plans to reinforce it. It served as a defensive fort against Filipinos who had not been brought into the Spanish fold. It was equipped with two cannons and manned by twenty-eight soldiers.

Fortress of Romblon was situated on the island of Romblon in the province of Panay. It was built of masonry and had an embankment. It received no assistance from Manila's treasury.

Fortress of Nuestra Senora del Rosario, at the port of Yloylo, in the province of Ogton, was used to defend against Muslim attacks from Mindanao and the Sulu Islands. It was a square construction with four bastions and was provided financial assistance by the Royal Treasury in Manila.

Fortress of San Pedro, stood on the island of Cebu in the town of Santisimo Nombre de Jesus. It was a triangular construction with three bastions and an enclosed stockade. One hundred soldiers manned the fort and it had its own pilot. Equipment included thirty-one bronze and iron artillery units of varying caliber, 16,000 cannon balls and gunpowder.

Fortress of San Jose, village of Cagayan in the province of Cebu was a square construction. It was supported by Manila.

Fortress of San Francisco Javier, Yligan was in the province of Cebu on the island of Mindanao. It was a star shaped masonry construction surrounded by a palisade. It had ten iron cannons of varying caliber and was manned by twenty-one soldiers eight of whom were Filipino Pampangans.

Fortress of Santiago, Dapitan, Mindanao was manned by fifteen soldiers and had two cannons. It was a small fortress surrounded by a stockade parapet and built high above a rocky reef. It was supported by funds from the Royal Treasury in Manila.

Fortress of San Jose, a triangular shaped fort, was supplied with weapons and maintained financially by Manila. Located in the village of Tandag, in the province of Carag, Mindanao, it was manned by eighty soldiers.

Fortress of San Francisco, Mindanao in the village of Catel, had a small palisade and was manned by ten soldiers.

Nuestra Senora del Pilar De Zaragoza was built in 1719 by Juan de Ciscara, a military engineer. An older fort, built in 1635, was originally constructed on the site and the new fort replaced it. Located in Zamboanga on the island of Mindanao, the fort was strategically important to the Spaniards as it defended the southern most outer reaches of the Spanish Empire in the Philippines. The design of the structure consisted of a square shaped fort of high stone walls and masonry construction with four main bastions, parapets, barracks, a well and the main gateway into the fortress, *Puerta de la Fuerza*. The fort backed onto a village, which also had its own palisade defense. It was well equipped with cannons, cannon balls, mortars, stone-throwers, hand weapons and gunpowder and was manned by 347 soldiers. It was more heavily armed and manned than many of the other forts in the islands. It was exposed to attacks by the Muslims of Mindanao

Shirley Fish

and from the neighboring countries, as well as by foreign enemies such as the English and Dutch who were operating in the region

Nuestra Senora de la Concepcion y Triunfo de Pangui was located in Mindanao. Valdes Tamon provided only a plan of the fort but mentioned that it was supplied and manned by soldiers.

Manila and Fort Santiago

Manila, the most fortified city in the Spanish controlled Philippines, had been steadily eroding due to the ill-effects of what Valdes Tamon referred to as the corrosive effects of *salty winds.* 5 To address the problem, he immediately began a program of repairing and strengthening the military defenses with the assistance of a resident engineer, a Spaniard born in the Philippines, Tomas Andrade. Although Andrade was highly esteemed by the governor, other than some repair work to Manila's main gate, *La Puerta Real*, little was accomplished.

The city's original wooden walls had been replaced in 1600 by a thick wall of massive volcanic blocks. The sturdier walls provided the residents of Manila with a greater sense of security, and they were convinced that the city was impregnable. But by the eighteenth century the city walls were beginning to show their age after years of neglect and exposure to the elements.

Manila had been built according to the successfully employed bastion system established in the Spanish colonies in the Americas. The city consisted of curtained walls interspersed by full and semi-bastions. Set within Manila's walls were twelve bastions, embankments, watchtowers, ravelin and crownwork. These included the Bastions of San Diego and San Andres located in the southeast and southwest portion of the wall. At the San Andres Bastion, Valdes Tamon ordered the construction of a much-needed gunpowder storage area.

Surrounding the city of Manila was a defensive canal with a drawbridge located at the city's main gate, *La Puerta Real*. This was the primary gate through which most individuals entered the city each day. The second busiest gate was *La Puerta del Parian* leading to the Chinese community. There were six other gateways into the city and four postern. The Parian gate allowed for easy access to the Chinese neighborhood and its many shops and restaurants just outside the city's walls. The area was under continuous military surveillance by soldiers placed in a watchtower atop the city's walls. The watchtower was apparently large enough to house an entire company of soldiers. Governor Valdes Tamon described the city's other defenses in his 1738-39 report.

"The external work consists of a crownwork which defends the gateway; a lower outer rampart which runs from the flank of the San Gabriel bastion almost as far as the gate, leading to a little bridge which connects with the aforementioned crownwork; a moat ... a covered path, parapet and stockade, with its platform, built to requirements, as far as the narrowness of the site permitted. At its foot there is a swamp which acts as an avant-fosse, at the end of which, running south along its outer bank, there is a large causeway which immediately joins up with another smaller causeway running between the avant-fosse and the river. Both join together at a little bridge, adjacent to a small fort built for the guard at the large bridge, which crosses the river beside it."

"The half-curtain moat is formed by the waters which flow upriver when the tide rises. It begins at the flanked angle of the San Gabriel bastion and runs very close to the Parian gate, with counterscarp, leaving it there to bear off towards the crownwork, which it leaves semi-isolated with a little promontory. After a small stretch, it flows straight into the avant-fosse, in the manner of a deposit. Not so its main body, which leads off to the right, depending on the waters it receives, following close alongside the large causeway, in as much as its meandering allows, until it reaches the walls, and there it ends, beside the San Diego bastion, where a boundary was imposed on it, undoubtedly to prevent the frequent flooding to which the contours would be subjected if it joined up with the sea." [6]

The city's defensive system was considered adequate to fend off an attack by the Muslims, Chinese or Asians. But it was thought that an attack by Filipinos was highly unlikely as there had never been a concerted effort to organize a large-scale offensive against the Spaniards until the advent of Diego Silang. Silang came to prominence when the British occupied Manila and Cavite in 1762. It was also presumed, that a massive attack by a European nation was completely remote, as almost all of their colonies in Asia were too distant from the archipelago to effectively mount an offensive against the Spanish possession.

According to Valdes Tamon, Manila's most vulnerable areas were those sectors facing to the North, along the Pasig River, and to the west along the beachfront. But he was still confident that a European power could never launch a successful attack against the colony. Given that premise he surmised that the city's defenses, such as they were, could tolerably protect Manila if attacked by an Asian country.

Within the city itself, in its northernmost section, a secondary line of defense was provided by the construction of a citadel, Fort Santiago. The triangular shaped citadel was located on a promontory bordered by the Pasig River to the north, Manila Bay to the west, and the city to its south. Above the fort's main entrance is a wooden relief of the Apostle James as he rides a galloping stallion. He is depicted as a warrior, brandishing a shield and raising a sword to attack the enemies of Spain. At the horse's feet are the defeated opponents slain and trampled in battle.

The site for the fort is the same location where in the sixteenth century Muslims had erected their own wooden fort which was then ruled by Rajah Sulayman and was defeated in battle by Legazpi on behalf of the Spanish crown in 1571. When Legazpi captured the city, he decided to retain the site for a future Spanish fortification. As it faced the river and bay on two sides with the creek to the East, he thought at the time that it provided a good defense of the city. Moreover, the creek could be widened to provide further protection.

The heaviest fortified section of the citadel was the side facing the villages to the south. Here, the citadel's walls and moat were strongly built to help defend the fort, as well as providing a last refuge for the city's residents if Manila was attacked. This area consisted of a stone curtained wall with an embankment, full and semi-bastions, guard posts, batteries, barracks, chapel, bombproof gunpowder storerooms, dungeons, water tanks and a moat, which was added in 1685 and was connected to the Pasig River. A tall tower was located near the entrance into the fort with batteries from which it was possible to provide surveillance of Manila Bay, the area beyond the fort's walls and the Pasig River.

However formidable the Spaniards considered their fortification in Manila, not everyone shared in that belief. For example, Le Gentil indicated that Manila's defenses left much to be desired. Unfortunately for the city, Spain was not prepared to undergo the necessary expense required to improve the capital's military fortifications.

"The city of Manila itself is very badly fortified and not capable of defense. It has no bombproof magazines or any shelter for the soldiers. After the war, the Engineer of Manila sent to Spain a plan of fortification based by the designer upon the Vauban System, but it was too elaborate. Bastions, demilunes, horn works, a double covered way – nothing had been omitted to make the place secure. It was really a beautiful project – but how much would it have cost? The fortification, furthermore, would have been worthless without soldiers to man them, for it is not fortifications alone which protect cities against the enemy – on the contrary, it is soldiers." 7

During the early years of the nineteenth century, another traveler to Manila, Zuniga, found that the Spaniards had attempted to make some improvements to the city's defenses by endeavoring to reinforce those sections of the city thought to be most vulnerable to attack. But he also pointed out, that even those meager improvements could not withstand a siege of great length or magnitude.

"*The city is surrounded by a stone wall with a good moat and an outer ditch. In those parts of the wall not surrounded by either the sea or the river, it is crowned with solid defensive structures. There are wall exits, two by the river and three on dry land all of which have defensive weapons, specially the land exits which have even embankments on both sides of the gate. In addition to these exits there is a one-leaf door near the Governor's palace which is always shut. The main gate formerly followed the direction of the main plaza and the Governor's palace, and it is where the provincial governors and Archbishops enter when they make their dramatic entrance ... The most exposed side of the wall is the most fortified. The special corner facing the coast has been fortified by a battery of defensive weapons which extends up to sea level to prevent ships form firing at the plaza. The Parian gate, which is where people pass to reach the bridge and all places in it, is defended by the fort of San Gabriel located at the corner of the wall facing the river quite near to the bridge. At the point where the river empties into the sea, there is a small fortress commonly called Fort Santiago. It has a door which opens toward the main plaza and a false door toward the river. It is moderately fortified but I do not think that it can withstand a siege of many days.*" 8

Fort San Antonio Abad

A mile and a half south of Manila in the village of Malate, was the small triangular structure known as Fort San Antonio Abad. In 1762, the fort stood on the beachfront facing Manila Bay. It was used by the Spaniards as a storage area for gunpowder and for this reason they referred to it as the *Polvorista* or a place where powder was kept. Here, gunpowder was also produced for use by Manila for its defense and for fiestas, as well as by the galleons and other vessels.

Above the fort's main gateway there is a stone relief depicting a coat of arms of Leon and Castille with two raging lions and two stone castles. The fort is constructed of massive stone blocks and high walls with semi-bastions, gunports and atop the walls there are areas for seven iron cannons.

Manila's Soldiers and Weaponry

By 1738, there were nine companies of 675 soldiers in the Spanish infantry serving at the Manila garrison of Fort Santiago. The soldiers were under the command of several officers who reported directly to the governor. The officers included a brigadier, a sergeant major and six captains. A second lieutenant and a sergeant in turn, further commanded each company.

In the lower ranks there were armor and standard bearers, as well as individuals who played the fife and drums. In addition to these individuals there were, *"thirteen halberdiers, the Governor Captain General's personal guard; two salaried adjutants, and seven supernumeraries; an artillery lieutenant general with his sergeant and 36 artillery gunners; a military engineer and a royal works quartermaster general; the foremen and corresponding officials for the artillery foundry, and for managing the forges and the gunpowder factory; and, all working in these offices, a Pampangan infantry company with its captain, second lieutenant, sergeant, standard-bearer and approximately 243 troops, depending on events."* 9

What is of particular interest is the fact that there were so few Spaniards or Mexicans recruited to serve at the Manila garrison. The small number of individuals of Spanish descent who served in the military were often sent to the archipelago as a punishment for crimes committed in Mexico. Consequently, the colonial government had no choice but to recruit Filipinos for the city's defense. With little military training and the lack of European weapons, Filipinos were quite vulnerable in warfare.

In addition to the deteriorating fortifications and a lack of weaponry and ammunition, Valdes Tamon found that the Manila garrison was sorely undermanned. This too was observed by Le Gentil, when he pointed out that in order to adequately defend the city, it would have been necessary to provide the colony with at least 6,000 European soldiers who were well-trained and could hold their own against a European army. He felt it was difficult to defend the colony against enemies such as the Dutch, Muslims and Asians.

Le Gentil pointed out that the Mexican soldiers found in the Manila garrison were only competent enough to fend off attacks by the Muslims. The colony was not able to protect itself against a massive attack by a European nation. However, when Valdes Tamon took over the post of governor, he found he had only a small number of soldiers with which to ward off attacks by the enemies of Spain, and most of these lacked formal military training.

Officers and soldiers were paid monthly wages in silver dollars with the exception of the governor, who received a fixed annual income, which was paid in three installments. In addition to a wage, each officer and soldier received a monthly allotment of rice. Salaries received were for example as follows: brigadier $167; fort commander, $66; sergeant major, $30; captains, $15; captain of the guard, $25; lieutenant general of the artillery, $25; military engineer, $25; lieutenant, $15; works quartermaster general, $20; salaried adjutants, $8; supernumeraries or assistants, $6; second lieutenants, $4; sergeants, $3; artillery sergeant, $8; a Spanish soldier, $2; Halberdiers, $3; artillery gunners, $2; drum major, $3; standard bearers, fife and drums at $2 each; Filipino captain, $4; Filipino second lieutenant and sergeant at $2 each; and Filipino soldiers received $1 a month.

Manila's weaponry included 43 bronze and 65 iron cannons of various calibers set within its bastions and semi-bastions. Additional weapons and arms included: 20,370 balls for the artillery; 18 bronze stone throwing engines with their chambers; five small iron artillery guns; four iron pinzotes (long-arm pistols); 458 matchlock harquebuses; 409 rifles, flintlocks and bayonets; thirty-four pairs of pistols; twenty bronze and iron blunderbusses; 2,267 rapiers, scimitars and wide bladed swords; 1,097 iron grenades; 50,342 lead balls; and gunpowder.

At Fort Santiago there were twenty-nine bronze and twelve iron cannons. Weaponry and arms included: 1,534 iron balls for the artillery balls; one 300-lb ball bronze mortar; ninety-five muskets; eighty-five matchlock harquebuses; 3,414 balls; 161 grenades; eighty iron bars; eighty lamps, fire and flint devices; 148 cutlasses, chuzos (armed pikes), mojarras (lance head), pikes, lances and forked rests; and gunpowder.

The city had its own foundry and a permanent forge to manufacture artillery, firearms, grenades and ammunition of various calibers. These were produced using imported metals.

Fort San Felipe - Port of Cavite

Second to Manila in importance was the port city of Cavite. Located on a promontory of land jutting into Manila Bay, it was considered the capital's first line of defense. For this reason, the Spaniards had every intention, from early on, of erecting a fort which would be far superior to the one they had constructed in Manila. But although the fortification followed the time-honored architectural designs established in the American colonies, it was never quite as formidable as Fort Santiago.

Constructed in 1609-16, Fort San Felipe was 5,100 feet long and 1,200 feet wide. As a quadrilateral, irregular construction with four bastions and orillions, the western curtained wall had a gateway and an outer rampart. The south curtained wall faced inland and was protected by twenty cannons.

In the fort there were barracks, an armory, gunpowder storage areas, water tank and offices. Outside its walls was the Filipino village of San Roque. A curtained wall of 540 feet with towers and a moat between the promontory and the mainland formed the fort's defenses, which meant that it was semi-isolated on one side whilst surrounded on the other three sides by Manila Bay.

As a naval yard, the Manila galleons, as well as a number of other vessels, were built and repaired here. Consequently, there were a number of individuals working at the port who were considered specialists in both the military arts and in shipbuilding skills. Additionally, there were seamen who were assigned to the various ships, as well as other employees who outfitted the ships with provisions. Governing the entire operation at Fort Felipe was the *castellan* or fort commander who reported directly to the governor in Manila. The fort commander was in charge of the port's financial, political and military affairs.

Due to its military importance for the defense of Manila, Fort Felipe was manned by a larger number of soldiers and weapons than any other fortification in the islands other than the capital city. It was equipped with 260 cannons and other weaponry. Tamon Valdes's report included a detailed description of the Cavite fortifications, which was captured by the British in 1762 when they invaded the country.

The fort was already in a state of decline and badly eroding when the British arrived in Manila Bay. Due to its location surrounded on three sides by the sea, rough waves and strong monsoon winds frequently battered it. *"Fifty years ago Cavite was a good sized place, but the sea has carried away part of it. In less than fifty years the action of the waves has destroyed the Franciscan convent, an entire row of houses, the hospital of San Juan de Dios, a considerable part of the wall, three forts, and a ravelin. To stop the sea a strong masonry sea wall has been constructed."* 10

An engineer was instructed by Valdes Tamon to build a new breakwater for the Cavite fort. Once completed, it was able to endure tropical storms and strong winds, as it was tall enough to withstand the highest tide levels. Ramparts, banquettes, bastions, semi-bastions, flanks and curtained walls were added to enhance the fortification's military capabilities.

In the fort there were 109 bronze and 251 iron cannons. Weaponry and arms included: two eight-ounce caliber small bronze artillery guns; four small iron cannons of the same caliber; 101 stone throwing engines with 216 chambers and iron slides; 16,905 iron balls for the artillery supply; 207 diamond point iron bars; sixty-five cloven iron bars; twenty-two iron angelotes; 190 iron grenades; 142 muskets; 221 matchlock harquebuses; sixteen rifles, some with bayonets; nine pistols; one blunderbuss; 6,772 balls (2,910 iron, sixty-two in ramada a measure of raw or crude material and the remainder lead); 480 hand weapons (cutlasses, dress swords, machetes, lances, pikes, halberds, double-edged halberds and halfmoon hatchets), chuzos, languinatas (pikes) and gunpowder.

Of the soldiers manning the fort, there were three Spanish infantry companies with one of these commanded by the fort's castellan. A sergeant major and a captain commanded the other two companies. Each company was composed of 180 soldiers consisting of a chief officer, an artillery captain with twenty-four artillery gunners, a lieutenant reporting to the fort commander, two artillery gun carriage carpenters and a war scrivener. There were also Filipino Pampangan soldiers with their own officers and 220 soldiers and 120 ship construction workers. Each of these men, except for the fort commander and the scrivener, received a monthly rice ration and a salary from the Royal Treasury in Manila.

In addition to the military officers and soldiers based at Fort Felipe, there were a number of naval senior officers at the naval dockyard. These included: a captain, naval second lieutenant, sergeant of the navy, four squadron corporals and petty officer, record taker and overseer of the royal harbor works, storehouse warrant officer, surgeon, galley skipper, chaplain, master of royal forges, master of rigging works, master of cask-making works, senior carpenter master and a works foreman.

Other dockyard employees included: 226 mariners (of which sixteen were ship's masters); 166 cabin boys; rigging makers; 152 scuttlers; sixteen cask-makers; fifteen seamstress; thirty-three clerks; 135 blacksmiths; thirty-one storehouse managers; sixteen carpenters; brace sawyers and shipyard carpenters (Filipinos and Chinese) and caulkers.

Even though the fort assisted in protecting Manila, it was recognized for its importance as a ship building port. In particular, it had become important for its ability to construct the galleons that plied the Pacific to Mexico. Eventually the construction of the galleons and other vessels became its main focus of attention. Here too, the crews manning the galleons were organized and cargo loaded onto the galleons for the ocean journey. Export goods arrived at the port from China and other Asian countries and were repacked and loaded aboard the galleons.

A typical galleon such as the *Nuestra Senora de Covadonga*, which served as a flagship, sailed with a full complement of officers, soldiers, craftsmen and individuals who provided other services. On board would be a rear admiral, two first officers, mates, artillery sergeants, petty officers, carpenters, caulkers, divers, scriveners, boatswains, surgeons, dispensers and water bailiffs. A galley such as the *Nuestra Senora del Pilar*, which carried the chaplains, would accompany the galleon. In addition, the galleon sailed with two coast guard vessels manned by gunners and marines.

By 1762, the commander of Fort Felipe and the other fortifications located across the archipelago reported to the governor, Archbishop Manuel Rojo in Manila. In his journal, Archbishop Rojo described the colony's military defenses and pointed out that there were twenty companies of approximately one hundred men each then serving in the various garrisons across the archipelago in September 1762. The soldiers were not Spaniards, but in many instances criminal deportees from Mexico. The total number of troops never exceeded more than 1,500 soldiers and when the British arrived in the Philippines, there were only 556 Spanish soldiers in the entire archipelago assisted by Filipinos who were unfamiliar in the use of weaponry and lacked military skills. Nevertheless, the archbishop had no choice but to hurriedly recruit as many Filipinos as he could with the assistance of the church friars to defend the colony against the British.

Chapter Seven
The British Invasion of Manila

"Make a vigorous attack on the place, and to exert your utmost efforts to become master thereof, together with all the defenses, fortifications, and works thereunto belonging. In case by the blessing of God upon your arms, you shall succeed in the reduction of Manila, possession is kept of the place. And though by our prerogative royal, we have an undoubted right to dispose of all places." [1]

King George III

When the fleet was about to sail to the Philippines, Brigadier General William Draper sarcastically described his military units as *"our little army."* [2] Despite the fact that his regiments consisted of a number of experienced British soldiers, he was obviously not pleased with the size nor with the composition of the military troops under his command.

He was disappointed that the East India Company in Madras had provided fewer soldiers than he had requested. Moreover, those released for the expedition had little if any experience or were unreliable French prisoners of war. Not receiving the sort of assistance he expected from the East India Company, the smaller army consisted of soldiers of such varying nationalities, religious beliefs and languages, that Draper wondered how in the world he was going to command them. Such an assortment of men led to his momentarily doubting the feasibility of the expedition.

"The troops allotted for this enterprise were the 79th regiment, and a company of the Royal Artillery. The auxiliaries furnished by the gentlemen at Madras, consisted of thirty of their artillery, six hundred Sepoys (Indians), *a company of Caffrees* (Africans), *one of Topazes* (Asian-Portuguese), *and one of pioneers; to which they added the precarious assistance of two companies of Frenchmen* (prisoners captured in the war with France in India), *enlisted in their service, with some hundreds of unarmed Lascars* (East Indian sailors) *for the use of the engineers and...of artillery. As a compensation for this feeble supply of men, they favored us with some very good officers in every branch of the service."* [3]

Arriving just off the island of Pulau Tioman, along the eastern coast of the Malayan peninsula in the South China Sea, the British fleet was joined by Captain Grant of the *Seahorse*. By 22 September 1762, they reached the Philippine archipelago and the coast of Luzon. On the 23 September, they sailed into Manila Bay and anchored off Cavite.

By this time, the commanders of the *Essex* and the *Falmouth* had carried out their orders in China and were able to join the fleet in Manila. Two ships were still missing, the *South Sea Castle* and the *Admiral Steevens*. The vessels had become separated from the rest of the fleet during the voyage to the Philippines. Captain William Stevenson of the Engineering Corps wrote of the easy voyage to Luzon and Manila Bay stating that, *"After an agreeable passage of eight weeks, the evening of the 23 of September we anchored in Manila Bay."* 4

That night, Rear Admiral Samuel Cornish dispatched several officers to survey the fortifications of Cavite's Fort Felipe. He was pleased to learn that Cavite could be easily captured solely using firepower from their ships. Manila Bay surrounded the fortress on three sides, and it appeared ill prepared for a defense against a sea attack. The wall encircling the citadel could be breached just using the ship's cannons.

In Manila, Acting Governor-General, Archbishop Manuel Rojo, was informed of the arrival of the rather large British fleet. He was momentarily stunned by the news and wondered why they had sailed unannounced into Manila Bay. Perhaps the fleet suffered some mishap and needed assistance he thought. But as he was unsure of their purpose, he assumed the worst and hurriedly ordered the reinforcement of the city's meager defenses. In his journal, he later described the surprising arrival of the British fleet

"At 5:30 in the afternoon a powerful fleet of thirteen vessels was seen. Although so unexpected a novelty caused the greatest surprise and the greatest astonishment, since no news of the war had reached Manila and it was not even surmised that it had been declared, we suspected, nevertheless, that this was a hostile fleet. Consequently, His Excellency, Archbishop Rojo, the Governor and Captain-General, at once issued the orders necessary and in accordance with the circumstances, to put the place in a state of defense, without forgetting to sent to Cavite the help needed there." 5

The Spanish forces then in Manila consisted of a solitary and weakened regiment reduced to that state by the desertion of soldiers, sickness and death. With little choice in the matter, Archbishop Rojo began to immediately recruit the city's merchants in order to augment the Spanish forces. He also dispatched messages to the provincial governors requesting that they send volunteers to help defend Manila.

As a member of the clergy, Archbishop Rojo had very little knowledge of military matters much less how to resist an invasion. Facing probably one of the most daunting experiences of his life, he tried to be as diplomatic as possible with the British commanders, whilst attempting to minimize the damage to the city or loss of life.

The archbishop had arrived in Manila on 14 July 1759, to assume his duties as the head of the Catholic Church in the Philippines. Once in Manila, he found that the colony was then under the governance of a Philippine born Spaniard, Miguel Ezpeleta, Bishop of the island of Cebu. Ezpeleta was acting as the temporary governor of the Spanish possession until Mexico could appoint a new governor for the colony. Ezpeleta's appointment had been a sudden decision by the Royal Audiencia as the former governor, Pedro Manuel de Arandia, died while in office in June 1759. Hence, as Manila awaited a replacement governor, Archbishop Manuel Rojo's arrival in the Philippines altered the political situation of the colony. Normally, when a governor died in office, the person selected to head the archipelago's colonial government until Spain could appoint a new governor was the archbishop, but in 1759 the archbishop's post was also vacant. When Rojo arrived in the city, he demanded that acting governor Miguel Ezpeleta turn over the governor's office to him.

Ezpeleta had no recourse but to comply with the archbishop's wishes. Through a *Royal Cedula* of 26 September 1760, Spain formally sanctioned Archbishop Rojo's position as Acting Governor of the Philippines. Consequently, it was Rojo, in office as governor for only two years, who was in the unfortunate position of having to make crucial decisions, which would affect the entire colony and how the Spaniards would confront the British forces.

Archbishop Manuel Rojo was born in Mexico in 1708 of Spanish descent. The son of a wealthy Mexican soldier and plantation owner and his Spanish born wife, Rojo became a scholar. He received a Bachelor of Arts degree in 1724 and a Bachelor of Canon Law degree in 1732. Whilst in Spain where he continued his studies, he received degrees in Civil Law and Theology. Considered as a highly qualified teacher, he was accepted for the position as Dean at the University of Salamanca. He became a judge and founded the *College of Lawyers* (Bar Association) in Madrid. This led to his being offered a position as an *oidor* (judge) by the Council of Indies to the Royal Audiencia (governing body of Mexico), but he turned down the offer. Ultimately, he made his way to Mexico where he was to serve in a number of positions in government and in the church. In Mexico City, he founded the College of Lawyers in 1758. On 22 July 1759, he accepted the position of Archbishop of Manila and in July 1761, he temporarily became the Acting Governor of the Philippines.

While the Archbishop later claimed that he was unaware of the Seven Year's War, he had, in fact, received news of the conflict through various sources. But those early warnings, he chose to ignore and they were casually dismissed. Several Armenian merchants, conducting business in Manila, informed the archbishop that the British were in the midst of preparing an invasion force in Madras. Rojo was also forewarned by a visiting Spanish priest who spoke of the European conflict, as well as receiving news of the war from other sources in China. However, by naively dismissing the important warnings of a possible impending invasion, he placed Manila in a terribly vulnerable position.

In the early morning hours of 24 September 1762, Admiral Cornish and General Draper sailed aboard a frigate and began cruising along Manila Bay where they, *"examined the coast, in order to fix upon a proper spot for landing the troops, artillery, and stores."* 6 From the ship, they could see the city's massive walls, bastions, parapets and cannons. They also noted the villages located just beyond the walls of the city and the sturdily built stone churches. A smaller fortification was spotted along the beachfront the *San Antonio Abad.*

While they continued cruising along the coastal areas of the bay, they were unaware that the archbishop was apprehensively observing them from atop the city's parapets. Rojo immediately decided to send an emissary to the British commanders with a message demanding to know who they were and what they were doing in Manila Bay. When the archbishop's emissary arrived aboard the admiral's flagship, Captain Stevenson described the events as they unfolded.

"This morning an officer with a Spanish flag came on board the Admiral's flagship ... with letters from the Captain-General of the Philippines desiring to know by what authority we entered their bay with such a force without previously advising him ... offering us at the same time all the assistance in his power if we were driven there by distress, but assuring us if we came in a hostile manner (which he could not think possible not having heard of any declaration of War between Spain and England), he was determined to defend the honor of the Catholic Crown to the last extremity." 7

Returning to his office at the governor's residence, Archbishop Rojo nervously paced back and forth, as he impatiently awaited the British commander's reply. He prayed that the British had arrived in peace and not with any other ulterior motive. The reply came swiftly. Two British officers were presented to the archbishop bearing a letter signed by both Admiral Cornish and General Draper. The two commanders explained the details of the European war and of Spain's involvement in the conflict as an ally of France. As they were operating under the direct orders of George III, they had been instructed by the king to invade and conquer the Spanish possession of the Philippines. While the two British officers were with the archbishop, Admiral Cornish had simultaneously sent two additional emissaries to the citadel of Cavite with a similar message. In both messages, they stressed the futility of any attempt to resist their demands and asked for an immediate surrender.

"The conduct of the Spanish Court having obliged His Britannic Majesty ... to conquer Manila of the Philippine Islands, and to convince the Spaniards that the most distant dominions of their Sovereign are not proof against the force and power of our King, or beyond the reach of his just displeasure...and desiring to avoid a sad extremity which must be the infallible and inevitable consequence of an ill-timed and fruitless resistance on your part, we demand in the name of the King ... the immediate surrender of the City and the fortifications and territories therein appertaining. You see well what means we have to enforce our demand. The Spaniards, unless they are totally lacking in judgment, must see that they must accept our clemency. We await a speedy reply. We are, with the highest esteem and consideration, your most obedient servants, S. Cornish, William Draper, On board His Majesty's Ship Norfolk, September 24, 1762" 8

But in reply, Archbishop Rojo informed the British commanders that neither the king of Spain nor the Mexican viceroy had related to him any of the details concerning the European war or of his country's involvement in the conflict. Furthermore, he had not been ordered to surrender the Asian possession to the British. *"I have no instructions from His Majesty to surrender it, but on the contrary am obliged ... to defend this Capital which His Catholic Majesty entrusted and delivered to my care. I shall do all in my power to defend it to last drop of my blood."* 9

By now it had become obvious to both Cornish and Draper that their abrupt arrival in Manila had completely taken the Spaniards by surprise. Meeting with almost no resistance and the archbishop's insistence that he was unaware of the hostilities between Britain and Spain, the two English commanders decided to act quickly. They altered their military strategy to take full advantage of the enormous disturbance their presence had created in the capital. At first, they had planned to attack and seize Cavite, but this idea was shelved. Instead, they decided to immediately launch a full-scale assault on Manila, knowing full well that if the capital fell the port city would soon follow.

"We anchored in Manila bay; and soon found, that our visit was unexpected; the Spaniards were unprepared. To increase as much as possible the visible confusion and consternation of the enemy, we determined to lose no time in the attack of the port of Cavite, that was at first intended, but proceed directly to the grand object, judging that our conquest there would of course occasion and draw after it the fall of Cavite." 10

In any case, the change in strategy came about, as the winds were not favorable for an attack of Cavite. Admiral Cornish was also of the opinion that attacking Cavite would have created a delay of at least two days before they could proceed to Manila and conquer that city. During the interim, the Spaniards might have had an opportunity to prepare a defense of Manila. Moreover, Cornish pointed out that the seizure later on of the port city would provide the East India Company with an excellent and convenient port for use by their own ships. The British were aware that the galleons and other vessels were constructed, refitted and repaired at the port and as such, it was deemed an exceedingly valuable prize.

The British commanders were still hoping that the Spaniards would surrender peacefully without the need to use force. But the Spaniards were adamantly opposed to giving in so easily to the British. They were determined to defend Manila no matter what was required even though they realized what they were up against. The British had far better trained and equipped soldiers who were eager for the offensive to begin.

Before any actual combat began, the British commanders sent their assurances to the inhabitants of the villages outside Manila, that they would not be harmed unless they made the unfortunate decision to join the Spaniards against them. In an attempt to gain their support, the British also informed the natives that if they were successful in seizing Manila, they would eliminate the tax system they had come to dread. Furthermore, the British commanders stated that they would allow Filipinos to continue practicing their religious beliefs without any interference or fears of reprisal. But, on the other hand, they were emphatic that if the Filipinos chose not to accept their terms, they would be severely punished. At the same time, they stressed the fact that all of Manila's residents would be respected and their homes undamaged.

When it became obvious to Archbishop Rojo that a conflict was eminent, he quickly convened a meeting with the city's most prominent Spaniards in both the government and in the military. They heatedly disputed how they planned to address the dilemma they now faced. At the end of their rushed meeting, almost all of the Spaniards had agreed to resist the threats made by the British and decided to defend Manila at all costs.

Realizing that the Spaniards were not prepared to surrender peacefully, Cornish and Draper began preparations to land troops near the small fort they had observed along the beachfront and which was a short distance away from Manila. With the intention of using the fort as their first camp, they would be able to later mount an attack against Manila from it. They planned to set up a battery across from Manila from which they would create a breach in the city's walls. Draper also decided to lower the long boats and as each boat was filled with soldiers, they would be ordered to sail across Manila Bay to the beach opposite the Filipino villages of Ermita and Malate.

While the soldiers were still in the preliminary sages of preparing to sail to the shore, Admiral Cornish was informed of an approaching Spanish galley. The ship was heading towards Manila Bay. He ordered three armed vessels to intercept the galley and capture her. The galley, the *Santa Gertrudis*, was already sailing into the bay when her captain spotted the British fleet. He was desperately trying to get as close as possible to the shore in an attempt to evade the British who were trying to capture his vessel. The Spaniards aboard the galley fought back with heavy gunfire, but in the ensuing confusion, the *Santa Gertrudis* ran aground. She was then easily seized, but before the British could board the vessel, many of her frightened passengers and soldiers, jumped overboard and began swimming to the shore.

Those individuals still remaining aboard the *Santa Gertrudis*, including the captain, Don Jose Cerezo, Ensign Ignacio Castro and Antonio Tagle, the nephew of Archbishop Rojo, were taken as prisoners of war by the British. The galley became the first prize seized by the British during the expedition. One Spanish source claimed that the British, after capturing the vessel, had helped themselves to $30,000 in silver found in the ship, as well as a number of other valuables.

With the seizure of the *Santa Gertrudis*, Cornish learned that the galley had been sent ahead by the incoming galleon the *Filipino*. The galley had been accompanying the galleon on its return journey across the Pacific from Mexico. At that very moment, the galleon was nearing its approach to the Philippine islands and was carrying more than $2,500,000 in silver. The silver was the payment for the goods sent to Mexico. Moreover, aboard the galleon was the annual subsidy of $250,000 sent by the Mexican viceroy to subsidize the colony's expenditures. Needless to say, as soon as Cornish and Draper learned of the approaching galleon, they were overjoyed and enthusiastically looking forward to seizing what was then considered the grandest prize of all – a Spanish galleon.

Unfortunately for the British commanders, they were unaware that the galleon had already reached the Philippines and that it was, in fact, anchored off the island of Samar. There, it had been awaiting the return of the *Santa Gertrudis*, which had been dispatched to Manila to fetch a pilot to guide the galleon through the *Embocadero,* the dangerous Straits of San Bernardino. This particular sea channel connecting the Philippine Sea to the islands of the archipelago was known by seafarers as an extremely hazardous stretch of water. To safely negotiate the straits, the captain of the galleon needed the services of a pilot who was familiar with the region. But as time passed and there was still no sight of the galley, the captain of the *Filipino* was already beginning to wonder why it was taking so long for the return of the *Santa Gertrudis* and the pilot.

Just prior to the capture of the *Santa Gertrudis,* Captain Cerezo was able to hand over some important letters to one of his sailors, who managed to jump overboard and escape capture by the British. The documents, signed by Captain Juan Sotomayor of the *Filipino,* were safely delivered to Archbishop Rojo. By this time, Rojo was already aware of the galleon's whereabouts and realized that it was only a matter of time before the British also located and seized the vessel.

To ensure that the silver aboard the vessel did not fall into the hands of the British, Rojo sent a message to the galleon's captain, informing him of the presence of the enemy's fleet in Manila and of the expected attack of the city. The captain was instructed to transport the silver inland for safekeeping and to destroy the galleon.

The Conflict Begins

That evening at 7 p.m., under heavy fire provided by the frigates *Argo, Seahorse,* and the *Seaford*, which were commanded by Captains King, Grant and Peighin respectively, Draper began landing his troops just opposite the Filipino village and church of Malate. This procedure involved three divisions of soldiers, which were commanded by General Draper with Lieutenant Colonel Scott, Colonel Monson and Major More. The vessels employed in the landing were commanded by Captain Parker of the *Grafton*, Captain Kempenfelt of the Admiral's flagship the *Norfolk,* and Captain Brereton of the *Falmouth.* The three divisions were purposely separated from each other to distract and confuse the Spaniards. The British soldiers had been instructed to join together at a predetermined location. Draper described the landing in his journal saying, *"The 79th regiment, the marines, a detachment of artillery, with three field pieces, and one howitzer, fixed in the long boats, assembled in three divisions under their sterns; the left commanded by Col. Monson, quartermaster-general; the center by me, with Lt. Col. Scott the adjutant-general; the right by Maj. More, the eldest field officer."* 11

The British continued to heavily fire from the ships towards Manila in an attempt to keep the Spaniards and Filipinos away from the landing troops. However, this did not have the desired effect as a number of people were already gathering atop the city's parapets and pouring out from the villages of Ermita and Malate to view the landing soldiers. Even though the British commanders were aware of the growing crowd of onlookers, they needed to address a far more problematic difficulty and this was the raging surf, which was becoming increasingly dangerous.

The long boats were tossed and turned in the heavy surf and several were damaged with a loss of ammunition, but with all the soldiers safely accounted for. Luckily, the Spaniards made no attempt to mount any sort of opposition to the landing troops. For the British commanders, this was an amazing turn of events, but not all that unexpected as the Spaniards had been taken by surprise and were not prepared to quickly retaliate. Instead, as the anguished Filipinos stood gawking at the landing troops they began to panic and rushed to set fire to their houses in the villages. The fires raged throughout the night.

Once on shore, the soldiers immediately made their way to the safety of the stone church of Malate. It was easily seized and turned into Draper's headquarters. Nearby, three additional churches were also seized in Ermita, Santiago and San Juan de Bagumbayan. British soldiers were placed at the small fort, *San Antonio Abad*. The night prior to the troop landings, the Spaniards had feverishly removed and transferred the gunpowder stored there to another location away from the city.

The small fort provided Draper with a convenient location to store ammunition, as well as providing a base from which to communicate with the rest of the fleet. One of the other buildings captured at this time was a convent in Malate, which prompted Archbishop Rojo to order the members of all the various religious orders in the colony to evacuate their cloisters. He also instructed the religious institutions to provide volunteers for the Spanish led military. Members of the clergy were recruited to fight the British, but it was left largely to the friars and priests in the provinces, to persuade Filipinos to assist in fighting the British.

The Filipinos had been told that the enemy's objective was to convert them from Catholicism to their own religion of Protestantism. Just this idea alone was enough to send the poor Filipinos into a frenzy of fear, as by this time many had converted to Catholicism and were faithful followers of the religion.

Under the orders of General Draper, Colonel Monson was instructed to seize the village of Ermita and to inspect the roads leading into the city. Ermita was the closest village to Manila's walls and its stone church provided Draper with a source of much needed cover, as the Spaniards were now beginning to fire their guns from atop the city's walls. Not only did the strongly built church provide a safe haven from the gunfire; it also provided shelter from the heavy rains that were beginning to fall. Draper, unfamiliar with the rainy season of the Philippines described the downpour as a "*deluge.*" [12] As the storm grew in intensity, the surf became increasingly hazardous. One officer, Lieutenant Hardwick, drowned in the heavy waves as he tried to make his way to the shore.

To assist Draper's troops, Cornish sent ashore a battalion of 700 seamen under the command of Captains Collins, Pitchford and Ourry of the

Shirley Fish

Weymouth, *America* and the *Panther* respectively. This battalion was positioned between the marines and the 79th Regiment.

In Manila, there was a rush of activity as Spaniards began to mobilize their soldiers and prepare their defenses. While British soldiers continued landing during the night, Spanish musketeers were sent to attack them. But the Spaniards were confronted by intense gunfire fired by the British soldiers already in possession of the Malate church and occupying a number of Filipino houses nearby. During the severe onslaught, the musketeers had no choice but to retreat back into the city. In addition to the musketeers the Spaniards began firing from the bastions of Manila. Although they wounded and killed several British soldiers, their return gunfire was not powerful enough to deter the British from their offensive.

On that first day of the invasion, Draper was full of praise for his troops. Even though he had not been sure as to how they would perform in battle or even cooperate with each other. Nevertheless, he was sufficiently impressed by their conduct and effort during this first day of warfare. Suddenly, he was a bit more hopeful that the invasion could very well succeed if his men continued to maintain their sense of unity and obeyed his orders.

The next day, at night, the Spaniards advanced from their garrison in Manila under the command of a Frenchman in their employ, Cesar Fayette. Archbishop Rojo mentioned in his journal that the city council had approved a decision to launch a *"vigorous sortie"* [13] against the British soldiers occupying the churches of Ermita and Malate. But the better-equipped and trained British soldiers had an advantage over the Spanish garrison of Mexican soldiers, who although armed, were unskilled in the military arts. Moreover, Filipino volunteers, armed with spears and arrows, augmented the Mexican troops and were ordered to fight the British. This was clearly an unequally fought confrontation as the simpler weapons carried by the Filipinos proved no match against the weaponry used by the British. However, the Spanish offensive did not achieve its goal of preventing the British soldiers from continuing to land their troops on the beach. Finally, after realizing that the British commanders had every intention of continuing their activities, Fayette retreated to the Bagumbayan church where he came under fire. In his journal, General Draper described the Fayette offensive.

"The Spaniards advanced out of the garrison, under the command of the Chevalier Fayette, with four hundred men, and two field pieces; and from a church, about two hundred yards to the right of that we yesterday took possession of, near the sea, begun a cannonade upon the right flank of our post. Some Sepoys, under Ens. Carty, who behaved very well, were first sent to skirmish with them, supported by three piquets of the 79th regiment, and one hundred seamen, all under the command of Col. Monson, who drove the enemy back into the town." [14]

In another description of the offensive, Le Gentil suggested that the Fayette assault had been simply ludicrous. He was astonished by the seemingly unrealistic Spaniards who apparently thought that their untrained soldiers were capable of taking on the formidable British troops. He said, that the offensive had been launched as a kind, *"...of boast and bravado, for how could one flatter himself, with at the most sixty men for I do not take any account of the eight hundred Indians and two small cannons that he could give any trouble to six thousand men of good troops, withdrawn into two or three citadels, which it would really have been necessary to have besieged in order to try to dislodge them; for the walls of these churches are made of cut stone, and are as thick as the walls of the royal observatory (in France), namely five or six feet thick."* 15

LeGentil was correct when he stated that the odds for a victory favored the British rather than the Spaniards. With only the loss of a few men, Colonel Monson was able to drive the Spanish soldiers from the Bagumbayan church. Draper once again, praised the conduct of his troops who so far had performed excellently and wrote in his journal of this and of a second ultimatum sent to the Spaniards demanding that they surrender. *"The superior skill and bravery of our people were so evident from this affair, that it occasioned a second summons to the Governor, but to no purpose: the answer was much more spirited than their conduct had been."* 16

The British began referring to the Malate church as their No. 1 Post and the Bagumbayan church as the No. 2 Post. From atop the stone towers of the churches, they now had an unobstructed and clear view into Manila. From this vantagepoint they could monitor all of the daily activities in the city, at its main gate, streets, parapets and the bastions. Consequently, they were now in a position to better prepare sorties against the city as they could monitor the movements of the Spaniards and Filipino soldiers.

In the second demand for surrender sent to Archbishop Rojo, Draper pointed out that if the Spaniards did not surrender soon he would not be able to control the actions of his soldiers who were eager to ransack the city. He was still hoping to avoid a drawn out and bloody confrontation and implored Rojo to see the sense of surrendering the city as the consequences were too dire to contemplate. In his letter Draper wrote, *"Your Excellency sees how unequal your people are to support this affair, I beg you therefore to consider your situation before it is too late. I have a multitude of most fierce people, who are unacquainted with the more humane parts of war; it will not be in my power to restrain them, if you give us more trouble. I am your Excellency's most obedt humble servant, William Draper"* 17

As he stood holding Draper's letter in his hands, Archbishop Rojo decided to hurriedly reconvene another meeting with the city's civic leaders and military officers. When they were all assembled, he read to them the contents of Draper's letter, but once again, they were all firmly against surrendering to the British. They were momentarily expecting fresh reinforcements from the provinces, and this gave them a sense of hope that they would be able to defend Manila against the European army. As a result, Archbishop Rojo proudly assured Draper that he and the other Spaniards were certain that their troops would be able to withstand the enemy's offensive. *"I consider my forces to be in no way inferior to Your Excellency's, nor the defenses and defenders of this Capital to the attackers I see arrayed before it."* 18

However, Archbishop Rojo was sufficiently troubled by the implications of Draper's threat. The statement that Draper might not be able to restrain his soldiers, who, as far as the general was concerned, were nothing more than a bloodthirsty and uncontrollable group of men, worried the archbishop. In another message to Draper, Archbishop Rojo stated that he was certain the commander had a greater influence upon his soldiers than he perhaps believed possible. He also assured Draper that he would do everything he could to guarantee that his Spanish-Filipino soldiers behaved well. *"It is surely not incompatible but most in keeping with the character of Your Excellency to know how to regulate and restrain the native ferocity of the auxiliaries accompanying the disciplined formations of British regulars, just as I assure Your Excellency I shall do with all the people under my command."* 19

While the British were well aware of the increasing number of Filipino volunteers the Spaniards were rounding up in the provinces, they also knew that most of the recruits were poor and inexperienced farmers who were completely untrained in the use of fire arms. But despite the obvious disparities between the two warring groups, the Spaniards were determined to fight on no matter what the cost or how many Filipinos they had to sacrifice in the process of defending the colony.

The Spaniards and British continued to fire upon the other – with the Spaniards firing from the city's parapets, and the British positioned throughout Malate and Ermita. Many buildings were damaged in the process and there was loss of life on both sides. Some of the British cannon balls, which had been shot into the city, measured eighteen inches in diameter, and these, the Spaniards reused, firing them back at the British positions.

The Archbishop's Nephew

On the 27 September, Archbishop Rojo sent another emissary to the British – this time bearing a white flag of truce. He apologized for the grievous actions committed by some of his Spanish and Filipino soldiers. At the same time, he requested the release of his nephew, Antonio Tagle, who was one of the passengers on the galley, which was captured by the British. Tagle was then in possession of important documents from Mexico for his uncle. The documents contained news of the Seven Year's War. Fortunately for the archbishop, Draper was willing to release Tagle and had replied to Rojo saying, *"I have the pleasure to acquaint you that your nephew is safe on board the Admiral's Ship, and that he will be sent on shore as soon as possible, till which time I shall give the strictest orders not to fire upon your city and suspend all hostilities."* [20]

The archbishop was delighted by Draper's decision, and he took this act of kindness as a hopeful sign that the hostilities would soon end. However, Rojo was bluffing when he followed this up by warning Draper that Manila was such a tremendously fortified city and not worth the bother of forcefully seizing it. Moreover, he said that he was also awaiting the arrival of Spanish and French forces, presumably implying that they would help defend the city. It is, however, possible that he already was aware of the French soldiers fighting for the British who were planning to desert when the first opportunity came about.

"What a hopeless undertaking it is to take by storm a city so strongly fortified and defended by such seasoned troops and auxiliary formations of infantry and cavalry, as this is. It seems a pity that a British officer of such distinction should waste so much time and effort and be the occasion of so much useless suffering. I am an archbishop and little instructed in warfare, but the best military experts have made me thoroughly acquainted with the strength of this city and these Islands, even apart from the imminent arrival of the Spanish and French fleets. I say this to you as a friend; as the head of an army, I am as ready for battle as you are, and prepared to resist to my last breath." [21]

Nevertheless, as Rojo awaited the arrival of his nephew, that young man, Antonio Tagle, wrote a letter to his uncle describing the conditions aboard the British ship where he was being held prisoner. He mentioned that the British commanders went out of their way to make him as comfortable as possible under the circumstances. *"On the 24th, while making for that city, at 9 o'clock in the morning, we were taken by the English ships, because the whole crew jumped overboard and fled. We are at present on board the flagship, Captain Jose Cerezo, Ensign Ignacio Castro, and myself with two of my servants; but the English officers, gentlemen that they are, have given us the freedom of the ship. We eat at their mess and they show us every courtesy. I write no more in order not to be troublesome. Your faithful servant, who kisses Your Lordship's feet, Antonio R. Sierra Tagle"* [22]

The archbishop's nephew was brought ashore accompanied by Lieutenant Fryer who was carrying a white flag. But no sooner had they landed on the beach, than they came under attack by several Filipino soldiers who were just then making their way towards the No. 2 Post. Lieutenant Fryer and Tagle were murdered on the spot. Both Cornish and Draper looked on in horror. Of the senseless murder of Lieutenant Fryer, Draper later wrote, *"The barbarians, without respecting his character, inhumanly murdered him, mangling his body in a manner too shocking to mention. In their fury they mortally wounded the other gentleman, who had endeavored to save Mr. Fryar. Our party received their onset with much firmness and bravery, and repulsed them with some loss on their side. As it was evident that the Indians alone were guilty of this horrid piece of barbarity, our soldiers showed them no mercy."* 23

Archbishop Rojo was equally mortified, but insisted that the Filipinos had obviously acted of their own volition, as they had not been ordered to slay the two men. The Filipino soldiers, on the other hand, claimed that the Sepoys, who were shooting at them, led to their return fire. But despite being ordered to halt all hostilities, while the lieutenant and Rojo's nephew made their way to the city's main gate, the Sepoys had disregarded Draper's orders and had continued to fire their guns.

The Filipinos stated that they had been attempting to take the No. 2 Post at the Bagumbayan church, when the Sepoys attacked them. In the ensuing confusion, Fryar and Tagle were killed. But if the situation had not already badly deteriorated, after the two young men were slain their corpses were horribly decapitated. With heartfelt sorrow, Archbishop Rojo later lamented, *"What has happened was totally unexpected, wholly unforeseen, and indeed utterly contrary to my repeated orders; a shocking thing, but quite within the capacity of many of these native tribes."* 24

Appalled by the senseless murders, Draper demanded that the archbishop turn over to him the individuals involved in the killing. He also requested the return of Fryar's head, which apparently was still being held by the Filipino soldiers and who were refusing to return it to the Spaniards or to the British. Draper angrily said that if his demands were not quickly met, he was prepared to execute the Spanish prisoners he was still holding. The archbishop quickly gave in to Draper's demands turning over to him the Filipinos who had committed the deed. Rojo even went so far as to ride on horseback to the British camp in an attempt to appease the English commanders.

For a short period of time the hostilities ceased until eleven that night, but were resumed soon after. During the interval, Admiral Cornish decided to send the *Panther* and the *Argo* in search of the *Filipino* galleon. The captains of the two ships were instructed to seize the treasure reportedly contained within the galleon once she was located and captured. Cornish and Draper, as well as the other officers of the fleet had agreed to share whatever prize money was found in the galleon. The question of prize money and booty had been a hotly debated issue back in India before the expedition set out for the Philippines. Now in the archipelago, it was again under discussion as to how the prizes taken would be divided amongst the officers and crew. Both Cornish and Draper, as well as the other commanders of the navy and military agreed to equally share in whatever prizes were taken at sea and on land.

"The officers of the navy very generously agreed to our sharing any prizes that might be taken in this cruise; as we had before consented to their sharing with us in any booty that might be taken at land; and the distribution to be made according to the rules his Majesty has fixed for the sea service." 25

Construction of the Battery

Draper's next move was to begin the construction of a battery. It would be built across from the city's walls on the other side of the canal separating Manila from the land to the south. When it was completed, a breach would be opened in the city's southwest wall next to the *San Diego Bastion* through which his soldiers would be able to enter and seize Manila. He informed Cornish of his plans for the breach and asked that several ships be positioned as near as possible to the walls in order to bombard the city with heavy fire and create a diversion while his men continued to work on the construction of the battery.

"The Admiral, at my request, ordered the Elizabeth, Commander. Tyddyman (Tiddeman)*, and the Falmouth, Captain. Brereton, to place themselves as near the town as the depth of water would permit, and second our operations, by enfilading the front we intended to attack; but the shallows kept them at too great a distance to answer the purpose effectually, though their shot struck much confusion and terror into the inhabitants. We continued our bombardment day and night."* 26

Draper selected the location for the breach after his officers had closely examined the city's fortifications in order to determine its most vulnerable spot. This turned out to be the wall to the left of the San Diego Bastion. The bastion was just opposite the land to the south and facing the narrow canal. The canal, which the British referred to as a ditch, was not well patrolled by the Spaniards and this fact led to its being selected as the perfect place from which they could enter through the city's walls.

"The negligence and omission of the enemy to post sentries in the covered way gave us an opportunity of sounding the ditch; which perilous enterprise was effected by a small party of the 79th regiment, under Capt. Fletcher, who begged leave to undertake it. The Spaniards fired from their

bastion, and killed or wounded three of our people. The depth of the water was only five feet, the breadth about thirty yards. As the great extent of this populous city made it impossible to invest it with our handful of men, two sides were constantly open to the Spaniards, to introduce supplies of men and provisions, and carry out their effects. They availed themselves of our weakness." 27

As the ships continued to fire at Manila, the shots were not directed at any particular target. The shelling was creating the diversion they desired, as the Spaniards were so preoccupied with the ensuing commotion, that they little realized a breach was being opened in the walls. Meanwhile, Archbishop Rojo seemed amused with the fact that to his mind, the British were inept as their ships' guns kept missing the city. He said that the, *"balls which were fired horizontally were all buried on the shore,"* while the rest flew over the city missing it completely. 28

By 30 September, as construction continued on the battery, the British officers and soldiers were momentarily jubilant with the arrival of the store ship the, *South Sea Castle.* The ship carried the spades, shovels and pickaxes, they needed to build the battery. Four hundred soldiers had been hastily producing replacement tools, as the whereabouts of the *South Sea Castle* was still unknown. But with the arrival of the ship, the proper tools required for the job were now available for their use.

During the night of 1 October, as a strong gale battered the fleet and especially the *South Sea Castle,* the ship was grounded near the small Spanish fort. The mishap was viewed with mixed feelings, as it was unfortunate that the ship had run aground, but it now allowed for easier transportation of its cargo to the shore. Previously, the ships had to take their supplies and weapons ashore using the long boats, and this led to a number of logistical problems as the surf was continuously rough. Moreover, the *South Sea Castle's* cannons now provided the troops with additional gunfire cover to protect their camps in Malate and Ermita, as well as the battery.

However, Admiral Cornish was concerned that the *Elizabeth* and the *Falmouth,* which were still firing on the city, might sustain some damage. As they were anchored too close to Manila in only four-fathoms of water, they could have sustained damage from the Spanish guns. But although they were tossed a bit by the gale that was hourly gaining strength, the ships managed to hold their own. The Spaniards had begun firing at the two vessels and towards the British camps and trenches. Large numbers of inexperienced reinforcements were beginning to arrive in Manila. These were mostly Filipinos who, although technically called volunteers, probably had very little choice in joining the Spaniards in their battle against the British. The Filipinos arrived armed with their homemade weapons.

Nonetheless, every attempt to dislodge the British soldiers was easily repulsed.

At last, the British battery was opened on 2 October. The twenty-four hour job of its construction was so flawlessly handled that the British soldiers were able to easily open a breach in the city's walls. Despite the fact that the soldiers continued building the battery while being pelted by heavy rain and wind, they rejoiced in having completed the job at hand.

Another battery was added opposite the *San Andres Bastion* to the southeast of the city's walls. The purpose of this battery was to quell gunfire from Spanish soldiers who were positioned at the bastion. *"On the afternoon of the 2nd, the seamen, with wonderful activity, brought up and mounted all the guns in the battery; which we masked."* On 3 October, *"One hundred seamen were appointed to assist the corps of artillery in this service. Our cannon, by the most excellent skill and management of Maj. Barker, and the officers under him, were served with such justness, quickness, and dexterity, that the twelve pieces on that face of the bastion were silenced in a few hours, and the Spaniards drove from them. We had but two men killed. At night we began a battery for three guns, on the left our place of arms, to silence those that were in barbet upon the orillon of the bastion of St. Andrew* (San Andres), *which annoyed our flank."* 29

The British continued firing towards Manila to prevent the Spaniards from making any attempts to repair the breach. Archbishop Rojo had to admit that the British battery had been, *"so well served, that at ten in the morning, all the parapet of that part, was on the ground."* 30

While the British bombarded the city from the battery, the Elizabeth and Falmouth increased their fire on the city with such a fury that along the shore and beyond the walls on the land side, the Spaniards were able to collect more than 4,000 twenty-four pound balls. The heavy fire from the British guns was beginning to weaken the Spanish defenses. Archbishop Rojo was growing increasingly agitated by his military's inability to protect the city from the onslaught. Faced with the intense fire from the British ships in Manila Bay and the soldiers at the battery, he still had to contend with the incessant fire emanating from the church towers of Malate and Ermita.

"But what molested us still was the musketry of the enemy, which was placed in the tower and church of Santiago, which they had arranged for that purpose by opening in all the roofs several windows so that they dominated us. They saw also all that occurred in the city, and although the greatest efforts and the most powerful attempts were made to batter down the church with our artillery, we were unable to do it, or to dislodge the enemy from that post. But it is incredible that our bastion open without a parapet on either side, it is incredible ... that the various officers who

sustained it, and of all the musketeers and artillerymen who were obliged to fire in barbet, there were killed only two artillerymen, two musketeers, and three pioneers, in spite of a desperate fire which all those suffered from five different parts. It is true that more than twenty wounded and maimed were taken out, among whom was a lieutenant belonging to the artillery who lost his right arm. The greater part of the officers were wounded and bruised from blows with stones, and had contusions, but that did not prevent them from sticking to the posts. The vessels ceased their fire at orisons. That of the camp continued all night with the same activity, so that the artillery of our bastion having been dismounted, they were obliged to abandon that post, leaving there only a few sentinels without shelter." 31

A Last Spanish Offensive

The Spaniards mounted one last major offensive to dislodge the entrenched British. They were able to gather as many as 5,000 Filipino recruits. Of this total, 2,000 men were chosen from the province of Pampanga. They were used to form a final sortie against the British on 3 October 1762.

The strategy consisted of the formation of three columns of Spanish and Filipino soldiers who were deployed to attack the British at three predetermined points. Don Francisco Rodriquez commanded the first column. His unit was ordered to attack the Santiago church where the British had a number of cannons and mortars in place. The second column, led by Don Santiago Orendain, was sent to assault the British camps in Malate and Ermita. Commanding the third column was a Filipino, Manalastas, who was to attack the British soldiers on the beach and the ships anchored near Manila's walls.

Additionally, musketeers under the command of a sergeant major from Cavite and two captains and four subalterns were ordered to provide support to the three columns. The Filipinos advanced from the walled city through the Parian gate just opposite the Chinese neighborhood. But to the consternation of the Spaniards, who were safely watching the advancing soldiers from atop the city's walls, the Filipinos began shouting as they approached the British camps. Their loud yells provided enough of a warning for the British who began rushing to repel the attack. Despite this, the Filipino soldiers were able to penetrate into one of the British positions killing several of their soldiers who were guarding the camp's perimeter. The British did not employ the use of their cannons, which were loaded with grapeshot, as they were afraid of injuring their own men. After a bloody battle, with much loss of life on either side, the Filipinos retreated back into Manila at 9 a.m., the next day.

At the end of the offensive, one of the most highly regarded officers of the fleet, Captain Porter, of the Admiral's flagship the *Norfolk,* had perished and others were wounded or killed. The mortality amongst the Filipinos was severe. According to Archbishop Rojo, the British retaliated for their losses by capturing more than sixty Filipino soldiers, who were later hanged in their camps. When news of the executions reached the Filipinos remaining in the Manila garrison, they realized the futility of continuing to assist the Spaniards when there was no hope of succeeding against the foreign invaders. The Filipinos fled to their respective villages, which further diminished the meager forces available to the Spaniards.

General Draper described the last Spanish offensive as being ill-timed as it had taken place during a heavy downpour. It was his contention that the Spaniards had probably thought that the inclement weather would have provided them with an advantage the British commanders had not anticipated.

"They were encouraged to this attempt by the incessant rains in which they flattered themselves our firearms would be useless. Their approach was favored by a great number of thick bushes that grew upon the side of a rivulet, which they passed in the night, and by keeping close, eluded the vigilance of the patrols. Upon the alarm, Col. Monson and Capt. Fletcher, with the piquet's, were dispatched to the assistance of the seamen, who very sensibly kept firm in their posts and were contented to repulse them till day break; when a fresh piquet of the 79th regiment appearing upon the Indians' right flank, they fled, were pursued, and dispersed, with the loss of three hundred men." [32]

The Filipino assault was the last major strike carried out by the Spaniards against the British forces even though smaller skirmages continued randomly. Nevertheless, Draper was sufficiently impressed by the aggressive and valiant Filipino attack, which could have caused severe damage had they been better armed or trained. *"Had their skill or weapons been equal to their strength and ferocity, it might have cost us dear. Although armed chiefly with bows, arrows, and lances, they advanced up to the very muzzles of our pieces, repeated their assaults, and died like wild beasts, gnawing the bayonets."* [33]

After this particularly harsh assault, the battery renewed its fire with increased intensity. As a result, the Spaniards were prevented from all attempts to repair the walls. Clearly by this time, they had been rushing to close the ever-expanding breach, but their efforts were completely futile.

Despite the failure of their last major offensive against the British, the Spaniards were still refusing to surrender. They remained stubborn to the end, which prompted Draper to write in his journal that the Spaniards were, *"obstinate, without bravery, or any generous resolution of defending the breach."* 34 Nevertheless, the British were now ready to enter Manila through the breach.

On 6 October 1762, at 4 a.m., while Major Barker continued a brisk fire towards the city from the battery, Draper's soldiers gathered in small groups so as not to appear too suspicious to the Spaniards. When a large group of Spaniards was spotted near the San Andres Bastion, Draper wondered if his plan to enter the city through the breach had been uncovered. If this was the case, he realized that he would have to contend with musketry fire and grapeshot sent his way. However, the British soldiers had little to worry about in this regard as the Spaniards soon dispersed when fired upon from one of the British trenches. At this point, as the Spaniards retreated from the bastion, Draper gave the signal to advance through the breach and into the city under the intense cover of artillery fire and mortars.

Chapter Eight
The Seizure and Looting of Manila

"On the 6th of October we took the capital by storm, after twelve days operation, which are detailed in my journal. Our loss upon this occasion would have been trifling, but for the death of Major. More, a valiant good officer; and it is with particular satisfaction I can assure your Lordship, that the firm bravery and perseverance of the troops could only be equaled by their humanity after victory." [1]

General William Draper

The entrance of the British into Manila spelled the beginning of the end for the Spanish held colony. It was a momentous and historic event, as it was the first time the Spaniards were ousted from their Asian colony by a foreign power. For the British, it was a victorious moment of jubilation. But for the Spaniards, it was a demoralizing, anguished filled moment difficult to comprehend. The Spaniards had never thought that a foreign power could successfully topple their regime in the archipelago.

With the British soldiers on the verge of seizing the city, the Spaniards were at a loss as to how to prevent them from doing so. But for the euphoric British commanders, the city of Manila, a great prize in itself, was about to become theirs.

"Sixty volunteers of different corps, under Lieut. Russel of the 79th led the way, supported by the grenadiers of that regiment: the engineers, with the pioneers, and other workmen, to clear and enlarge the breach, and make lodgments, in case the enemy should have been too strongly entrenched in the gorge of the bastion, followed: Col. Monson and Maj. More were at the head of two grand divisions of the 79th: the battalion of seamen advanced next, sustained by the other two divisions of the 79th: the company's troops closed the rear. They all mounted the breach with amazing spirit and rapidity. The few Spaniards upon the bastion dispersed so suddenly, that it was thought they depended upon their mines. Capt. Stevenson had orders to make a strict search to discover them; but our precautions were needless. We met with little resistance, except at the Royal gate, and from the galleries of the lofty houses which surround the grand square. In the guardhouse over the Royal gate one hundred of the Spaniards and Indians, who would not surrender, were put to the sword. Three hundred more,

according to the enemy's account, were drowned in attempting to escape over the river, which was very deep and rapid." 2

In a final meeting with Manila's leading residents, members of the religious institutions and military commanders, and Archbishop Rojo, a decision was reached as to their next course of action. The military were in favor of surrendering, as they now realized the uselessness of continuing to oppose the British. However, the city's most prominent merchants were against this idea as they were expecting new recruits from the provinces. Knowing this, they were filled with a renewed sense of hope and believed that there still was a chance of dislodging the British.

However, they remained unsure as to how long they would be able to maintain control of Manila. It was agreed to at least evacuate the women, children and the elderly to a safer location outside of the city. They also decided to transfer the government's revenues to the provinces and away from possible seizure by the British. There was the realization that at some point their military officers would have to abandon Manila. In that case, only the archbishop was to remain in the city to prepare a surrender document once the British captured Manila.

For the Spaniards who fled the city, seeking refuge in the city's suburbs was easier said than done. The Spaniards encountered groups of angry Filipinos, who for so long had harbored deep-seated resentment towards the colonial government. As they searched for sanctuary, irate Filipinos vented their anger against the Spaniards. The Spaniards had few friends amongst the Filipinos and when they most needed assistance they instead found hatred.

One of the last decisions reached by the Spaniards before surrendering the city to the British was to appoint the judge, Simon Anda, a principal member of the Royal Audiencia, to the position of Lieutenant Governor. He was to act as the colony's governor while operating clandestinely in the province of Bulacan, where unbeknownst to the British, an interim Spanish government was established. The Spaniards were in agreement that they could not leave the colony without someone to govern the land in the name of the Spanish king. Consequently, while the Spaniards had very little choice but to finally surrender Manila to the British, in reality they had every intention of continuing to maintain a Spanish government in the provinces.

The British Enter Manila

Once the British soldiers had physically entered the city, Archbishop Rojo realized that there was little else to do but to begin drafting the surrender document. Within the terms and conditions he began writing, he planned to at least gain as many concessions as he could for the Spanish community. In his journal, he provided an insight into the events as they then unfolded and according to the Spanish point of view. As the remaining citizens of the city had been thrown into a panic and fled as quickly as they could from the British, Rojo described the day when the British invaded the city.

"At dawn ... the enemy began to fire shells into the city. They set fire to several of the buildings, and together with the shot from the mortar batteries and the fusillade from the tower of Santiago (church), which resembled a shower of hail, threw the garrison and the inhabitants into great consternation, which gradually increased. All the day ... and the following night, were passed in this perplexity, no means being found by which to escape the danger. Although orders for the ditches and the defense of the breach were renewed, in order to prevent the assault, and activity was redoubled and the necessary efforts made, yet there was no means of executing any of those things, because of the continual and deadly fire of the enemy. Consequently, there was no means of getting the bearers of fascines to work. Finally, at six o'clock in the morning, the enemy's troops left their posts in three columns. The first directed its course toward the breach; the second toward the royal gate; and the third marched along the highway surrounding the covered way, toward the east and bordering on the plaza de armas."

"The few soldiers left us occupied the gorge of the bastion of the foundry, the royal gate, the flank of the bastion of San Andres, and the curtain joining them. The enemy were supported by their batteries and by the fusiliers of the tower of Santiago, who poured in a steady fire. Consequently, it was impossible for ours to occupy the breach in order to defend the approach. The approaching columns discharged two rounds with their muskets, by which they sweep the two collateral bastions, the curtain, and all the posts which could oppose them. Finally, all together, they mounted the breach, and seized the bastion of the foundry. At the same instant they attacked the royal gate, which they battered down with axes and iron levers."

"After some slight opposition on our side, some officers who were there, not being able to defend those posts, the enemy fired from there on the other posts which they seized also following the cordon, and went to present themselves before the fort whither the governor and captain-general retired. At that moment, the militia, the regular troops, and the Indian who were in the fort threw themselves in disorder from the top of the walls. Many threw themselves into the river, where a number of them were drowned. Consequently, when the captain-general reached the fort, he found only the castellan, Monsieur Pignon, his second, and one artilleryman. The few

troops that he found were in confusion and were throwing themselves from the wall. The enemy's column, which entered by the royal gate, directed its course toward the plaza de armas and seized the palace. That which marched by the highway, took the small fort which defends the bridge across the Pasig River. Thence it went to the city, entering by the Parian gate." 3

By 6 October 1762, the British were in full possession of Manila. Archbishop Rojo dejectedly made his way to Fort Santiago, but found that the citadel was almost completely empty. Alone with only a few remaining soldiers, he ordered his men to raise a white flag of surrender. He retreated to his office where he began drafting the surrender document or the *capitulation* as it was then referred to.

Two British officers arrived before him and demanded the immediate surrender of the city and its military fort. Rojo indicated that he was ready to surrender Manila to the British and that when they had entered at his office he had been in the process of drafting the surrender document. He requested a meeting with the English commanders, which was quickly arranged. Extending all due respect and cordiality they could muster to each other under the circumstances, the three leaders, General Draper, Admiral Cornish and Archbishop Rojo discussed the details concerning terms of the surrender.

Admiral Cornish was completely satisfied with the outcome of the final incursion into Manila. He was now eager to discuss the terms with Archbishop Rojo, as he was intent on not only gaining the capital city, but also the port city of Cavite. Moreover, he expected that the final surrender document would also cede the entire archipelago to the British Crown. Another condition, he and Draper insisted upon, was the demand of a ransom of four million dollars to protect the city from looting. Admiral Cornish later wrote of his actions once Manila was seized. *"I immediately went on shore, and, with the General, had a meeting with the Spanish governor, and some of his principal officers; when a capitulation was agreed on, that the town and port of Cavite, with the islands and forts dependent on Manila, should be given up to his Britannic Majesty; and that they should pay four millions of dollars for the preservation of the town and their effects."* 4

Captain Dupont of the 79th Regiment and one hundred soldiers were now in possession of the city. Spanish officers and members of the city council were imprisoned. But to gain the affections of the Filipinos, those individuals recruited by the Spaniards to fight the British were released and allowed to return to their homes. Nonetheless, the British victory was bittersweet. They lost one of their most valued officers, Major More. An arrow killed him instantly as he stood near the Royal Gate of the city.

The Spaniards Surrender

Archbishop Rojo's surrender document called for a number of concessions. These included military honors for the Spanish troops, religious freedom to practice Catholicism, and that the lives and property of the city's inhabitants would be respected. Furthermore, he requested that the British pay the salaries of the Spanish military. He assured the Englishmen, that Spain would reimburse England for this expenditure. Rojo also asked that the Spaniards be allowed the freedom of movement in the city and offered one million dollars to protect Manila from being looted. However he insisted on retaining the city's main citadel, Fort Santiago. When Draper and Cornish reviewed the archbishop's proposals, they found them totally unacceptable.

Colonel Monson had warned Archbishop Rojo that the fort was to be unconditionally surrendered or the hostilities would continue. Draper again stressed that before any terms of surrender could be considered, Fort Santiago had to be immediately surrendered. The archbishop finally complied with Draper's wishes. All of the remaining Spanish soldiers became prisoners of war with the exception of the archbishop. But despite the fact that they had been imprisoned, the Spanish officers were allowed to retain their swords as an act of courtesy to fellow commanders. According to Draper, the captured Spanish commanders were provided with the respect that they merited as high-ranking military men. *"The Spanish officers of every rank shall be esteemed as prisoners of war, upon their parole of honour, but shall have the liberty of wearing their swords; the rest of their troops of every degree and quality must be disarmed and disposed of as we shall think proper; they shall be treated with humanity."* [5]

As to the four million dollar ransom demanded by the British commanders, the Spaniards thought it was too severe. Despite this, they realized that they had very little choice in the matter but to pay whatever they could towards it. They decided to turn over to the British a partial payment of $2,000,000 in cash and valuables collected from the Spanish community. Archbishop Rojo had assured Draper and Cornish that the Spanish Royal Treasury in Madrid would pay the remaining balance of $2,000,000. Ultimately, the Spaniards were only able to raise $546,000. To make up for the difference, the British commanders demanded that the approximately $2,500,000 Mexican silver dollars carried to the Philippines from Acapulco aboard the *Filipino* galleon be turned over to them. But the Spaniards did not tell the English commanders that the silver had already been transferred to Simon Anda's camp in Bulacan.

The Looting of Manila

While the surrender document was still under discussion, British soldiers began looting the city. How long the looting of the city lasted is still open for debate. According to the British, it lasted for three hours and not for forty as has often been stated in many renditions of the incident. However, it is true that Manila was looted and ransacked. Soldiers wildly looted the houses and churches of the city. They took whatever they thought might be of some value.

Archbishop Rojo finally begged Draper to end the madness. Draper tried to stop the ransacking by issuing orders to his men to immediately end the looting, but the crazed soldiers seemed unstoppable. In the end, he shot one of his soldiers who continued to disobey his orders. Three of the looters were hanged and others were threatened with death if they did not obey the General's orders. Draper ordered the return of all items looted from houses and churches including the vestments used by the clergy, with which the Sepoys had adorned themselves and were then parading down the city's streets clothe in the religious garments.

The archbishop assumed that the British commanders had given their soldiers permission to loot the city. Later, of course, it was learned that Draper gave no such order and that the ransacking had erupted spontaneously amongst the restless men who were bent on taking whatever valuables they could find. When the looting began, the archbishop placed guards at the convent of Santa Clara and the nunneries, to protect the women from the rampaging soldiers. But as far as the Spanish historian Zuniga was concerned, the Filipinos recruited by the Spaniards to help defend the city, as well as those in their employ had committed much of the looting.

"These dispositions being made, the city was delivered up to the pillage, and the soldiers spreading themselves over the town, plunder and robbery ... was accompanied by those atrocities which are usual with victorious troops although, to say the truth, there was no reason to complain of the English soldiers, as they were sufficiently moderate in comparison to what generally place on such occasions. The Indians (Filipinos) *were much worse than they, for they discovered where the riches of their masters lay, in order that they might participate in the plunder."* 6

According to various Spanish sources, the British soldiers entered the houses of the Spaniards and the religious institutions, all the while looting and destroying property. Women were raped, churches ransacked, holy images vandalized, government and church archives were destroyed. It was true, however, that at first Cornish and Draper did very little to stop the frenzied soldiers. It was only after Archbishop Rojo's pleas for an end to the looting that the British commanders made an effort to stop the ransacking. The Spaniards were astonished by the ferocious and unruly behavior of the soldiers. One Spanish woman, who was victimized, later described her experience.

"I, Feliciana de Arriola, widow of Ensign Marcos Pisarro, do swear to God and upon a cross, in due form, that I was plundered by the English and Sepoys; that I am a poor widow who earned my living with my shop selling cocoa, lard and oil and lending money on pawn; that the total value of what was plundered from me, including my clothing and that of my children, my own jewelry and that of others which I had on pawn, is about 1,500 pesos; and that I have been left with nothing to wear nor half a rial with which to buy something to eat. And because it is the truth I make this statement on oath and affix thereto my hand. Arroceros, 3 February 1763" [7]

As far as Draper was concerned, he was not surprised that the soldiers under his command had looted the city without his permission. Considering that his little army was composed of men from all walks of life, nationalities, religions and included French prisoners and mercenaries, maintaining some sort of order amongst such a varied group of soldiers was not an easy task. For many of the soldiers, looting and plundering a captured city was the only opportunity they had to take prizes. When the soldiers turned into a wild mob, breaking into private homes and churches, they felt justified in their actions as they had captured the city and it was now theirs to do with as they pleased.

"We entered Manila by storm on the 6th of October 1762 with an handful of troops whose total amounted to little more than two thousand; a motley composition of seamen, soldiers, Sepoys, Cafres, Lascars, Topases, French and German deserters. Many of the houses had been abandoned by the frightened inhabitants, and were burst open by the violence of shot or explosion of shells. Some of these were entered and pillaged. But all military men know how difficult it is to restrain the impetuosity of troops in the first fury of an assault, especially when composed of such a variety and confusion of people, who differed as much in sentiments and language as in dress and complexion. Several hours elapsed before the principal magistrates could be brought to a conference; during the interval the inhabitants were undoubtedly great sufferers ... That several robberies were committed after the capitulation was signed is not to be denied ... But that the place was pillaged for forty hours, and that pillage authorized and permitted by me, is a most false and infamous assertion." [8]

Draper was able to recover some of the looted valuables of gold, silver, jewels, objects of art, and family heirlooms. While the total value of the items stolen had allegedly amounted to $26,623, the Spaniards later claimed that the soldiers had taken more than one million dollars in valuables. What

Shirley Fish

eventually happened to most of the items looted still remains a mystery. Clearly, the officers were involved in some of the looting in one manner or the other, as Draper was later found to have in his possession valuables from the city which included the city's flags and eight copper plates used to print the Murillo Velarde map of 1743. These, he later donated to his alma mater, Cambridge University when he returned to England.

In addition to the demands for the ransom, Draper and Cornish were still insisting that the archbishop provide them with an official document stating that the entire archipelago and all of its islands held by the Spaniards would be ceded to the British Crown. To this demand, the Spaniards eventually agreed. But at this point the quibbling over the amount to be paid in ransom to protect the city from ransacking was subject to controversy as the city had already been looted. Whether the ransom amounted to one million or ten million the damage had already been done.

The final capitulation agreement was signed by the British and the Spaniards in Manila on 7 October 1762.

"Article I – That the effects and possessions of the inhabitants shall be secured to them, under the protection of His Britannic Majesty, with the same liberty they have heretofore enjoyed. Granted."

"Article II – That the Catholic, Apostolic, and Roman religion be preserved and maintained in its free exercise and functions, by its pastors and faithful ministers. Granted."

"Article III – That the families, which are retired into the country, may have free liberty to return unmolested. Granted."

"Article IV – That the same indemnification and liberty may extend to all persons of both sexes, inhabitants of this city, without prejudice or molestation to their interior commerce. (They may carry on all sorts of commerce as British subjects.)"

"Article V – Having great confidence in the manners and politeness of their excellencies the Britannic Generals, hope they will use their best endeavors in preserving peace and quietness in the city and suburbs, chastising all people who shall dare to oppose their superior orders. Granted."

"Article VI – That the inhabitants of this city may enjoy the same liberty of commerce as they have had heretofore, and that they may have proper passports granted them for that end. Answered by the 4th Article."

"Article VII – That the same liberty may be granted to the natives of the country, for bringing in all manner of provisions, according to their usual method, without the least opposition or extortion, paying for them in the

same manner as hath been heretofore practiced. Granted. (Note – Anyone coming in with arms, will be put to death.)"

"Article VIII – That the ecclesiastical government may be tolerated, and have free liberty to instruct the faithful, especially the native inhabitants. (They must not attempt to convert any of our Protestant subjects to the popish faith.)"

"Article IX – That the authority, as well as political as civil, may still remain in the hands of the Royal Audiencia, to the end that by their means, a stop may be put to all disorders, and the insolent and guilty be chastised. (Subject to the superior control of our government.)"

"Article X – That the use and exercise of the economical government of the city, may remain in its same freedom and liberty. Granted."

"Article XI – That the ministers and royal officers, their persons and goods, may be in full security, and be maintained in their honours, with a stripend sufficient for their support, his Catholic Majesty being answerable for the same. Upon these conditions, for the above mentioned Ministers will be under the protection of his Britannic Majesty, in the same manner as the rest of the inhabitants. (His Catholic Majesty must pay for their support.)"

"Article XII – That the inhabitants may have liberty to reside within or out of the city as shall be most convenient for them. (Still subject to the revocation of our government, if they find it necessary. Done in the city of Manila, the 7th of October, 1762. Signed by Rojo, Cornish, Draper, Villacorta, Ventura and Viana.)" 9

Setting Up the New British Government of Manila

Admiral Cornish and General Draper decided that Archbishop Rojo would be allowed to continue governing the day-to-day activities of the colony, while they maintained control of all military and naval matters. By taking this course of action, Cornish and Draper tried to minimize the influence of Simon Anda's rogue government in the provinces. The archbishop had enthusiastically accepted the British offer and even went so far as to try to convince Anda to accept the sovereignty of Great Britain. But Anda adamantly opposed the presence of the British in the archipelago and refused to go along with the archbishop's pleas for cooperation with the new regime.

With Rojo's acceptance of the capitulation, the port city of Cavite was also turned over to the British. The archbishop agreed to hand over the silver brought to the Philippines aboard the *Filipino* galleon. He said this despite knowing that it had already been transported to Anda's camp. He also assured Draper and Cornish that Spain would pay whatever outstanding sum remained of the ransom. But the two commanders stated that if they succeeded in capturing the galleon before the entire ransom had been paid the valuables and cash taken from the vessel would not be included as part of the ransom payment.

The British eventually located the whereabouts of the *Filipino*, but the silver had already been removed from the ship. Angered by this, they began to incarcerate the residents of Manila. They were aware that many of the city's Spaniards and some Filipinos continued to oppose their presence in the Philippines. These same individuals were in sympathy with Anda and had joined his resistance movement. The fact that the silver had disappeared from the galleon only served to confirm the fact that the Spaniards were doing all they could to create difficulties for the British.

"Opposition to British rule and support of Anda increased by the day. The new rulers reciprocally augmented their harsh measures, which only proved impolitic, for they served to further kindle the flame of resistance. Many Filipinos managed to express their adherence to the nation's cause by secretly sending gunpowder, lead and other war materials to Anda's camp in the provinces." 10

Even though the Spaniards were resisting the demands that they provide a document stating that they had surrendered the entire archipelago to the British, they finally agreed to do so. Using a bit of coercion on their part, the British eventually obtained the valuable document signed by Archbishop Rojo and the Royal Audiencia ceding the entire archipelago to Great Britain on 29 October 1762. All the while, the archbishop and his officials were continuously doing whatever they could to obstruct and delay all attempts by the British to take full possession of the country.

Cavite and the Santissima Trinidad Galleon

As the colony's main port, Captain Kempenfelt with the *Seaford* and the *Seahorse* were ordered to take possession of Cavite on 10 October 1762. With the seizure of the port, they were in possession of a large quantity of naval stores found at the citadel of Fort San Felipe. They also discovered that the naval yard was well equipped for the construction of a variety of ships and boats including the galleons.

Admiral Cornish proudly reported to the British Admiralty on 31 October 1762 that, *"By this acquisition we are in possession of a very large quantity of naval stores; and beside the advantage of almost every convenience for refitting a squadron, the people are supplied with fresh meat and vegetable in great plenty."* 11 No doubt, he was elated by the possibility that in the future, British ships could be constructed, refitted and well-provisioned at the fine port.

In addition to the loss of Manila and Cavite, another blow suffered by the Spaniards was the seizure of their galleon the *Santissima Trinidad*. Two British frigates, the *Argo* and the *Panther* intercepted and captured the galleon on 31 October 1762, as it sailed through the Straits of San Bernardino. The 1500-ton galleon was slowly making its way back to Cavite for repairs after having been caught in two severe storms off the Mariannas. During the second storm, her main mast was destroyed.

A battle ensued between the galleon and the two British frigates. The Spanish ship was manned by a crew of 800 men and carried sixty guns. The heavily damaged *Argo* eventually had to return to Manila Bay for repairs, whilst Captain Parker of the *Panther* carried on alone against the galleon. He was finally able to seize the galleon after a five-hour battle.

As one of the largest galleons employed in the Manila-Acapulco trade run, the ship was fully laden with cargo. It had departed from Manila for its journey to Acapulco on 3 September 1762, just prior to the arrival of the British in Manila. The loss of the ship and valuable cargo was a massive financial setback for the Spanish and Chinese investors of Manila.

In his report to the British Admiralty and John Clevland dated 10 November 1762, Admiral Cornish described the capture of the galleon. He and the other commanders were euphoric with their success in capturing the vessel and seizing the vast cargo she was carrying to Mexico. He spoke of the surprise of finding out that the galleon was not the *Filipino*. They were, nonetheless, exhilarated by the capture of the magnificent prize and her cargo then valued at three million dollars.

"The enemy made but little resistance, trusting to the immense thickness of the sides of their ship, which the Panther's was not able to penetrate, excepting her upper works. Capt. Parker was no less disappointed than surprised, when the General came on board, to find, that instead of the Saint Philippina (the *Filipino* galleon)*, he had engaged and taken the Santissima Trinidad, who departed from Manila 1st of August* (the correct date is 3 September 1762) *for Acapulco, and had got 300 leagues to the eastward of the Embocadero* (Straits of San Bernardino) *but meeting with a hard gale of wind, was dismasted and put back to refit."* 12

One of the passengers aboard the *Santissima Trinidad* was Don Pedro Calderon Henriquez. A Spaniard by birth, he served as a judge in Manila for twenty-five years. He was returning to Spain with his family when the British captured the galleon. In a petition he presented to the British government of Manila on 25 September 1763, he requested a refund for the valuables and cash amounting to more than $30,000, which he claimed he had lost when the galleon was seized. Don Henriquez provided an interesting description of the events of October 1762 when the ship was intercepted by the British warships.

"As we were returning to these islands, we were taken in the Embocadero by two English ships, one carrying thirty and the other 64 guns. After a combat that lasted five hours ... we were brought to the port of Cavite. I was denied liberty to go with my family to Manila, but after having been detained for nineteen days they granted me leave to come hither. Being obligated in both places to live upon charity as they are actually under the British dominion, and this city plundered, nothing has been allowed towards my maintenance, though I have lost above 30,000 dollars in said ship, I have made representations upon different occasions concerning this matter." 13

Don Henriquez suggested in his petition that the galleon could not lawfully be considered a prize as it was taken after the capitulation had been finalized. He also pointed out that one of the conditions of the capitulation ensured that Manila would be spared and not plundered, which was not the case. Additionally, the security and possessions of the city's inhabitants were to remain secure, which they were not. Consequently, the British, as far as Henriguez was concerned, had broken the very conditions they agreed to in the capitulation.

"With much more reason should there be an allowance made to me in consideration of the large fortune that was taken from me in the ship, sufficient to maintain me directly, according to my rank. I qualify, being it is notorious, and being without the least doubt that the Santissima Trinidad is not a lawful prize which would be contrary to what their excellencies the British generals had promised in the first article proposed by the illustrious captain general of these islands and his magistrates and agreed to by their excellencies and signed by the 10th day of October."

"In it they expressly promised the inhabitants the security of their effects and possessions, but as this ship the Trinidad was not taken before the 30th of the month, she should in no means be looked upon as a lawful prize neither does it avail saying that the fourth condition (of the Capitulation), that their excellencies required, concerning the 4 millions of dollars, which were to paid by way of Contribution. As these conditions were made the 5th day of October (the 6th of October according to the British) *and all four, with the necessary and absolute condition that the city of Manila should be preserved from being plundered; but as this condition has not been complied with as the place has been plundered with the utmost rigour for more than forty hours (which these are few examples of especially in places of no more than two hundred citizens such at Manila), said conditions are no longer of any weight, and all impositions, imprisonments, embargoes, and other proceedings put in practice against the Spanish and Indians relating to any contribution, have been notoriously against the law and public faith and their excellencies knowing that according to the laws of*

war, there could not be any contribution exacted from a place that had been plundered left out of the article, in what was capitulated the 10th of October, which is the only formal agreement that is met with in form of proposals with the answer to each one, agreed or denied or limited according to the common custom of Capitulation, and it cannot be imaged nor presumed that the English nation will fall off from their promise in what they agreed to." 14

In his statement, Don Henriguez said that Admiral Cornish ordered his men to unload the galleon without notifying the individuals who owned property in the ship. All jewels found in the ship were confiscated without the owners having any say in the matter. *"My desks, bundles and chests were broken open and many things of great value taken out of them."* 15

With the British now firmly in control of Manila and Cavite, Admiral Cornish wrote to the Secretary of the Admiralty, John Clevland. In his letter, Cornish described the navy's role in the capture of Manila.

"The siege, though short, was attended with many difficulties, and great fatigue, in which both the officers and men exerted themselves with the utmost cheerfulness. We had constantly fresh gales, a lee shore and consequently a high surf, to contend with, which made it always difficult, frequently hazardous, and sometimes impossible to land with boats. The rains fell very heavily, and our little army were surrounded and harassed by numerous bodies of Indians, who, though undisciplined, armed only with lances, bows and arrows, yet by a daring resolution and contempt for death, they became not only troublesome, but also formidable. I have the satisfaction of acquainting their Lordships, that throughout the whole expedition, the most perfect harmony and unanimity had subsisted between his Majesty's land and sea forces." 16

While the British commanders were basking in the joy of their success, they little realized that they were about to occupy a land where they would face a number of obstacles to their rule. The first British colony of the Philippines, under the auspices of the East India Company, would be immobilized by a hostile Spanish community, which resented the new regime, as well as by conflicts within their own ranks.

An Account of the Number of Seamen and Marines Landed from His Majesty's Squadron and Those Killed and Wounded during the Attack of Manila 17

Norfolk (Flagship) - Rear-Admiral Cornish, Capt. Richard Kempenfelt, 2 commissioned officers, 12 petty ditto, 96 seamen landed, 2 seamen killed. 1 ditto wounded.

Elisabeth - Commodore Tiddeman, Capt. Isaac Curry, 1 commissioned officer, 2 petty ditto, 76 seamen landed. 1 seamen killed. 5 ditto wounded. Marines 2 commissioned officers, 3 non-commissioned ditto, 21 privates landed.

Shirley Fish

    Grafton - Capt. Hyde Parker. 1 commissioned officer, 3 petty ditto, 100 seamen landed, 2 seamen wounded. Marines, 2 commissioned officers, 6 non-commissioned ditto, 32 privates landed. 1 private wounded.

    Lenox - Capt. Robert Jocelyn. 1 commissioned officer, 5 petty ditto, 119 seamen landed, 4 seamen killed, 2 ditto wounded. Marines. 3 commissioned officers, 4 non-commissioned ditto, 38 privates landed, 1 private wounded.

    Falmouth - Capt. William Brereton. 1 commissioned officer, 2 petty ditto, 50 seamen landed, 2 seamen killed. Marines, 2 commissioned officers, 1 non-commissioned ditto, 11 private landed.

    Weymouth - Capt. Richard Collins. 3 commissioned officers, 7 petty ditto, 80 seamen landed, 1 seaman killed, 1 ditto wounded, Marines, 2 commissioned officers, 6 non-commissioned ditto, 26 privates landed, 2 privates killed.

    America - Capt. Samuel Pitchford. 2 commissioned officers, 2 non-commissioned ditto, 61 seamen landed, 1 seaman killed, 1 ditto wounded. Marines, 1 commissioned officer, 4 non-commissioned ditto, 22 privates landed, 1 private killed.

    Panther - Capt. George Ourry, acting Captain. 1 commissioned officer, 2 petty ditto, 50 seamen landed. Marines, 1 commissioned officer, 5 non-commissioned ditto, 24 privates landed.

    Argo - Captain Richard King. Marines, 2 commissioned officers, 3 non-commissioned ditto, 22 privates landed.

    Seahorse - Captain Charles Cathcart Grant: Marines, 1 commissioned officer, 2 non-commissioned ditto, 26 privates landed.

    Seaford - Captain John Peighin. Marines, 1 commissioned officer, 2 non-commissioned ditto, 18 privates landed, 2 privates killed.

    Officers killed and wounded, etc. belonging to the:

    Norfolk, Lieutenant. Peter Porter and Mr. White, surgeon's second mate, killed."

    Lenox, Thomas Spearing, Second Lieut., of the Marines, wounded.

    Total officers, seamen, and marines: landed 1017, killed 17, wounded 17. The surgeons, armourers, and other officers are not included in the above account."

Chapter Nine
The Troubled British Government of Manila and Cavite

"I do myself the honour of sending you the returns of our little army employed in the siege and conquest of Manila and have the additional satisfaction to inform you that we took it with trifling loss, excepting the death of my first major; More, a valuable, good officer. The Spaniards did not defend it with that virtuous and laudable bravery that might have been expected from men who were fighting pro aris et focis and so rich a prize. The strength of the place, its great numbers of people and warlike stores might have bid defiance to an army of ten times our force, had they known their business, but as it was their first war, their inexperience was accordingly." 1

General William Draper

The East India Company in Madras, planned to install a fellow civil servant as the colony's new governor. If anything, the decision to maintain the colony's status quo was clearly seen as an indication that neither the Company nor General William Draper and Admiral Samuel Cornish had any intention of retaining the Spanish possession once a treaty was signed with Spain at the end of the Seven Year's War. No doubt, the British understood that they would be occupying the Spanish territory for a short period of time. With this foregone conclusion, they had obviously no wish to implement any drastic alterations to the governance of the colony. The only major condition they stipulated was the requirement that all Spanish residents of Manila pledge their allegiance to George III, and this was carried out on 25 October 1762.

While Draper and Cornish were making the earliest decisions concerning the newly acquired colony, it was the East India Company's civil servant, Dawsonne Drake, who was appointed to the position of deputy and provisional governor of Manila. As the first British governor of the colony, he had arrived in the Philippines with the fleet. He remained aboard one of the British ships until Draper captured Manila. Four days after this event, he came ashore for the first time.

Shirley Fish

Dawsonne Drake – First British Governor of the Philippines

Little is known about Dawsonne Drake other than the fact that he lived most of his life in Madras. Born to George and Sophia Drake in 1724, his father may have also been employed by the East India Company in India. At the age of eighteen, he was hired as a civil servant by the Company and served as a writer in Madras. In 1755, at the age of thirty-one, whilst employed as the manager of the East India Company post at Devilotai, he became entangled in a dispute with the Company's directors. Apparently, when ordered to a new posting in Sumatra, where he was to assist in sorting out various administrative irregularities, he refused to move to the island. Claiming ill health, he was dismissed. His refusal to leave India for Sumatra was based upon the fact that that he had learned that the island was then considered an extremely unhealthy place. It was difficult for Europeans to survive the rigors of the climate and the environment. But despite the fact that he refused to leave India and had temporarily hurt his career, he was later reinstated possibly due to the assistance of influential friends or relatives employed by the Company.

According to the instructions Draper received from the directors of the Company in Madras, he was to turn the capital over to Drake once the invasion had been successfully completed. It was not until the passage of twenty-five days that Draper was finally prepared to carry out the wishes of the Company. However, during a meeting with Draper, the new governor insisted that he and the members of the Manila Council would be given complete control of the colony's government and the military. The Manila Council, assigned by the Company directors to support the newly established British trade post, consisted of fellow civil servants, Henry Brooks, Claude Russell, John Lewin Smith and Samuel Johnson, who was also appointed to the position of secretary for the Council. Draper consented to Drake's request, as the Company had not instructed him otherwise. He could not foresee any difficulties arising by agreeing with Drake's wishes. However, the hastily made decision set the stage for a multitude of misunderstandings, which occurred later on between the governor and members of the Manila Council, as well as with the commanders in charge of the navy and the army.

A lavish ceremony was arranged to install Drake as the colony's deputy governor. The ritual followed a similar protocol established in India during the installation of highly placed officials to prominent positions within the Company hierarchy. Draper, Cornish, Drake and members of the Manila Council marched to the Governor's Palace where British soldiers fired a 15-gun salute for the dignitaries. The entire British military corps attended the ceremony along with Archbishop Rojo, the Royal Audiencia, as well as the principal members of the Spanish community.

But just as soon as the ceremonies ended that very festive day, Drake began to experience the first of a long list of difficulties, and these were to plague his entire term as governor. Not only was he confronted by angry Spaniards in Manila, who refused to accept his authority as governor of the colony, but he also had to contend with the rogue Spanish government operating in the provinces under the command of Simon Anda. Early on, he had an inkling that managing the colony was going to be more difficult than he had anticipated. There were Spaniards in the government and in the military, as well as civilians, who were supporting Simon Anda's efforts to destabilize and oust the British from the country. They were supplying Anda with provisions and information concerning the day-to-day activities of the British naval and military forces. Many Spaniards fled to Anda's camp where they joined in guerrilla activities organized against the British.

In addition to the obstacles posed by Spaniards in the government, military or civilians, an especially disrupting force turned out to be the Spanish clerics. Even though they had initially agreed to cooperate with the British according to the terms of the surrender agreement, they soon did everything they could to undermine Drake's ability to govern the colony. The friars and their activities against the new administration were particularly problematic. Friars could be found in the numerous towns and villages of the archipelago where they had the most influence and held sway over the sentiments of the native population. Through their resistance activities, they were able to rally Filipinos to support their efforts to destabilize British rule in Manila. The friars fomented an environment based on fear by telling Filipinos, who by that time had become devoted Catholics, that the British were intent on eliminating their religious beliefs.

But no matter how disturbing the activities of the Spaniards posed for the new governor, what was to cause him the most grief was his frustrating relationship with his fellow Englishmen. As Drake had never had any military training, or a basic understanding of the men who chose a career in the military or navy, this became a sore point amongst the British officers. Consequently, Drake was seen as being a man from a different world and opposite to everything the officers stood for as career naval and military men. However, Drake was now in control of both the military and navy, with the blessings of General Draper. Those English officers still remaining in the colony were acrimoniously angered by the impropriety of the governor's jurisdiction over them. Disagreements arose on a daily basis between the governor and the officers. These, in turn, became a source of growing aggravation for Drake and his perceived inability to properly govern the colony. But as Archbishop Rojo was still managing the daily activities of running the government of the Philippines, Drake's position as deputy governor may have been perceived as being one of show rather than substance.

The East India Company in Manila

Nonetheless, Drake was determined to turn the colony into a profitable venture for the East India Company. He organized the first British civil government of Manila, placing Peter Poveny to the position of Mayor of Manila, while Lieutenant MacKane was his adjutant. William Stevenson was appointed City Engineer and an Englishman who was a resident of the Chinese community for twenty years, James Kennedy, was appointed the Administrator of the Parian. Kennedy had become quite friendly with the residents of the Parian and was very familiar with the culture of the Chinese living there. With approximately 7,000 Chinese inhabitants in the Parian, Kennedy retained the system of governance the Chinese already had in place, but appointed a number of Chinese officials or *Cabecillas* who served as constables and reported directly to him.

The Manila Council monitored the governor's activities in the colony and reported back to the President and Council of Fort St. George in Madras. As Drake governed Manila and Cavite he had almost complete authority in the two cities. However, in certain matters, he still needed to share authority with the Manila Council. Three committees had been created to oversee the governance of the colony and these included the Committee of Accounts, Committee of Works, and a Committee of Appeals. A number of junior civil servants served within the committees and these included William Goodlad, Francis Jourdan, John Nodes, Nathaniel Barlow, Richard Fyfe, Rector Mackay, Quintin Crawfurd, John Spratt and Henry Parsons.

Moreover, several of the Council members assumed other duties in the governance of the colony. For example, Quintin Crawfurd was in charge of Manila's sanitation and had the responsibility of making sure the city's streets and buildings were kept in a state of tidiness. There were three Frenchmen residing in Manila who were also assigned to positions in the government. One of these, Francis Allegue, formerly employed by the Spanish government, was hired to assist the Engineer William Stevenson. The other two Frenchmen, Edouard Wogan and a gentleman by the name of Guion, were hired as interpreters. A special court known as the *Choultry* was established to handle petty cases of less than one hundred dollars. Three councilors were assigned to oversee the court's activities and cases were heard every Wednesday.

The East India Company settlement had two primary objectives. The first was to establish and promote trade in the archipelago and throughout the region. Secondly, it was to add to the Company's profits. But these two goals became difficult to attain as the invasion had essentially ended, if only temporarily, the Manila galleon trade. And this trade had become up to that point the main business of the Spanish colony. Thus, by demanding the four million dollar ransom, the city's coffers were emptied and the Spaniards had relinquished their valuables and cash in an attempt to fulfill the ransom demand. Even the city's charitable funds had been turned over to the Manila Council by the religious institutions. In addition to the inability to obtain the full ransom and concentrate on expanding trade, the British also had to contend with Anda's resistance movement, which was becoming increasingly problematic. Consequently, the country whilst under British rule, was not able to conduct as much trade as was initially anticipated.

An effort was made to encourage trade in the Philippines especially amongst the Chinese merchants who were the main businessmen in this field. The Manila Council appointed one of its members, John Smith, who was later replaced by Henry Parsons, to act as the colony's Customs Collector. In March 1763, the Council removed an impediment to trade by reducing the customs duties to a fixed amount of five percent. But the measure meant that the Council had to make do with lower revenues for the daily expenses of the colony. By 1763, the total customs duties received amounted to $4,324. In comparison, the Spaniards had annually received approximately $29,920 in combined customs duties and anchorage fees. Nevertheless, the measure was heartily received by the Chinese merchants. Additionally, a commercial treaty was signed with the Sultan of the Sulu Islands to foster trade with the Muslims.

The governor encouraged a growth in trade between the Philippines and China. In a letter to Thomas Fitzhugh, of the East India Company in Canton, Drake requested that the Chinese merchants there resume their trade with Manila. In reply Fitzhugh said, "We *have been informed by the Chinese of the benevolent treatment of their countrymen met with when the place was taken and assured them that their Junks from Amoy or any other Ports in China will have all possible encouragement in their trade to Manila and find many advantages they were strangers to, while it was in possession of the Spaniards."* 2

The governor prepared a list of the commodities available in the archipelago, which could be sold in markets across the Asian region. These included wheat, tobacco, cacao, rice, coconuts, various types of wood products, cotton, pepper, cordage, indigo, sugar, and gold. Drake pointed out that while the islands did not produce large quantities of spices, these could be cultivated in the archipelago. The East India Company was already aware that some spices grew wild on the island of Mindanao from reports provided by Dampier and Dalrymple, so there was the possibility of developing a spice industry of their own in the islands. With regard to the cordage, Drake pointed out that this product was the best of its kind and used in India. Another valuable product was indigo, which had never been produced in large quantities by the Spaniards. On the other hand, the British were aware of its potential as an export from the Philippines.

To further boost trade and increase the production of commodities, the governor set up a number of monopolies. They were allowed to operate for one year at a time, and the monopolies had been offered to the highest bidder. Monopolies were established for the sale and production of commodities such as betelnut, wine, and pork. All three products were then the major exports from the Philippines. Two of the bidders for the monopolies were Chinese Christians, Miguel Onguison and Diego Poqua, who were both allowed to trade in the sale of wine and betelnuts. Nevertheless, the revenues the Manila Council derived from the monopolies was small compared to the revenues previously collected by the Spaniards.

During the earliest months of British rule, only a minimal amount of trade was conducted with this new East India Company settlement of Manila. Four Chinese junks arrived from Amoy with a cargo of iron pans, inferior chinaware and fruits. No customs duties had been imposed upon the cargoes of the vessels to encourage other Chinese merchants to travel to Manila. Later, merchants arrived from Madagascar with a cargo valued at $2,000. Other vessels arriving from the Asian region with trade goods had to pay similar customs duties as those imposed in Madras.

Trade with Madras was conducted on a limited basis with a small quantity of Indian fabrics shipped to Manila by the East India Company. In May 1763, a consignment of sundry goods arrived in the Philippines – shipped aboard the *Houghton* by Nicholas Morse for Francis Barnewall in Manila. A number of other ships began to regularly arrived in Manila from Madras, but the vessels mainly carried Company dispatches, military supplies, medicines and food items including Madeira wines, beef and butter for the Englishmen, as well as funds to help pay for the colony's expenses.

Monthly expenditures had been steadily increasing due to a number of factors including the maintenance of the garrisons in Manila and Pasig, as well as the costly repairs of various vessels at the Cavite naval yard. Cavite's paymaster, John Nodes, reported that the repairs and the provisioning of vessels had become a drain on the Manila Council's treasury. During the period from May to October 1763, a total of $12,960 had been spent on repairs and provisions for the ships.

Adding to the increasing expenditures was the need to organize military forays against Simon Anda's army in the provinces. These had turned into costly ventures, but were absolutely essential in order to check the movements of the resistance movement. Anda had become a threat to the security of the British settlements in Manila and Cavite. The Manila Council had also inherited the expenditures of operating the Spanish government in the archipelago. Prior to the arrival of the British in Manila, the colony was already hard pressed for funds to cover its annual expenses. As the British failed to capture the *Filipino*, the subsidy sent aboard that vessel could not be used to pay their increasing expenses.

Initially, the Manila Council had to make due with the 100,000 rupees supplied to them by the Madras Presidency to cover the costs of running the Philippine government. As this sum was soon exhausted, they had no choice but to make a list of all the taxes, customs duties, anchorage fees and other charges which had been previously supplied to the Spanish Royal Treasury in Manila, and which they now hoped to collect to finance the colony's expenses. The Spanish government had derived its revenue from the taxes received from the Spanish estates and mostly paid by Filipinos, the issuance of gaming licenses, and the production of areca, betel nuts and wine. As Draper stated while still in the colony, he proclaimed that the Filipinos would no longer be subjected or required to pay taxes while the British administered the colony. As a result, the Manila Council was aware that it could not expect to receive any revenues from that sector, consequently, it had to locate alternative sources of revenue.

The estates and houses of the Augustinian friars, who opposed the British, were confiscated. Forty-four houses were seized and leased to new occupants. An attempt was made to rent out the estates, but it was impossible to find tenants. No Spaniard was willing to risk the ire of the friars by becoming a tenant of land previously owned by the clergy. Ultimately, the British allowed Filipinos to farm the land. A Spaniard, Juan de la Puga, was hired to manage the estates for the British.

Another drain on the Manila Council's revenues was the fact that Archbishop Rojo had again requested that the British pay the salaries of the Spanish civil and military personnel employed by the Spanish government. Bills had been issued to the British indicating that the Madrid government would reimburse the East India Company for the financial outlays. During the months of February 1763 to September 1763, Rojo requested a total of $24,190 from the British to pay the salaries of government employees.

To check the spread of counterfeit Spanish currency, Governor Drake and the Manila Council issued copper coins bearing the East India Company's coat of arms. These were used as the main currency in the colony, but Indian rupees were also introduced as a mode of exchange for goods to counteract the effects of the fake coinage proliferating in Manila.

In order to raise additional funds for the government's treasury, Drake sold the colony's surpluses of beef, salted fish and rice, which were kept at the city's storehouses. The storekeeper, William Goodlad, sold sacks of rice to Chinese traders for $5,985, which was then turned over to the treasury. Moreover, the property of other Spaniards loyal to Simon Anda, including Mexican soldiers, Spaniards such as Leandro de Viana, Francisco Villacorta and the Marquis de Montecastro, all of whom had fled to join the resistance movement were confiscated and sold.

The contents of the libraries of the Augustinian convents were sold off at public auctions. Books and other items confiscated from the convents were sold for $1,000. In one instance, various documents were not auctioned off, but later turned up in the hands of the East India Company civil servant, Alexander Dalrymple. In his possession were a number of important documents and collections of papers from the seventeenth and eighteenth century related to the Philippines and the Roman Catholic missions in Asia. These had been originally seized from the Augustinian convent of San Pablo in Manila.

Funds were also borrowed from East India Company ships anchoring at Manila Bay in route to Canton. The Manila Council approached the captains of the *Hector, Houghton,* and the *Hawke* for loans. In another letter to the East India Company representative at Canton, Thomas Fitzhugh, the governor mentioned that 600,000 rupees had been borrowed from the captains to meet the expenses of the Manila Council until June 1764. In addition to obtaining loans from the ships' captains, the Manila Council resorted to borrowing funds from private individuals including merchants.

"In June 1763, Francis Barnewall, the supercargo of the Sabut Jung, a country trading vessel, advanced a loan of 12,000 Spanish dollars. The Manila Council again obtained from Barnewall and his associate, Luis Carvalho, the amount of 3,850 Spanish dollars to be paid at Madras at the rate of ten pagodas per Spanish dollar with 'an additional 5 percent premium.' On another occasion, the Armenian merchants in Manila loaned 40,000 Spanish dollars to be paid at Madras within thirty days upon the presentation of a bill of exchange at the rate of 15 ½ Spanish dollars per ten pagodas." [3]

Although Drake tried to increase the colony's foreign and domestic trade, he was continuously confronted by a number of daily obstacles, which jeopardized his plans. His administration's shaky start had evolved into a contentious relationship with Admiral Cornish. When Cornish was informed of the governor's plan to select a new commander for Cavite, the admiral was enraged. Cornish had become quite comfortably entrenched at Cavite, where he was essentially running the fortification and port. No one had questioned his activities there, so the news of the governor's intentions was not only surprising, but also demeaning.

The governor had completely disregarded the admiral's presence and activities at the port city. In a letter to the governor, Cornish indicated his willingness to continue as commander of Cavite. Finally, the governor, probably at the insistence of the Manila Council, agreed to allow Cornish to remain as the commander of port city. But despite this, the admiral had felt slighted by the disagreeable inference that someone of Drake's choosing would be selected to replace him. No doubt, his anger was also compounded by the disturbing factor that he too was compelled to take orders from a civilian.

Annoyed by the incident, the admiral informed the governor that General Draper had acted too soon when he turned the colony over to him. Moreover, the decision had been prematurely made without his consent. According to Cornish, the East India Company had clearly stipulated in their instructions to the commanders that the colony was not to be handed over to Drake until the entire country had been conquered, which he rightly claimed was not the case. As only the cities of Manila and Cavite had been captured, the rest of the country still remained completely out of their control. Moreover, the provinces were in the hands of the rebellious Simon Anda.

While they had been successful in seizing Manila and Cavite, the invasion of the country had not been completed. Perhaps in his own way, Admiral Cornish was attempting to inform the governor that technically, he was not in a position to dictate orders to the military or naval officers given that premise.

While the matter was still under dispute, another area of contention arose between the admiral and the governor. This time Cornish heatedly addressed the question of the still unpaid ransom. When it came to actually paying the ransom, the Spaniards were conspicuously stalling as long as they could. They insisted that they did not have the resources to pay the remaining ransom. They also claimed that the British would have to wait for the *Filipino* galleon to arrive in order to receive the remaining ransom balance.

Even though the amount was agreed to in the surrender agreement signed to by both parties, the Spaniards were reluctant to pay any additional funds to the British. It is likely that their reluctance to pay the ransom was due to the seizure of the outgoing galleon, *Santissima Trinidad* as the Chinese and Spanish investors incurred massive losses with the capture of the galleon and seizure of her cargo. The cargo had a value of more than three million dollars, which was confiscated by the British. Given this, the total value of the cargo could have been included, as part of the ransom, but this was not the case. The British commanders refused to consider the seized ship and cargo as part of their ransom demand.

The archbishop collected cash, jewels and other valuables from the Spanish community, but Drake was still exasperated by the smaller than expected amount offered to him. In a strongly worded letter addressed to the archbishop, the Spanish citizens of Manila and to the various religious orders, Drake urged that they immediately comply with the surrender terms and pay the ransom balance. The letter succeeded in obtaining an additional $20,771, but this was still far from the amount demanded by the Manila Council. The governor then decided to meet with Archbishop Rojo and other leading members of the Spanish community and religious orders where he insisted upon knowing, why they continued to refuse paying the entire ransom due to the British. *"Their reasons for such behavior and what measures they propose failing upon to comply with that part of the capitulation representing to them at the same time their great backwardness on this occasion is but a bad return for the Generous and Mild Treatment they met."* 4

The Manila Council appointed Thomas Parry and Charles Pimbla of the British Royal Navy with the responsibility of collecting funds from the Spaniards. They managed to collect an additional $459,420 in cash and valuables from the archbishop, the Cathedral of Manila, the churches of St. Dominic, Quiapo, Ermita and the religious orders of Saint Francis, Saint Augustan and Saint Dominic. Funds were also received from the Obras Pias (Misericordia), the Society of Jesus and the funds belonging to an individual by the name of Varela. An additional sum of $48,797 was also collected from various Spanish families.

By early January 1763, Admiral Cornish was losing his patience. He insisted that forceful measures were needed to convince the Spaniards to pay the ransom. He felt that they had the resources to do so no matter what excuses they gave. The admiral thought that by threatening to send his soldiers to once again loot and plunder Manila and Cavite, it would force the people especially the Chinese to contribute a larger share of the ransom.

The residents of the city and suburbs had already suffered tremendously as a result of the rampaging soldiers and when their homes were first looted. As far as Governor Drake was concerned, the possibility of allowing this to happen once again seemed unreasonable. The governor managed to convince Admiral Cornish to instead accept Archbishop Rojo's proposal that the balance would be paid by the Spanish Crown and the Royal Treasury in Madrid and whatever they seized aboard the *Filipino*, would go towards the ransom payment. The Manila Council was also looking forward to seizing the treasure once the ship was located, but this was a factor that would allude them. In any case, the Spaniards made an additional payment to the Manila Council of $23,853 in valuables and $7,000 in silver.

By this time, Admiral Cornish was anxious to leave the colony and return to Madras. He was needed in India to assist in the protection of the Company's settlements there, but no doubt, he was also eager to get as far away as possible from the troublesome governor. With this in mind, he sought to resolve the ransom dilemma as quickly as possible. He offered a number of ideas on how to compel the Spaniards into paying the remaining ransom, but the governor adamantly opposed each of his suggestions. The admiral then offered a plan whereby the Chinese residents of the city would be forced to contribute a larger share of the ransom, but the governor once again objected as he refused to create any type of disturbance within the Chinese community.

With no further reason for remaining in the country and the growing animosity between the two men, the admiral rushed to prepare his fleet for its return journey to Madras. By this time, the governor, realizing that the admiral had every intention of taking his entire fleet back to India, urgently requested that Cornish at least leave a few ships in the colony for its defense. But Cornish testily replied, "*I have this moment received your very extraordinary letter ... without giving the President and Council leave to judge of my zeal for the public service I am to acquaint you that in consequence of my Instructions, when the squadron is refitted, I shall proceed with my whole force to Madras."* [5]

The governor was all too aware of the fact that if he was to retain and protect Britain's fragile hold of the colony, it was necessary to give the appearance of its having a strong military presence. But how was he to retain the colony if the admiral insisted upon taking his entire fleet back to Madras? The dilemma was resolved when Admiral Cornish changed his mind at the last moment and decided, to the relief of the governor, to leave a small contingent of naval ships and soldiers to defend both Manila and Cavite.

But the small force was not large enough to effectively extend Britain's influence to the regions beyond the capital and port city. In fact, the British soldiers remaining in both Manila and Cavite, were barely able to defend the two major cities. Only a few villages located just outside Manila and Cavite had been seized, and the British were not able to expand beyond these two captured areas to the provinces or other islands as they lacked soldiers and weapons.

A preliminary attempt was made, however, to set the stage for the establishment of trade settlements in Mindanao and the Sulu Islands. With this in mind and to foster friendlier ties with the Muslims, Drake signed a treaty on 23 February 1763 with Sultan Alimud Din I. The sultan had become a prisoner of the Spaniards prior to the arrival of the British fleet. The treaty provided the Sultanate of Jolo in the Sulu Islands and the East India Company with a mutually binding agreement to assist each other defensively.

In addition, the treaty contained the following points. The sultan and his successors would provide the East India Company with land upon which they could establish an outpost consisting of factories and forts. The East India Company would acknowledge the sultan's sovereignty and show respect for the Muslim culture and Islamic religion. Muslims would allow the British to conduct free trade in the Sultanate of Jolo. And if the sultanate was attacked, the British were expected to come to their assistance. Conversely, the sultanate stated that they would provide soldiers to the British, if they continued to occupy Manila and were attacked by an enemy.

Archbishop Rojo objected to the treaty as he claimed it was counter to the surrender agreement signed by the Spaniards and the British. It was the archbishop's contention that the Spaniards had already signed an agreement of their own with the sultan prior to the arrival of the British. In that treaty, the Muslims had agreed to turn over to the Spanish colonial government the islands of Palawan and Basilan, as well as the northern section of Borneo. Nevertheless, the British were intent on establishing trade settlements in Mindanao and in the Sulu Islands.

The Cesar Fayette Incident

Another dilemma faced by Cornish and Drake concerned the Frenchman, Cesar Fayette. He had been in the employ of the Spanish government, where he was involved in efforts to defend the capital against the British offensive. Due to his role in the conflict, Cornish felt that it was necessary to take some sort of legal action against him. But the admiral also had a personal grudge against Fayette, which led to his pursuing the matter. He was informed of letters Fayette wrote to two acquaintances in the Dutch colony of Java in which he had made some disparaging remarks about the admiral. According to the historian Zuniga, Fayette had referred to the admiral as being nothing more than a pirate or criminal. The admiral was incensed and ordered the immediate arrest of Fayette. Cornish had every intention of transporting Fayette to Madras to be tried. But by this time, Fayette had become a personal advisor to the governor and was under his protection at the Governor's Palace in Manila.

When the admiral became aware that the governor was harboring the Frenchman at his residence, Cornish was so infuriated that he considered creating an incident, which would impact upon the governor's ability to govern the colony. One idea he considered carrying out was to create a disturbance in the Chinese community, but after calming down a bit, he decided to concentrate on getting the fleet ready for its return to Madras. Rather than being continuously involved in one squabble after the other with the governor, Cornish thought it prudent to leave the colony as soon as possible. Once back in India, he would officially accuse Drake of misconduct and request that the East India Company begin an immediate investigation into the governor's activities in Manila.

Prior to returning to Madras on 2 March 1763, Admiral Cornish placed Captain Brereton of the *HMS Falmouth* in charge of the Cavite squadron. Unfortunately for Captain Brereton and Major Fell of the 79th Regiment and commandant of Manila, the two officers were destined to inherit the Fayette problem, as well as the continuing saga of difficulties with the governor.

Immediately upon arriving in Madras, Admiral Cornish notified the directors of the East India Company of the need to arrest Fayette and bring him to justice. This was followed up with instructions being sent to Drake by the Company directors in which, he was ordered to arrest Fayette and to hand him over to Captain Brereton. The captain acknowledged that he too had received instructions to arrest Fayette and requested the governor's cooperation in the matter saying in a letter to him, *"If you have any Honor, or hope to have Your Word given any Credit to, I expect you will immediately cause the said Mr. Faillet* (Fayette) *to be given up."* 6

However, instead of complying with Brereton's appeal for the governor's cooperation, Drake was angered by the request and chose to verbally insult the captain. In a fit of pettiness, Drake did not reply directly to Brereton but instead wrote to another naval officer where he stated, *"You may tell Captain Brereton that when he learns how to write with more politeness and respect and as becoming a gentlemen to another, he may expect to have letters answered and paid some attention to, but till he does he may expect that himself and his correspondence will be treated with the contempt they deserve."* 7

Captain Brereton and Major Fell agreed that if given no choice in the matter, force would be used to arrest Fayette. Major Fell ordered Captain DuPont of the 79th Regiment to arrest Fayette, but as soon as he was informed of the arrest order, Drake had it rescinded. The governor hurriedly convened a meeting of the Manila Council where it was decided to arrest Major Fell and replace him with Captain Thomas Backhouse.

That same evening, Major Fell, accompanied by his soldiers went to the Governor's Palace to arrest Fayette. As he ascended the palace staircase, he met the governor who was on his way down. The two men began arguing over the arrest of Fayette and Drake became so violent that he took his sword and was about to attack Major Fell. Stumbling backwards along the staircase, Major Fell had just missed the governor's lunge. In one rapid move, the major was able to quickly take a musket from one of his soldiers and was about to shoot the governor, when the two men were separated by the accompanying soldiers. During the scuffle, several of Major Fell's soldiers had already found Fayette, who was hiding in one of the upper

Shirley Fish

rooms of the Governor's Palace. He was immediately placed under arrest and was taken away to Captain Brereton's ship for transport to Madras.

Soon after the Fayette incident, the governor sent his soldiers to Cavite to arrest Major Fell. The governor intended to send the major to Madras to be tried, for as far as he was concerned, it was Major Fell who had furiously attacked him. He angrily said that the major's actions were unpardonable and *"carry mutiny throughout."*8 Major Fell, on the other hand, was already beginning to regret having been provoked by the governor. He realized that his counter-attack against the governor, albeit in self-defense, would be condemned back in Madras by the Company's directors.

Due to the ensuing disputes over the Fayette matter, and disappointed with his inability to come to Major Fell's aid when arrested by the governor's soldiers, Captain Brereton resigned from his post as commandant of Cavite. He was still the commander of the *HMS Falmouth,* anchored in Manila Bay, but from that point onwards he extended as little cooperation as he could to the governor. His actions also ensured that the British Royal Navy would remain a separate entity whilst in the Philippines. No doubt, the governor and the Manila Council were frustrated and annoyed by the stance of the naval officers as both continued to dictate policies to the uncooperative naval officers, which were largely ignored.

Thus, with Admiral Cornish, Major Fell and Captain Brereton out of the way, Governor Drake was now in complete control of Manila and Cavite. He was essentially free to do as he pleased without any opposition except by the Manila Council. But his difficulties continued. The military and naval officers disagreed with Drake's controversial methods of governing the colony. As each officer and the governor tried to outmaneuver the other, the tense, hostile situation festered throughout the entire period of British rule in Manila and Cavite. This environment of mutual antagonism ensured that very little of any consequence was established in the colony.

Simon de Anda y Salazar's Resistance Movement

As a member of Manila's Royal Audiencia, where he served as a judge, the fifty-three year old Simon Anda reported directly to Archbishop Rojo. Born in the town of Subijiana, province of Alva, in Spain on 23 October 1709, Anda's full name was Simon de Anda y Salazar. His parents, Juan de Anda and Francisca Lopez de Armentia, were members of the Spanish aristocracy and as such, were in a position to provide their son with an exceptional education. He received a doctorate from the University of Alcala in Civil Law and began practicing his profession in Madrid. The Spanish king appointed him to the position of judge for the Philippines where he arrived in Manila on 21 July 1761.

The news was quickly spreading throughout the British ranks, that Simon Anda was amassing an enormous army in the provinces. This had become a worrying factor for the British in the capital. But in reality, the number of professional soldiers in Anda's army was greatly exaggerated and the men recruited by the Spaniards, albeit with little choice in the matter, were mostly simple farming folk. However, the British had no way of knowing this, and prepared where they could their defenses for the worst possible scenario.

Simon Anda had succeeded in frightening Filipinos and Spaniards by claiming that the British were intent on ridding the country of Catholicism. He urged them to join his resistance movement in order to prevent this from happening. Anda made an effort to ensure peace in the provinces and especially in those communities where Filipino and Chinese sympathies leaned towards the British. The various revolts launched by these two groups were met with opposition from Anda's forces.

To appease the disgruntled Filipinos, who would otherwise join the British, he regulated the salaries of laborers and fixed the prices for commodities and, *"He discouraged the manufacture and sale of wines and imposed heavy penalties on drunkenness. He issued directives to the troops prohibiting looting, extortion, and immoral conduct. He outlawed cockfighting, card playing, and other forms of gambling, and prescribed the death penalty for theft. He imposed severe penalties on persons caught collaborating with the enemy, counterfeiting the currency, and chipping the silver pesos. Moreover, he stopped the collection of tribute, the imposition of forced labor, and welcomed monetary and material contributions to the cause as well as volunteers to fight for God and the king."* 9

According to Anda, once Manila was seized, the archibishop had essentially become a prisoner of war. Therefore, he no longer recognized Rojo as the legitimate governor of the colony. Consequently, on 6 October 1762, Simon Anda issued a public notice in which he proclaimed that he was the legitimate Spanish governor and president of the Royal Audiencia of the Philippines.

Under the circumstances, Anda felt justified in taking this course of action based upon the Spanish Laws the *Recopilacion de las Leyes de Indias*, established in 1620-29. In the laws it was stipulated that the governance of the colony could be conferred upon whoever was left in the government, even a judge, if the governor died while in office or was absent from duty. As the other judges, Villacorta and Galban were similarly under imprisonment by the British in Manila, it was only Anda who remained to organize and manage the Spanish government in the provinces. There were several Royal Decrees of 1720, 1731 and 1761 overriding the laws established in the seventeenth century whereby the rule of government would have passed to the Filipino born Spaniard, Bishop Miguel Lino de Espeleta, but Anda ignored this fact. Espeleta, based in Cebu, had already served as a temporary governor in Manila until the appointment of Archbishop Rojo assumed the post.

Anda's proclamation was received with mixed blessings. For the Filipinos of Pampanga, a courageous people although rounded up by the Spaniards for their army whether they wanted to or not, the Spaniards were thought as not having provided much of a defense for their soldiers. As a result, the better-trained and equipped British soldiers were basically in a position to annihilate the Filipinos. It had been only through the persistence of the church friars, that the Filipinos were persuaded to fight on behalf of the Spaniards.

"Many Spaniards, too, joined his cause. Most of the Spanish friars, including Augustinians, Dominicans, and Franciscans, supported him. Many distinguished Spaniards who accepted the terms of Manila's surrender and pledged never to take up arms against the British, violated their word of honor by secretly escaping from Manila and joined Anda's camp in Bacolor. Among them were two oidores of the Royal Audiencia, Francisco de Villacorta and Manuel Galban; Royal Fiscal Francisco Leandro de Viana; Jose Pedro Busto, Spanish engineer in the iron mines of Angat (Bulacan); and Marques de Monteclaro." [10]

But no matter how persistent Anda was in his attempts to convince the British that he was the legitimate governor of the Spanish colonial government, he was never accepted as being so by the English commanders. Instead, to the Manila Council, Anda had become an outlaw and placed a bounty on his head of $5,000 for his capture. Even though he insisted on being called by the title of governor, the British refused to acknowledge Anda's claim. This in turn, became a source of continuous annoyance to Anda. The British addressed Anda as simply a member of the Royal Audiencia, the Visitor of the Provinces and the Lieutenant of the Captain-General and Governor Archbishop Rojo. In retaliation for the reward for his arrest, Anda offered $10,000 for each of the men responsible for issuing the bounty for his capture. This included Governor Drake and the members of the Manila Council, Smith and Brooks.

Frustrated by the British policy of consistently ignoring his claims of legitimacy, Anda announced that this was due to the fact that English officers knew nothing of Spanish laws. Nevertheless, as the East India Company had already installed their own civil servant as governor in Manila, this meant that the archbishop had become subservient to the British even though he continued to administer the daily activities of the colony. Archbishop Rojo still reported to Governor Drake and to the Manila

Council. They decided all the major decisions for Manila and Cavite, or at least in those areas that they were controlling.

The Manila Council asked Archbishop Rojo to try to convince Anda to surrender to them. But the archbishop's pleas to the rebellious Spaniard went unheeded. Instead, Anda now looked upon the archbishop as a traitor to Spain. After this last communication between the two men, their relationship remained hostile and this continued until Archbishop Rojo's death in January 1764.

While Simon Anda was in Pampanga, he came into possession of the silver from the *Filipino* galleon. With a value of $2,253,111, the treasurer who was employed by the Spanish colonial government, Nicolas de Echauz, delivered the silver to Anda's camp, whilst the British were in the process of seizing Manila.

But it is highly improbable that the galleon's captain would have released the silver for use by the resistance movement. More than likely, the silver was held for the Spanish and Chinese investors in payment of their shipments sent to Mexico the previous year. However, Anda was unquestionably in possession of the subsidy sent to Manila each year by the Mexican viceroy for the colony's expenses. These funds may have been used for military purposes such as purchasing weapons from Chinese merchants. Just how much was actually spent on buying weapons is unclear as the evidence indicates that most Filipino soldiers continued to fight the British using bamboo bows, arrows and spears. Despite this, Anda was able to raise an army of approximately 10,000 men, the majority of whom were totally inexperienced. Two thousand of the recruits in Anda's army had been allegedly armed with European weapons. The military units, composed of natives were commanded by Filipinos such as the Marshal of the Camp, Francisco de San Juan and Colonel Santos de los Angeles, who were appointed to the positions by Anda.

Although the British commanders might have been concerned about the large number of Filipino soldiers in Anda's army, what worried them the most was the threat posed by the 300 highly trained French soldiers who deserted their garrisons to join Anda. The British, during the Anglo-French wars in India, captured the Frenchmen. When the French prisoners were recruited for the campaign in the Philippines, they had no sense of loyalty towards France's longtime enemy, Britain. During the siege of Manila, they were already planning to desert the British camps. They intended to become aligned to Anda in a bid to gain their freedom. Unfortunately, some of the first French soldiers to flee from Manila to Anda were intercepted by Filipino soldiers who were unaware of their plan to escape from the British army. When they encountered the fleeing French soldiers, the Filipinos attacked and killed them.

"A French sergeant, a very clever and intelligent man, informed Anda of the friendly intention of the Frenchmen. He replied that he would facilitate their desertion; but Anda neglected to act in the matter, with the result that the first men who undertook that perilous enterprise were slaughtered, almost under the walls of the city, by Anda's native troops, who did not recognize them and gave them no quarter. One may well imagine that this mishap considerably dampened the ardour of the others. The sergeant complained to Anda that he had evidently failed to give orders so that the deserters, upon leaving Manila, should be met by natives to guide them in safety to his army."[11]

As Draper became aware of the French soldiers' plan to desert his army, he kept them under close surveillance to prevent their running away. When Manila was taken, it was only then that an opportunity arose for the Frenchmen to carry out their plans. They had been assigned to patrol and guard duties and these assignments provided a chance for them to flee from the British camps. With regard to the French desertions, Draper commented, *"the troops belonging to the East India Company who were sent to compose a part of these garrisons of Manila and Cavite being mostly Frenchmen have deserted in great numbers to assist malcontents who are in arms in the country and the rest."*[12] He had suggested that the Frenchmen be removed from the islands leaving only British soldiers in the Manila garrison.

But before the Frenchmen could desert their posts, the British officers mustered the entire army, with the remaining 130 French soldiers positioned at the center of the assembly. They were quickly disarmed and their uniforms stripped away. The French soldiers were then taken aboard one of the British ships for transport back to Madras. In addition to the French soldiers, 312 Mexican soldiers (prisoners), and Sepoys were transported to India. The Sepoys had also been periodically deserting the British army as they were angered by their low wages.

One of the French soldiers, who managed to escape to Anda's camp and was a chief organizer of the desertion plan, informed the Spaniard that he was prepared to encourage the Sepoys to also desert the British. But Anda rejected the offer. He was not interested in recruiting the mostly Muslim Indian soldiers. To his mind, they fell into the same category as the Muslims the Spaniards had bitterly fought against in the Spanish peninsula. Anda refused their assistance even though his resistance movement could have benefited by adding the militarily trained Sepoys to his army. While Anda's decision was based on purely religious differences, the Frenchman realized that with the loss of the Sepoys the British commanders would have been dealt a far greater blow than any other strategy employed by Anda. Without the Sepoys, the British could not have retained the colony. Nevertheless, the Spaniards were totally against an alliance with the Muslim Indians.

In order to prevent further desertions, Governor Drake and the Manila Council enforced a number of emergency measures. Based on the advice of Major Fell and Captain Backhouse, this entailed sending Chinese soldiers who were assisting the British to patrol the Pasig River. They were ordered to intercept and capture deserters. To appease the Sepoy and Lascar soldiers, their wages were increased. A reward of $200 was offered for information on individuals urging the desertion of the soldiers in the British army. But even with the new measures in place, the number of men in the British military and navy in the Philippines were beginning to dwindle. Adding to the weakened state of the British forces in Manila and Cavite was the fact that a large contingent of soldiers and sailors had returned to Madras with Draper and Cornish. The governor and the Manila Council had retained what they considered were just enough men to hold the two cities until Madras could send out fresh reinforcements.

But another difficulty was the fact that the military and navy were continuously saddled with desertions, sickness and death of the troops due to poor diets and diseases. Many could not cope with the intense and humid heat of the tropical climate found in the archipelago. Clearly new recruits were desperately needed, but the East India Company in Madras, largely ignored the requests for reinforcements. The British military and naval garrisons found that they were left with no choice but to remain on constant alert for fear of a sudden reprisal by Anda's troops.

"With a little more time, it would have been difficult for them (the British) to have maintained their position much longer, so greatly had the number of troops at their command been reduced at the end of fifteen months' possession of Manila. Drunkenness killed a lot of their men. The intense heat, strong drink, too much fruit – particularly bananas – and abuse of women, more easily obtained in Manila perhaps than in any other place in the world, all contributed to wear them down little by little, and would have finally destroyed them ... they were kept constantly on guard for fear of a surprise. Two or three musket shots fired by the people outside the walls (of Manila) were sufficient to throw the whole city into a state of alarm. The general call to arms was sounded and in an instant all the men were in the batteries and under arms."[13]

It was likely that given more time, Anda could have raised an even larger and better-trained army. But there is no evidence that he had such a grandiose plan in mind. One point in his favor was the fact that he had the overwhelming support of Spaniards who continued to express their loyalty to the Spanish king and they, in turn, supported his plan to oust the British.

Anda's military strategy consisted of preventing the British from spreading beyond the confines of Manila and Cavite. To accomplish this and to create a state of confusion wherever possible, whilst avoiding any major confrontations with the European army, he used guerrilla tactics to engage the enemy in skirmages. He launched a number of sneak attacks against the British at Bulacan, Laguna, Rizal and Batangas. The English officers had assumed that the Spaniards were incapable of mounting any major campaigns against them, but Anda continued to wage one engagement after another without any let up.

Another ploy used to incapacitate the British was to prohibit Filipinos from provisioning their garrisons. The prices paid for the foods sold to the British garrisons by Filipino vendors had been continuously rising and was a source of much welcomed profits. Filipinos were reluctant to obey Anda's orders as the Englishmen paid handsomely for their goods. Consequently, the British set up an outpost in the town of Pasig to monitor the supply of foods destined for Manila and originating from the Laguna Bay region. To ensure that the provisions would be continuously supplied to Manila, the Pasig River was patrolled by armed vessels to thwart any attacks by Anda's soldiers.

The Manila Council fixed the prices for a number of products including rice, sugar, tobacco, salt, beef, pork, fish, milk, bread, fowls, wax, and vegetables, as well as for earthenware and shoes. The price list was posted throughout Manila and in the neighboring towns for all to easily see. The Company's civil servant, John Spratt, was assigned to monitor the activities of the Manila market and to curb black-market activities. Henry Brooks was appointed by the Manila Council to organize and manage the storage of supplies for the Manila garrison and residents to ensure a steady flow of provisions for at least a three-month period.

An offensive was launched against Anda on 8 November 1762 by Captain Thomas Backhouse. The British soldiers marched from Manila and were confronted by Anda's aide, formerly a Spanish engineer, Jose Pedro Busto and his troops at Maybunga. However, Busto's forces proved no formidable opponent and soon retreated to Marikina. Captain Backhouse made his way to Pasig, capturing the town after a conflict with many of its inhabitants. At this time, he was able to recapture the Muslim prisoner then being held by the Spaniards, Sultan of Jolo, Alimudin I.

Captain Backhouse and his soldiers then marched to Cainta and Taytay occupying both areas. At Cainta he left a contingent of Sepoys, the descendants of whom can still be found in the area. During this campaign, he learned that the cargo from the galleon the *Filipino* had been transported across land to Bantangas and Laguna. He headed in that direction in an attempt to seize the prize, but despite the fact that the Filipinos were able to block the entrance to Laguna Bay with a number of boats, this did not prevent the captain from carrying on with his mission. He encountered some resistance at Pagsanjan, and in anger the captain ordered that the town be set afire. Marching to Batangas, he soon discovered that the galleon's silver was already in the hands of Anda. In a fit of disappointment the town of Lipa was plundered and set afire.

Another English officer, Captain Slay, marched to Bulacan with a force consisting of 400 English soldiers, 2,000 Chinese, and 300 soldiers from Malabar. At Bulacan, they met with some resistance, which was easily subdued. The town was seized, plundered and the church burned. Busto's army of 8,000 men then confronted Captain Slay. The Spanish army arrived in the area and launched skirmages against the British forcing the English soldiers to retreat to Manila.

Even though the British made further inquiries into the state of affairs in the other provinces surrounding Manila, they did little to conquer these outlying regions. Without the resources of having a larger army at their disposal, the British officers could not organize any campaigns to seize the other provinces or islands. Nevertheless, they made an effort to seize the entire country if only in writing by requesting a signed statement from Archbishop Rojo, which in effect turned the entire Spanish possession over to the British crown. Once in possession of this statement, and as far as the British were concerned, this was all they needed to confirm that the entire Spanish possession was now under British rule.

In any case, as the organizers of the campaign were aware that they would eventually have to return the Philippines to Spain, there was little need or incentive to spread their influence into the provinces. Consequently, the lack of a large-scale invasion of the territories beyond Manila and Cavite provided Anda with the time he needed to organize his army. Whilst waiting for the British to conduct forays into his territory, he was able to further secure his position in the provinces as the legitimate Spanish governor of the colony.

Chapter Ten
The Filipino and Chinese Supporters of the British

"There were besides many Chinese Christians in the Parian and scattered over the provinces and almost all of them declared for the English. The moment they took possession of Manila these Chinese gave them every aid and accompanied them in all their expeditions." [1]

Zuniga

The difficulties the British experienced with Simon Anda's resistance movement had been somewhat relieved by a number of uprisings in the country. This surprising turn of events led to an interesting development as some Filipinos and Chinese decided not to support Anda's government in the provinces, but instead to become aligned to the British. One British sympathizer was the Filipino, Diego Silang.

When the British had so easily toppled the Spanish government in Manila, Silang was stunned by how rapidly the invasion and seizure of the capital had occurred. Up until that point in the history of the colony, many Filipinos had taken for granted the assumption that the Spaniards were invincible. But suddenly, they were no longer in power and this incredible development coupled with the colonial government's inability to protect its possession left many individuals such as Diego Silang completely bewildered.

It should be noted that during the entire Spanish colonial period in the Philippines, there was never a completely amicable relationship in existence between the Spaniards and the Filipinos. At best, the relationship between the two groups had been uneasy and even uncomfortable. At worst, Filipinos felt great anger and bitterness towards the Spaniards who they considered their oppressors. Filipinos resented having to pay the excessively high annual taxes imposed upon them, as well as the harsh system of arbitrary recruitment for their various work projects in the government, military and within the religious institutions. Consequently, after the British success, Filipinos began venting their anger towards the Spaniards. Some Filipinos so strongly resented the colonial government that they readily supported the British hoping they would permanently rid the country of Spanish influence.

"The natives do not appear to be fond of the Spaniards, as they have shown on a number of occasions, and quite recently during the last war, when the English came to besiege Manila. The Spaniards themselves say

now that they know it from experience. Trusting to the loyalty of the natives, almost all Manila, upon the arrival of the English, left the city to take refuge in the provinces, especially in the vicinity of the Laguna de Bay. Wherever they went they were ill treated by the natives. They were robbed, even beaten, and the women insulted to such an extent that I heard some Spaniards say that if the English were ever to come again to Manila, they would prefer to remain inside the walls." 2

Whilst at Cavite, Captain William Brereton came into contact with the Filipino leader Diego Silang and his reform movement. The two men were able to amicably discuss their mutual struggle against Simon Anda's forces. Until the advent of Diego Silang, there had never been as forceful or as charismatic a Filipino leader in the Philippines. He was able to organize a powerful and widespread campaign to oust the Spanish regime. Rousing large numbers of Filipinos to fight the Spaniards, Silang was a visionary who sought a better future for Filipinos. In essence, he had become the first Filipino to launch an independence movement even if it meant becoming aligned to the British to reach his objective.

The British-Filipino Alliance

Diego Silang was born on 16 December 1730, Ilocos Sur in the northern province of Vigan. Losing both his parents at a young age, he was raised and educated by a Spanish friar in his hometown. As an adult, he became a courier carrying important documents from the provinces to the Spanish government and church officials in Manila. When the British captured Manila and Cavite, Silang asked the Spanish government in Vigan to end the unpopular tribute tax system, as well as urging them to organize an army to confront the British interlopers. According to Silang, as Spain was unable to protect the colony, he found it necessary to raise an army to defend the country against the British invaders. The Spanish authorities were astonished by his effrontery and were strongly opposed to all of his suggestions.

To the Spaniards, Diego Silang had clearly become a disruptive element in their midst. They quickly arranged to have him arrested. He was imprisoned for only a short period of time, but once he was away from the Spanish authorities, he began to organize his fellow Filipinos against the Spanish regime. When he was arrested, Silang became embittered and enraged that he had been imprisoned after only trying to assist the colonial government in its defense against the British.

By 14 December 1762, he and his followers were able to oust the Mexican governor of the province of Ilocos, Antonio Zabala. Setting up an independent government of his own making, Silang installed a priest, Tomas

Millan, as the new governor. He then proclaimed an end to the annual taxes paid by Filipinos and the enforced labor system. The city of Vigan, became the center for his revolutionary activities and from his headquarters there, he began spreading his influence to other areas in Pangasinan and Cagayan.

The British soon learned of Diego Silang's success in overthrowing the Spanish government in the northern province of Ilocos. They were eager to communicate and meet with him as they viewed this as an opportunity to possibly join forces with the Filipino leader against Simon Anda.

Lieutenant William Russell was instructed to assist Silang and his forces by bringing to the Filipino twenty European soldiers and thirty Sepoys to aid in his efforts against the Spaniards. But by this time, Silang was troubled by a number of Spanish attacks launched against him. Moreover, Anda had demanded Silang's immediate presence in Bacolor, where he was to explain his seditious activities. However, Silang chose to ignore the order and by doing so, he became increasingly apprehensive. His sense of dread was due to the fact that many of his own followers were becoming intimidated by Anda's threat of treason against him. His followers were also concerned about his growing ties with the British. Perhaps they feared that they may have been trading one oppressor for another. Nevertheless, in order to defend his cause and provide greater protection for the Filipinos still loyal to him, Silang agreed to cooperate with the British.

In a letter to Silang dated 6 May 1763, Captain Brereton, on behalf of the British forces, offered their pledge of military support to the Filipino leader. As part of their mutual defense agreement against Simon Anda, the captain stated that the British would send one of their ships, under his command to protect Silang and his followers. Captain Brereton acknowledged that he was aware of the injustices the Filipinos had suffered under the Spanish regime. He was also pleased by Silang's decision to work with the British in their efforts against the Spaniards and, *"to humiliate the sovereignty of so cruel a nation."* 3

Respectfully addressing Silang as *"Your Grace,"* Captain Brereton went on to say in his letter, *"In a short time, your Grace will have troops and war supplies. This dispatch is to assure your Grace of our friendship and my satisfaction at receiving your letter, and because of your loyalty. In order that your Grace may communicate it to all the people, especially to those under our command, I am sending your Grace a small bronze cannon in token of my affection."* 4 But unlike Brereton's offer of support, Captain Backhouse objected to sending the much-needed soldiers to Silang, as the British troops were more urgently required in Manila to protect their garrisons there.

By now the Spaniards had come to consider Diego Silang, as not only being a traitor, but also a tyrant. They felt that Silang was using the British presence in the country as an excuse to plunder the estates of the Spaniards and kidnap civilians and members of the clergy. Silang was demanding a ransom of one hundred dollars for each of the victims he kidnapped, which was then a considerable amount of money.

The historian Zuniga pointed out that during this same period of time, Silang sent two boats to the British in Manila, which had been filled with booty plundered from the Spaniards he had attacked in the provinces. He also stated that although Anda demanded Silang's immediate presence at his headquarters, the Spaniards had few available soldiers to go out and search for the Filipino and arrest him.

To solidify his relationship with the British, Silang vowed his allegiance to George III. In a letter to Governor Drake, Silang requested that his province of Vigan be placed under the king's protection. The governor's response was to send, *"a vessel bearing dispatches and a present to Silang, and conferred on him the title of Alcalde Mayor, which he directly made public, to the great regret of the Indians, who had urged him to deliver them from the English, and now saw themselves subjected to them to more vexations than they ever suffered before; at the same time that they no longer dared to express their sentiments."* 5

But unfortunately for Diego Silang, he had become too powerful and this meant that the Spaniards feel threatened by him. They decided they had no choice but to have him assassinated. A Spanish mestizo and a friend of Silang's, Miguel Vicos, volunteered to murder the Filipino leader. As a personal acquaintance of the leader, Vicos was able to easily enter his camp where he shot Silang on 28 May 1763.

Despite the fact that their leader had been slain, his followers continued to confront the Spaniards. Under the sway of Silang's wife, Gabriela, Filipinos fought for their rights and to be free from the oppressive Spanish regime. Eventually, Gabriela and the remaining Filipinos in their dwindling army were captured. The Spaniards executed Gabriela Silang before a multitude of Filipinos in Vigan's main square.

Another Filipino who followed a similar path as Silang was Juan de la Cruz Palaris. On 3 November 1762, he led a revolt against the Spaniards in Binalatongan. Palaris demanded the removal of a number of Spanish mayors and judges who were accused of corruption and excessive abuses against the Filipino people such as the dreaded tax system. Anda dispatched a squad of soldiers to quell the uprising, but they only managed to subdue Palaris in July 1764. At one point, Palaris had as many as 6,000 followers who all managed to escape death when the uprising was suppressed.

In addition to the support of the Filipinos, the Chinese community also aided the British. If given a choice between the Englishmen and the harsh measures imposed upon them by the Spanish regime, the Chinese preferred a continuation of the British occupation. For this reason, they supported the invaders including going so far as to become soldiers in the British army in order to help fight Anda's forces.

Chinese Support the British

When the Spaniards invaded and then ruled the Philippines in the sixteenth century, Chinese merchants were regularly arriving in the Philippines to trade goods with the Filipinos. They brought to the Philippines a variety of goods including silks, ceramics, cotton, and metals. After the Spaniards occupied the archipelago, they allowed the Chinese to continue trading with the Filipinos. They were also permitted to settle in the area just outside of the city walls of Manila in the Parian.

By 1580, there were approximately 10,000 Chinese living in the city. In contrast, there were only about 1,000 Spaniards in the whole country and they were scattered throughout the islands with a larger proportion in and around Manila. The Chinese community continued to prosper and grow and by 1748 there were 40,000 Chinese settlers in the country. Consequently, the rising number of Chinese inhabitants in the country had become a major concern of the smaller minority of Spaniards.

As the Spaniards attempted to govern the colony, they felt increasingly fearful of the Chinese. It was becoming so difficult to monitor the movements of the Chinese in the surrounding areas of Manila, that the Spaniards felt compelled to impose restrictions upon them. As early as 1581, the Chinese were restricted to the Parian. In the Parian, the Chinese were free to have their homes and operate their businesses. They were free to move about Manila and the other suburbs during the day, but they were at first, completely restricted from conducting business activities or residing anywhere else but in the Parian. With the passage of years, the Chinese began to settle in areas outside of the city and in other provinces.

The Spaniards nervously feared an uprising by the Chinese, as it was not uncommon for them to revolt against the colonial government. The area across the Pasig River, opposite to Manila and known as Binondo, became part of the area where the Chinese were allowed to settle and operate their businesses. Again, this area was continuously monitored by Spanish soldiers positioned atop the city's stone walls with cannons at the ready at the first sign of trouble.

After the British seized Manila and Cavite, the Chinese, both Christian and non-believers, became aligned to the English forces against the Spaniards. After being subjected to decades of Spanish oppression and the harsh imposition of fees and taxes on just about everything they did, the Chinese community eagerly welcomed British overtures of friendship and of a mutually beneficial relationship. They readily joined the British in their military campaigns against Anda's forces.

"During the whole of the 18th century the Chinese fought the government only once. This was on the occasion of the British invasion – when they fought on the side of the British forces. This time unlike in the past, both Christian and non-Christian Chinese fought the Spaniards. The Chinese paid dearly for their collaboration with the British. Many of them were hanged once the British evacuated Manila. Restrictive and harsh measures were soon ordered against them, including expulsion from the islands, limitation as to residence and occupation of those who stayed, and payment of higher taxes. These tax measures proved excessive to most Chinese who chose either to go back to China or to live in the provinces as agriculturists, thereby abandoning their merchandile trade. Taxes required of agriculturists were quite mild. It was not until the governor in 1778/87 that the restrictions were gradually lifted and once more the Chinese came to the islands in larger numbers. The governor then, Basco, wanted the Philippines to be economically progressive and he knew that the Chinese assistance on this matter would boost his plans." [6]

On 23 December 1762, approximately 900 Chinese from the province of Pampanga amassed an army of 5,000 men. They planned to attack the Spaniards on Christmas Eve while they attended an evening church mass. But Anda discovered the plot. He traveled to Pampanga with soldiers and confronted the Chinese at the military fort they had constructed and which was armed with cannons. A battle ensued, leaving many wounded, killed or captured by the Spaniards. Those captured were later executed. Some Chinese survived the conflict and fled to the mountains. After this incident, Anda urged a measure which had been used in the past by the Spanish regime whenever they had had some difficulties with the Chinese, and this was to insist on their being expelled from the archipelago. But often times the orders to expel the Chinese were not carried out. As the Chinese were large contributors of taxes to the Royal Treasury each year, as well as providing all the services, skills and goods the Spanish community needed, they had become indispensable to the continued economic activities of the country.

The Chinese were the artisans, tradesmen, printers, blacksmiths, booksellers, masons, ship builders, apothecaries, shoemakers, tailors, and carpenters. Moreover, as shop merchants they provided the residents of Manila with a variety of Asian goods such as silks, cotton, linen, lace and household items including pottery, ceramics and furniture. They owned the restaurants and food shops, which provided Manila with its daily provisions, and a host of innumerable services which the Spanish and Filipinos both enjoyed.

The Spaniards appointed Chinese to prominent positions in the government of the Parian. Thus, they became the captains, lieutenants and policemen who governed their own community. But the position most coveted by the Chinese in the Parian was that of *"chief."* As a chief one had the authority to collect taxes, and skim a bit off the top for oneself, before handing the remaining funds over to the Spanish Royal Treasury.

Although the Spaniards attempted to restrict the number of Chinese settling in the Philippines to 6,000 individuals, the measure was never carried out. The Chinese had become a major source of revenue for the Royal Treasury. In addition to the yearly taxes they were compelled to pay to the Spanish government, they were charged immigration and residence fees, as well as for trade licenses imposed upon their businesses. Moreover, in the same manner as the Filipinos, they were often recruited, albeit reluctantly, for various work projects designated by the Spanish government.

The practice of extending loans to Chinese businessmen, became another source of revenue for the Spaniards. The loans were provided at high interest rates. To curry favorable relations with the Spaniards, the Chinese often resorted to providing them with gifts of usually money. Thus, while the Filipinos lived a hand to mouth existence, the prosperous Chinese became a major source of revenue for the government and its corrupt officials. Without the presence of the Chinese in the archipelago, the Spaniards would have been hard pressed, as they gradually became dependent upon the interest payments they received from the Chinese.

"In the old days it was a common practice in Manila to give money to the Chinese, imposing upon them the obligation of returning so much at the end of the month as interest on the loan, or furnish the lender the necessary daily provisions in his house. A rich Spaniard, a judge at that, gave so much money to a Chinaman as capital in business; in return, the celestial was to take care of providing the house of the lender with daily needs of beef. He gives another sum to another Chinaman with the latter's obligation to provide the fowls needed by his household. A third furnishes vegetables under the same terms." 7

It was General Draper, while still in Manila during the latter months of 1762, who placed the Englishman, James Kennedy, in charge of the Chinese community. Kennedy had managed to live in Manila for twenty-five years and had become quite familiar with the day-to-day activities of the Parian. After Draper's departure from Manila, Governor Drake retained the services of Kennedy. He served as an intermediary between the East India Government in Manila and the Chinese community, but even here misunderstandings soon erupted between both groups and these were mainly due to cultural differences.

When the Chinese decided to give Governor Drake a monetary gift, Kennedy objected and withheld some of the funds. This led to conflicts between Kennedy and the governor. By this time, Governor Drake had grown corrupt and greedy and was readily accepting bribes in the form of gifts from the Chinese.

"He is charged with having received $2,000 as a gift from the Chinese and applying for the remainder of the $5,000 voted by them; with receiving $2,500 for the contract for the rent of the Arrack Farm, and that he received money for granting a monopoly for the sale of pork. But these charges were not due to the Chinese alone, for Kennedy, when examined says, 'I then remember that the above gentlemen (Smith and Brooke) and Capt. Stephenson animated me much not to spare you (Drake). They must have suspected that I knew of some malpractice's of yours, but I told them as I now declare I never knew of any.' The committee which investigated Drake's conduct says also that the 'veracity of the Chinese is little to be regarded.' Mr. Jourdan, one of the members of the Council, which brought on such a dispute that the council informed the governor 'that if he persisted in adopting such measures as they could not approve of he must be governor alone, which he informed them he would,' and Kennedy adds later in summing up his treatment by Drake, 'it's incredible the things I've heard of the triumvirate that I must say governed much in Manila without regard to honor or honesty, to the discredit of the Nation and the honorable Company." [8]

Difficulties continued between the British naval commanders and the governor. At one point the governor requested that a British naval vessel be sent to cruise off the island of Corregidor in Manila Bay. He was informed that a ship was about to arrive from China containing a cargo of weapons for the Spanish rebels. In answer to the governor's request, Captain Brereton replied that the governor's suspicions were unfounded and that he was not prepared to send a ship in search of the Chinese vessel saying, *"I think it vain to look for this Trumpery Vessel."* [9] When the governor requested that the captain attend meetings of the Manila Council, Brereton refused and said, *"I have no kind of ambition to be in your councils."* [10] Captain Brereton had been tampering with the governor's Chinese policies and had threatened to inform the East India Company directors in Madras of Drake's inappropriate activities in Manila.

Angered by the captain's threat, the governor ordered his Deputy Paymaster in Cavite, a Mr. Nodes, to find some incriminating evidence, which could be used against Captain Brereton. Nodes eventually reported back to the governor that he discovered that the captain was involved in illegal gambling and in the sale of alcohol. In his report to the governor Nodes stated, *"I cannot, Sir, at present call to mind any further particulars,* *nor can I add anything further on this head, only to assure you that his (*the Captain's*) common conversation seemed always to estimate that you were fools and idiots and know very little how to act in your stations."* 11

In response to Nodes' comments, the Manila Council urged Drake not to take any further action against the captain. But the governor claimed that the captain was often seen in the Chinese Parian, where he and the Spaniards were conspiring against him. Drake said that Captain Brereton was known to, *"libel me and accuse me."* 12

The governor had some cause for alarm. It was true that Captain Brereton was continuously maligning the governor to whomever and wherever he could. Eventually the Manila Council forced the governor to resign. And this meant that Captain Brereton's campaign to have the governor removed from office had been successful. Drake said of Brereton at the time, *"I am concerned to find any man so inveterate against another as Captain Brereton seemed to be against me. And that the spleen of Captain Brereton has hurried him beyond the bounds of civility among men and his bitter revenge made him run about like a devouring lion seeking by means and motives the most unjustifiable to ruin my character."* 13

Chapter Eleven
Colony Returned to Spain

"An English frigate arrived with the armistice which had been agreed by the powers of Spain, France and England. In any other part of the world hostilities would have ceased, and the chiefs of the contending parties would have been anxious to exchange reciprocal civility and kindness the moment such intelligence was received; but in the Philippines, such were the misunderstandings which had arisen that the armistice which in Europe had been carried into effect was here of no avail." [1]

Zuniga

The hostilities between Britain, France and Spain came to an amicable conclusion with the signing of the *Peace of Paris Treaty* on 10 February 1763. The countries, which had been turned into battlegrounds during the Seven Year's War, enthusiastically embraced the political solution to the conflict. But due to the slowness of communications then in existence between England and its settlements outside of the country, news of the treaty arrived only some months later in India. This same news took even longer to reach Manila, but it had eventually arrived in the archipelago when the East India Company ship the *Houghton* sailed into Manila Bay on 24 July 1763.

The seizure of Manila and Cavite by General Draper and Admiral Cornish did not play a major role in the final terms and conditions of the treaty. Even though the East India Company had early on expressed an interest in retaining Mindanao at the end of the war, it was not able to achieve this objective. When the treaty was signed, the countries involved in the war had no inkling of Draper and Cornish's success in the Philippines.

The news of the capture reached Madras on 7 January 1763, when it was delivered to the Company directors by the captain of East India Company vessel the *Osterly*. And it was only in April of that same year that General Draper, arriving in England aboard the *Seahorse* and accompanied by Captains Fletcher and Kempenfelt, was able to personally report to the Admiralty of his success in the Philippines. But his report arrived too late to be of any use to the British government when negotiating the terms for the treaty.

Whilst the return of the occupied territories to the Spaniards had not actually brought any benefits to the East India Company in Madras at the war's end, the British government was more successful as it had acquired new territories as part of the terms of the treaty. Spain ceded Florida to Britain in exchange for the return of Havana and the island of Minorca in the Mediterranean. In North America, France ceded Canada to Britain in exchange for fishing rights and her islands in the West Indies. In the Caribbean, the islands of Grenada, St. Vincent, Tobago and Guadeloupe were now under British rule. In India, France recognized Britain's commercial supremacy in the Carnatic and in Bengal.

The War's End

When he learned of the peace treaty, Governor Drake relayed the information to the commanders of the navy and the military. They welcomed the dispatch from Madras, as did Archbishop Rojo who was elated by the news. The archbishop had, in turn, notified Simon Anda of the war's end, but to his dismay the Spanish rebel refused to accept the legitimacy of the peace treaty. Anda suspected that this was a plot by the British to thwart any of his attempts to capture the enemy's garrison in Manila.

Instead of seizing the olive branch extended to him in a bid to establish peaceful ties with the British, Anda obstinately insisted that the hostilities against the enemy continue. However, to his chagrin the Spanish citizens of Manila, who were convinced that the treaty was genuine, begged Anda to accept the authenticity of the document and prevent any further bloodshed. Acting as mediators between the British and Anda were Padre de Luna of the Franciscan Order and Padre Pazuengos of the Society of Jesus. Both men urged Anda to accept the treaty and end the hostilities. But in reality, the reason why Anda refused to accept the news of the treaty was simply that the report had not been conveyed directly to him by the British, but instead to Archbishop Manuel Rojo. Anda was still annoyed by the fact that throughout the entire British occupation, the English commanders had refused to acknowledge his position as the self-proclaimed governor of the Philippines.

When a second vessel the frigate *Hector* sailed into Manila Bay on 27 August 1763 with the *Preliminaries of Peace,* the British informed both the archbishop and Simon Anda. But once again, Anda continued to stubbornly insist that the peace treaty was a fabrication of the British commanders in Manila. On 19 September 1763, an ultimatum was issued by the British calling for Anda to end all hostilities according to the treaty.

On 15 October 1763 another East India Company vessel arrived from Madras the *Admiral Pocock.* The captain of the ship brought to Manila copies of the peace treaty itself. In the documents, which had been modified to reflect the return of Havana to Spain, there was no mention of the Philippine capture. In the meantime, the British commanders were already preparing to return to India, when there was some concern that a civil war was about to erupt between soldiers loyal to the archbishop and those in Anda's camp.

As far as the British were concerned, they were planning to turn over the seized territories to Archbishop Rojo. It was the archbishop who was the deputy governor when they had first arrived in Manila back in September 1762, and as such, they had every intention of returning the colony to him. To prevent a civil war, Rojo considered asking the British commanders for soldiers to help protect the city from Anda's army until the Spanish king could determine who was the legitimate governor of the colony.

However, with the untimely death of Archbishop Rojo on 30 January 1764, any fears of a civil war had suddenly ended. According to Zuniga, the archbishop had come to regret the difficulties he experienced with Anda. Their friendship had ended badly and Archbishop Rojo had begun referring to Anda as a *"usurper"* [2] and his enemy. *"The Archbishop had suffered so keenly over the loss of Manila and his bickering with Senor Anda so greatly aggravated his sufferings, that he died before the English had taken ship."* [3]

Next in command of the colony after the archbishop's death was, after all was said and done, Simon Anda. Even though Rojo may have had his differences with Anda and he felt that the rebellious Spaniard was power hungry, he had acknowledged the fact that he had been instrumental in the role the Spaniard was playing in the provinces. After all, Rojo had approved Anda's appointment to head a secondary Spanish government in the provinces whilst the British occupied Manila and Cavite. Consequently, Anda was only carrying out his orders as instructed by the governor and the Royal Audiencia and as such he had remained loyal to the Spanish king.

Cooperating for once after all the conflicts they had been involved with, the British commanders and Anda joined together to provide Archbishop Manuel Rojo with an extravagant funeral. Those Spaniards viewing the ceremonies were left speechless, as they had not expected the British to be as respectful as they were to the deceased archbishop. *"As the Spaniards were unable to render the military honors due to his rank, the English undertook to do so; and they discharged this duty with grandeur and magnificence. All Manila was amazed, said the Spaniards, that the English, whose religious beliefs were so contrary to their own, and who had always shown an implacable hatred for priests and particularly for bishops, should have done this."* [4]

After the archbishop's death, the British commanders turned their attention to Simon Anda. They now acknowledged Anda as the legitimate governor of the Spanish colony and it was with him that they continued the preliminaries for the peaceful return of occupied territories.

But Anda was still refusing to accept the war's end. However, his attitude changed with the arrival of the British ship the *Revenge* on 8 March 1764. The captain of the vessel brought with him a document which was signed by George III, and contained the *King's Orders for Restitution of the East Indies*. Based upon Articles 23 and 24 of the peace treaty, the document indicated that the British Royal Navy and the military were to evacuate Manila and Cavite and return to India. With the arrival of the king's orders and his own initiatives to ascertain the validity of the document through his sources in Canton, Simon Anda was finally convinced of the war's end and the authenticity of the peace treaty.

"Article XXXIII of the Treaty of Paris of February 10, 1763, states that 'all countries and territories, which may have been conquered, in whatsoever Part of the World, by the Arms of their Britannick and Most Faithful Majesties as well as by Those of Their Most Christian and Catholick Majesties, which are not included in the present Treaty either under the Title of Cession or under the Title of Restitution shall be restored without Difficulty and without requiring any Compensation." 5

Drake's Last Days as Governor of Manila

Captain Backhouse replaced Major Fell as commander of the 79th Regiment on 3 October 1763. By 10 March 1764, with the arrangements completed to return Manila to the Spaniards, the governor requested that Captain Backhouse transport a portion of the 79th Regiment to Madras and leave the remaining soldiers behind to guard the Sepoys who were deserting the British garrisons. The captain refused the request as he stated that he had not received orders from Madras to comply with the governor's wishes. As this was yet another annoying incident with Drake, both Captain Backhouse and Captain Brereton decided to ignore the governor's request and continued to prepare the ships for their return to Madras.

The English commanders decided to return Manila to the Spaniards even though the governor had adamantly objected to the captain's decision. Sometime later the governor was informed that the two captains were preparing to evacuate the city according to their discussions with the Spanish representatives involved in the operation. The governor demanded an explanation from Captain Backhouse as to the evacuation activities then underway. But Captain Backhouse replied that his orders had come directly from the British monarch his, *"Royal Lord the King with regard to this Conquest."* The governor then ordered the arrest of Captain Backhouse for his *"refusal to obey and his many other illegal and extraordinary proceedings."* 6

On the night of 25 March 1764, Lieutenant Richbell of the 79th Regiment dragged Captain Backhouse from his bed and placed him under arrest. The lieutenant was bribed by the governor to carry out the order. The captain would remain imprisoned until the Manila Council ousted the governor from office on 28 March 1764. Once freed, Captain Backhouse returned to his ship from where he continued to direct the evacuation plans for the capital and port city. In a report he submitted to the Secretary of War concerning the unsettling relationship between the naval and military officers and the governor he later lamented, *"Give me leave my Lord to assure you, that the command of His Majesty's troops in Manila with Mr. Drake was a hell too severe to be endured by human nature; where anything good reigned in the composition, there a heart the least tinctured with honour, honesty, or the love of his country, must have been ever upon the rack, by the arbitrary scenes of injustice and oppression incessantly practiced by Mr. Drake."* 7

Consequently, during the entire period of Governor Drake's administration, he found that he was at the center of an acrimonious environment of his own making. Everyday, he was confronted by a number of unhappy military and naval commanders who were opposed to his controversial methods of governing the colony. Even though the officers and members of the Manila Council managed to maintain a cordial relationship with the governor, he was clearly seen as a problematic figure from the start.

The earliest members of the Manila Council, who had been employed by the Company in India, had resigned after serving with Drake for only a short period of time. Samuel Johnson resigned on 16 December 1762, and Claud Russel followed on 18 December 1762. Both men claimed ill health as the reason for having to return to Madras. Russel complained that his feet were swollen in the tropical heat of Manila and that his liver was severely weakened.

In his letter to Governor Drake and the members of the Manila Council, Claud Russell wrote, *"Gentlemen, you are all sensible how much I have lately suffered with the old complaints in my liver and breast that with great care and three tedious ounces of medicine I had happily once got over after labouring under them for several years and trying change of climate. The danger of being now again in the very same situation together with swellings of my feet which I have ever been a stranger to until our arrival here, is too evident not to alarm me and as I have sufficient reason to suppose greatest part of my liver already consumed, I should be wanting in duty to myself were I not to entreat the favour of your permission to go to the coast when I may have the assistance of the physicians who before attended me and being the only persons acquainted with my constitution and nature of my disorder are the most likely to administer relief."* 8

On 20 February 1763, Lewin Smith resigned due to ill health and on 28 February 1763, Henry Brooke used his loyalty to the Company as an excuse to get away from the governor. He asked for the governor's permission to return to India, as he claimed that the Company's affairs were in a terrible state and needed his inestimable assistance.

Three new civil servants had been selected to replace the original members of the Manila Council. However, they too were soon trying to do everything possible to return to Madras and flee from the governor. Captain Brereton described the uneasy relationship between the members of the Council and the governor saying, *"The four Councilors who were appointed by the Presidency of Fort St. George (Madras) left very soon, being quickly tired of their President, Mr. Drake."* 9

But as far as Governor Drake was concerned, the second batch of Manila Council members, Francis Jourdan, William Stevenson and Henry Parson, were nothing more than inexperienced *"spoiled boys."* 10 Nevertheless, by the end of March 1764, the Manila Council formally ordered the governor to appear before them. At this meeting, the Manila Council members read an extensive list of charges brought against Drake. He was asked to resign his post as governor on behalf of the East India Company and to return to Madras aboard one of the Company's ships. The governor realized that there was little else he could do, and promptly resigned. Of his forced resignation, Drake blamed Captain Brereton as being the mastermind behind the entire episode. *"The whole proceeding was entirely a plot of Captain Brereton which was executed by my counselors to their eternal shame, having served as instruments or tools to bring about his malicious purposes."* 11

The Madras Council appointed Alexander Dalrymple, who was then in Manila, as Drake's replacement. It was Dalrymple and the two captains who continued the evacuation of the British forces from the Philippines and who were to eventually return Manila and Cavite to the Spaniards and in particular to Simon Anda. When he received the occupied territories, the rebellious Spaniard had finally received the recognition he so long desired.

Manila Returned to the Spaniards

To ensure that the return of the occupied territories was smoothly carried out, Anda sent his representatives Francisco Xavier Salgado, Don Mariano Tobias, Don Raymundo Espanol and Don Nicolas Echuaz to negotiate with the British governor and commanders. Representing the British side were William Stevenson and Francis Jourdan. The meeting proved difficult and little was accomplished. It was only with the arrival of the newly appointed Spanish Governor Francisco Javier de la Torre, that any definitive decisions were made on the return of the colony to Spain and the timeframe planned for the British evacuation. The new governor, resting after the long sea journey from Acapulco aboard the Spanish frigate the *Santa Rosa*, had arrived in the Philippines on 17 March 1764.

The Mexican viceroy had especially chosen Colonel de la Torre for the job of governor of the Asian possession. Awarded the title of *Teniente del Rey* (king's lieutenant), de la Torre's appointment had been a political move by the viceroy. It was no longer deemed necessary or wise to allow clerics to act as deputy governors of the Philippines should the duly appointed governor die while in office or become incapacitated for some reason. Instead, a military man, de la Torre, had been selected to temporarily govern the colony and begin its reconstruction after the British evacuation. In the interim, the Royal Audiencia had named Simon Anda the deputy governor of the Philippines. But he was to hold the position for only a short time before de la Torre officially took over the reigns of power in the colony.

In deference to Simon Anda and to acknowledge all he had endured during the siege and occupation of Manila, de la Torre allowed Anda to reap the joys of accepting the return of Manila to the Spaniards. On that festive day, the governor claimed he was indisposed and remained in Bacolor. Anda was, therefore, allowed to proudly stand at the head of the Spanish retinue where he officiated as the legally recognized governor of the Philippines.

Consequently a lavish ceremony was arranged by the British and Spanish officials on 31 May 1764. There, the British officially returned the occupied territories to the Spaniards and to Simon Anda. At the head of the procession of Spaniards and Filipinos was Anda triumphantly riding a white horse along the streets of Manila. Alexander Dalrymple officiated at the ceremony held on the patio of the Santa Cruz church. Accompanied by marching music, the ceremony consisted of raising the Spanish flag followed by a gun salute and the ringing of church bells. The Spaniards gave a banquet for the former Governor Alexander Dalrymple and the commanders and other civil servants. The British later reciprocated by providing a dinner for the Spaniards on 4 June 1764. The jubilant Spaniards hailed Simon Anda as their liberator and were, no doubt, pleased that the British occupation of Manila and Cavite had finally come to an end.

But whilst the Spaniards were celebrating the return of the colony to their control once again, the British were continuing to feverishly prepare their ships for the journey to Madras. During this time, they made sure to confiscate whatever they could from the colony including all of the Spanish sailing vessels then at the port of Cavite, cannons, arms and ammunition. A letter written by a Manila Spaniard, Don Vela, to his brother Antonio

Gonzalez, who was living in Spain, alludes to the return of the Spanish possession. *"The letter which you wrote from Madrid arrived together with that of this place, but no other has arrived. By the same boat also came (news of) the peace, whereupon the English again delivered the place to our governor. It was almost bare of cannon, as the English had taken them. For eighteen months were we under the rule of the heretic, with sufferings greater than can be imagined there. They acted toward us worse than do the victorious Turks toward those whom they conquer. However, Manila well deserved it, not indeed, because of its total lack of all Christian procedure, but singularly because of its cursed neglect of politics, as if the whole world had to respect and fear us because of our boasting that we are Spaniards."* [12]

The British sailed for Madras on 10-11 July 1764, ending the occupation of less than two years. The troops sailed aboard the Royal Navy ships the *Falmouth* and *Seaford*, as well as on the Company's vessels *Revenge, Admiral Pocock, London, Squirrel* and the *Cumberland*. They also commandeered the Chinese and Spanish vessels the *Siam* and the *Ilocos*. In total, the number of soldiers returning to India amounted to: 60 Royal Artillery, 37 East India Company Artillery, 513 soldiers of the 79th Regiment, 110 East India Company troops, 703 Sepoys and 45 Nawabs (Anglo-Indians).

Don Francisco Javier de la Torre was officially installed as governor and captain general of the Philippines, but he only served in that position for one year. At the time and quite unsurprisingly, Anda turned over to the new Spanish governor the sum of two million dollars he managed to keep out of the hands of the British commanders. He kept the funds in his possession even though he claimed that the war against the British had been very expensive.

There are two possibilities as to the origins of the large sum of money. Firstly, it may have been the silver brought to the colony by the *Filipino*, which would have been turned over to the investors in the trade. As the galleon brought to the Philippines the sum of $2,253,111 of which $250,000 was the yearly subsidy for the colonial government's expenses. Anda may have used the subsidy to maintain the rogue Spanish government and army in the provinces. The payment for the goods sent to Mexico the previous year, would have in all likelihood, been returned to the original investors in the trade. Secondly, when Anda fled to the provinces, he took with him the funds from the Royal Treasury for safekeeping, and this may have been part of the money he turned over to the new governor.

With the new governor now administering the colony, there was no reason for Simon Anda to remain in the Philippines. He returned to Mexico and from there journeyed to Spain in 1767. When he arrived in Spain,

Charles III warmly received him. To the Spaniards, he had become a hero. As a reward, the king appointed him to his prestigious *Council of Castile,* and gave him the title of *Knight of the Royal Order.* On 12 April 1768, Anda submitted a memorial to the Spanish king detailing the difficulties he had encountered whilst in the Philippines. These he stated were mainly caused by members of the various religious institutions.

"The greater part of Anda's memorial pertained to the abuses of the friars, which were as follows: 1) interference in the affairs of the government; (2) neglect to teach the Spanish language to the Filipino people; (3) greed for material wealth, as evidenced by their acquisition of vast fertile agricultural lands and their participation in business and trade; (4) their opposition to canonical visitation by the archbishop or bishop; (5) neglect of their spiritual duties; (6) hostility to Spaniards who wish to trade or visit the provinces; and (7) maltreatment of the Filipino natives and local officials." 13

To correct the problems he had encountered in the Philippines, Anda suggested that a number of measures needed to be implemented. This included curbing the activities of the clergy in the Spanish possession. He believed that members of the various religious institutions operating in the country should not be permitted to own private estates. Additionally, the clergy should be prevented from interfering in political matters. To assist in curbing the abuses and corrupt practices of the clergy, he also suggested that they not be allowed to engage in trade. It was Anda's contention that the religious institutions should concentrate on religious matters and the conversion of Filipinos to Catholicism, as well as education and enabling them to learn the Spanish language. Other measures included developing the economic conditions of the archipelago including opening the mines, issuing new coinage, improving the laws covering trade and commerce and reorganizing the government with increased prowess extended to the governor. All future governors would be selected based upon the criteria that they be honest, entitled to the position, and have the credentials to handle the appointment with integrity.

The king was so impressed with Simon Anda that on 3 October 1769, he appointed Simon Anda to the position of governor and captain general of the Philippines and president of the Royal Audiencia. A few months prior to his return to the Philippines, and as was then the custom before one departed on a long and treacherous sea journey, Anda made his last will and testament on 12 December 1769. In the will he mentioned the living members of his family - his son Tomas and daughter Maria. He was then a widower following the death of his wife, Dona Maria Cruz Diaz de Montoyo y Vallejo. His son was married and his daughter had become a nun at the convent of Santa Cruz de Bernardez Recoletas. Anda noted in his will that his life's savings consisted of a grant from Charles III of $36,000 and a $12,000 payment for his overseas services in addition to a $3,000 pension. He returned to the Philippines arriving in July 1770.

Known for his honesty, courage and sensitivity towards the plight of Filipinos, Simon Anda displayed characteristics his fellow Spaniards in the Philippines did not come to appreciate. He soon garnered a fair share of enemies due to a noble desire to elevate the lives of the Filipino people whilst he was in office as governor. As he attempted to protect the native population from the corrupt and abusive members of the clergy and government officials, he incurred the anger of the Spaniards. He became the focus of their resentment and malice. On 30 October 1776, at the age of sixty-seven, Simon Anda died at the hospital of Fort San Felipe in Cavite.

In India and in England, General Draper and former governor Dawsonne Drake faced charges brought against them for their questionable activities whilst in the colony. The East India Company in Madras began adding up the expenses they had incurred in the preparatory phase of the expedition and the occupation of the territories in the Philippines. They later claimed that they had suffered great losses through their participation in the enterprise. After reviewing the large sums of silver and valuables seized in the archipelago through looting and confiscation of other property, it clearly becomes obvious that the East India Company and the commanders of the venture had enormously benefited financially from the entire episode.

Chapter Twelve
Following the Money

"The conduct and bravery of the officers and troops have done great honour to themselves and the nation and will entitle them to every good office in my power which extends no further than to request for them your patronage and protection and a favorable representation of their services to His Majesty. But although I have so much reason to be pleased with their behavior, mine, I fear has not been equally pleasing to them. My method of dividing the prize money has given much offence and made me very unpopular with the captains and subalterns." [1]

General William Draper

Although the East India Company had less of a contributory role in the supply of men, ships and provisions for the Manila expedition than General Draper or Admiral Cornish had anticipated, by December 1763, the Company was already busily tallying up the expenses it had incurred during the venture. Years later, an official document entitled *Expenses for the East India Company Invasion of the Philippines,* [2] was issued by the East India Company on 28 June 1775. In the document, which was addressed to the Lords Commissioners of His Majesty's Treasury, the Court of Directors of the United Company of Merchants of England trading to the East Indies, a list was provided detailing the various charges incurred by the Company during its participation in the expedition.

The directors stated that when asked by George III to extend their cooperation to the commanders of the expedition for its eventual success, they had been assured that they would be reimbursed for any expenses they incurred in this endeavor. Moreover, it was their understanding that if a peace treaty had been signed before the Company realized any benefit from the expedition, that the king would ask Parliament to provide the East India Company with recompense for its expenses.

Clearly the East India Company was trying to receive compensation for its participation in the venture even though William Draper initiated the original plan on their behalf when in England in January 1762 at the Admiralty meeting. The Company directors pointed out the risk involved to their settlements in India, but that they had agreed to participate in the expedition despite the fact that there were several directors who were opposed to the Company's role in Draper's plan. Their cooperation was nonetheless extended as it was deemed essential by the Earl of Egremont,

Secretary of State that they participate in the military expedition and cooperate with Draper and Cornish.

"That the parting with any Troops from the Coast of Choromandel exposed your Memorialists Trade and Possessions in India to so great Risks and Dangers, that the said Expedition was opposed by Major General Lawrence their Military Commander, and by some of your Memorialists Council at Fort St. George, yet your Memorialists President and the Majority of the Council there determined to send such a number of Troops as were required for the said Expedition, and in consequence thereof there were embarked from the Coast of Choromandel of your Memorialists European Forces, Commission and Noncommissioned Officers included 330 Men, Black Troops consisting of Caffres and Sepoys 1504 and Lascars 372 with Military and other Stores amounting to upwards of (pounds) 12,000 and two of your Memorialists trading Ships were employed as Transports on the said Service." 3

Expenses, Prizes and the Ransom

The directors of the East India Company in Madras claimed that their expenses in the campaign totaled 163,243 pounds. The list of expenses was submitted on 10 February 1768 to the Treasury requesting that the government reimburse the Company for its expenditures. The Company received an initial payment of 28,365 pounds on 2 November 1762, but since then, it not received any additional reimbursement funds from the government.

"Your Memorialists beg leave to assure your Lordships that they engaged in the Expedition at the risk of their own safety, solely in compliance with His Majesty's Requisition, and in confidence of the Assurances contained in Lord Egremont's Letter respecting the reimbursement of their Expenses." 4

The expenses absorbed by the Company included charges for the military, garrisons, hospital, salaries, diet, merchandise, garrison provisions and those provisions, which had been lost or decayed. Other charges included the purchase and maintenance of their horses, loss of Madeira wine, interest on borrowed money, loss of grain, expeditions to the Pasig area outside of Manila and to the Bay of Laguna and Bulacan. They had also to maintain their garrison at the port of Cavite with additional repairs to the fortification and to other structures. At one point, they had to refit one of their vessels the *Revenge*, for its journey from India to Manila. They provided housing of Manila prisoners in Bombay. They asked for a repayment of naval stores lost at Cavite, rupees stolen from Mr. Jourdan (a member of the Manila Council), payment to an arrack farmer for jars, military stores unaccounted for, a loan made to an individual by the name of George Roberts for $200, rents, and arrack shipped and sold in Canton.

But what has been omitted from the report is the sum the East India Company received as its share of prizes and booty in silver, gold, jewels and other valuables, as well as from the confiscated properties, ships, ammunition, weapons, cannons, all of which were later sold. The total sum they acknowledged in prize money amounted to $636,514, which included 43,280 Indian Pagodas. This sum was divided into three portions of a third each. The East India Company received more than $212,171 as its share of the prizes taken or sold. This implies that the Company's profit amounted to $48,928. The remaining two thirds were divided into eight portions. One portion of more than $53,043 was divided between Draper, Cornish and Tiddeman with each man receiving a share of more than $17,681. The remaining seven portions went to the other officers and soldiers who participated in the expedition.

At the time, a yearly salary of one hundred pounds was considered a good income. The purchasing power of this amount could provide a small family with a comfortable life. Hence, the shares Draper, Cornish and Tiddeman received meant that they each had in their possession substantial sums in return for their participation in the expedition.

However, the amounts distributed were not consistent with the estimated value of the property seized in Manila or taken from the captured galleon and galley. The value in silver dollars of these prizes had been estimated at totaling approximately 4.5 million dollars or greater if the sailing vessels, ammunition, weapons, and other confiscated prizes had been factored into the total seized property taken by the British. In reality, the sum may have been as high as ten million dollars given the fact that much of the property was not mentioned in the document submitted to the Treasury for reimbursement of the Company's expenses.

What is known is that in the years after the Seven Year's War, both Draper and Cornish were each living comfortable lives as apparently very wealthy men. Property taken from Manila reappeared at Cambridge University in England, the British Museum and was also discovered at the home of Dawsonne Drake when he died and his estate was being settled. Just how much of the property of the Spaniards was actually taken from Manila and Cavite and its environs may never be known. Everyone connected to the expedition was paid some proportion of the proceeds down to the non-commissioned officers and soldiers even though they received a much smaller percentage of the prize money.

When a request was submitted in January 1764 to the Spanish monarchy for the balance of the ransom of four million dollars, the Spaniards, understandably, refused to make any further payments to the British government. At the East India Company offices in London, the issue of the Manila ransom was still being heatedly debated with the matter still lingering on until 1767. The Spanish government continued to refuse paying the ransom balance. The matter became so contentious that the King of Prussia suggested that he would be happy to serve as a mediator between Spain and England, but his offer was rejected.

At one point, the British government considered linking the Manila ransom with another diplomatic issue then under discussion. This concerned the retention of the Falkland Islands, a matter, which was under dispute with France. However, when the British retained the Falklands, they decided not to pressure Spain into paying any additional funds towards the ransom.

The ransom had originally been demanded soon after the capture of Manila and whilst the Spaniards and the English commanders of the invasion, Draper and Cornish, had been preparing the terms and conditions for the capitulation agreement with Archbishop Rojo. It was then thought that the capitulation would in effect protect the city and its inhabitants from any harm or looting, after all, that was one of the conditions of the surrender document. But despite the fact that discussions were still underway, the British soldiers ransacked the city. It was ludicrous to pay a ransom to protect a city from looting if it already had been plundered. Nevertheless, Draper argued that as he had never given his soldiers permission to loot Manila, and that the full force of his troops had not been at liberty to plunder the city. If he had, indeed, given his permission to loot the city, the ransacking would have been more severe and drawn out for a longer period of time.

"Manila, my Lord, was in this horrid situation; of consequence the lives of the inhabitants, with all belonging to them, were entirely at our mercy. But Christianity, humanity, the dignity of our nation, and our own feelings as men, induced us not to exert the utmost rigors of the profession, against those supplicants; although my own Secretary, Lieutenant Fryar, had been murdered, as he was carrying a Flag of Truce to the town. The Admiral and I told the Archbishop and principal Magistrates, that we were desirous to save so fine a city from destruction, ordered them to withdraw, consult, and propose such Terms of Capitulation as might satisfy the fleet and army, and exempt them from pillage, and its fatal consequences." 5

With regard to the length of time the looting of Manila took place, it has been suggested in various histories describing the British invasion that the ransacking occurred over a forty-hour period. But according to Draper the looting only lasted for three hours. He also stated that the ransacking had erupted spontaneously amongst a group of soldiers in his small army. The men came from every walk of life, nationality and religion, and had been restless and impatient to receive their share of prize money for participating in the capture of Manila.

"Several hours elapsed, before the principal Magistrates could be brought to a Conference; during that Interval, the Inhabitants were undoubtedly great Sufferers. But, my Lord, this Violence was antecedent to our Settling the Terms of the Capitulation, and by the Laws of War, the Place (Manila), with all its Contents, became the unquestionable Property of the Captors, until a sufficient Equivalent was given in Lieu of it. That several Robberies were committed, after the Capitulation was signed, is not to be denied; for Avarice, want, and Rapacity, are ever insatiable. But that the Place was pillaged for Forty Hours, and the Pillage authorised by me, is a most false and infamous Assertion." 6

On the other hand, Archbishop Rojo's stated in his journal that the looting had continued for forty hours even though he had objected to the pillage after the passage of twenty-four hours. The looting continued, he said, even though Draper had ordered the soldiers to immediately end the ransacking of the city.

Draper was well aware of the maxim then prevalent in warfare, where vanquished territories were left open to the mercy of the conquerors and who could do what they willed with a seized territory. The opportunity to amass wealth by plundering a captured territory or seizing prizes on the high seas had become the primary reason why so many officers and soldiers participated in dangerous military and naval campaigns. Thus, in the case of the Manila offensive, the soldiers felt justified in their actions even if viewed as extremely objectionable by those individuals who were victimized. As Draper stated, *"It is a known and universal Role of War amongst, the most civilized nations, that places taken by storm, without any Capitulation, are subject to all miseries that the conquerors may choose to inflict."* 7

To comply with the ransom demands, Archbishop Rojo tried his best to raise the amount demanded from the colony's Spaniards in cash and valuables, He was, however, not able to raise the entire amount. It was then that he assured Draper and Cornish that the Spanish Royal Treasury in Madrid would pay the balance. Although the war had ended and the British government had continuously requested the ransom balance, the Spanish Crown sent a Memorial to George III regarding the matter. The document was hand delivered by the Spanish ambassador to the British court, and indicated a number of points arguing why Spain was not obligated to pay the remainder of the ransom. The Memorial was apparently a personal attack against William Draper and his role as the commander of the invasion. Draper was no doubt troubled by the Spanish comments attacking his behavior and actions during the Manila campaign.

"The calumnious and envenomed attack upon my own character, demands the most public justification: being described both at home and abroad, as a man void of all faith, principle, or common honesty; and so, indeed, I should be most deservedly thought, were I guilty even of the smallest Part of what the Spanish Memorial accuses me. A Day in Tunis, or Algiers, would blush to make use of so black an instrument of perfidy and piracy. I owe, therefore, this open vindication of my conduct, both to my Sovereign, and to my country, whose representatives were pleased to honour me with their public thanks, the greatest of all rewards, and indeed, the only one I have received, for my late services." 8

As no individual can be pleased being accused of piracy and plunder, it is not surprising that Draper claimed he was innocent of any wrongdoing whilst in the Philippines. But as the commander of the land forces, the looting occurred during his watch and the Spanish held him responsible for the ransacking of the city. Although he, Cornish and Rojo were still in the process of discussing the details of the surrender agreement, it was unfortunate that the impatient soldiers, poorly paid under the best of circumstances, turned unruly and began thrashing the city. In his defense, Draper noted that several Public Orders had been issued concerning the activities of his troops whilst in Manila, which proved that he had made every effort to protect Manila and restore order in the city.

"The following Extracts from the Public Orders, given out the very day we entered the town, will sufficiently convince your Lordship, of my constant attention to the preservation of those ungrateful people; who have taught me to believe, that humanity and compassion are crimes. Extracts. October 6th, Manila The utmost order and regularity to be observed. All persons guilty of robberies, or plundering the churches and houses, will be hanged without mercy. The Guards to send frequent patrols both day and night, to prevent all disorders. The drummers to beat to Arms, to Officers to assemble with their men, and call the rolls. The Adjutants to go round the town, and take an exact account of the safeguards, posted for the protection of the Convents, Churches and Houses. October 7th – All the inhabitants of Manila are to be looked upon and treated as His Britannic Majesty's Subjects: They having agreed to pay Four Millions of Dollars, for the Ransom and Preservation of their city and effects. The criminals executed for robbery and sacrilege, to be buried at sunset. I hope the foregoing Extracts are sufficient to vindicate my character. Moreover, the strictest search was made on board the Squadron by the Admiral's Orders, and amongst the troops, to recover what had been stolen and secreted; and all the money, plate, and jewels, so recovered, were put into the Treasury, and allowed, and accepted as part of the ransom." 9

It was also claimed by the Spaniards that the surrender agreement had been unlawfully obtained, as the British used force to compel the Spaniards into signing the document and that they were, *"threatened to put to the Sword, in case of refusal."* 10 According to the British version of the events as they unfolded, their commanders had extended every courtesy to the archbishop and other dignitaries of the Spanish government in Manila. They had insisted that Archbishop Rojo voluntarily sign the agreement. Nevertheless, the Spanish government claimed that the agreement was invalid, as the archbishop had not received the approval of the king of Spain, Charles III, to sign the document on his behalf. This, of course, was a ridiculous assertion, as it would have taken months and perhaps years for the document to arrive in Spain and for a reply to reach Manila. And even then, it may or may not have been approved by the Spanish king given that the war was about to end. As time was of the essence, the archbishop had no choice in the matter but to add his signature to the surrender document in order to protect the city and its inhabitants from further attacks or looting.

"Therefore the said Capitulation ought to be void, because it was signed by force; and because General Draper first violated and broke the Capitulation, by permitting the City to be pillaged. Consequently, that Capitulation only, which was proposed by the Governor, accepted of, and signed by Admiral Cornish and General Draper, upon the Seventh of October (1762), ought to be considered and respected in this affair." 11

The Spaniards, however, did have a point when they stated that the British had already helped themselves to much plunder in silver, jewels, artworks, and other valuables, which were worth far more than the four million ransom they demanded. The soldiers looted the homes of the rich Spaniards, as well as the religious institutions (monasteries and churches), and colleges scattered throughout the city. Most of the valuables were allegedly returned to the residents of the city by order of General Draper. But how much was truly returned remains a mystery.

Still, the partial payment Archbishop Rojo was able to collect from the Spanish community had been turned over to Draper and Cornish. Additionally, the Englishmen had obtained the cargo from the *Santissima Trinidad*, which was valued at more than two million dollars. When the ship was seized it contained a cargo of gold, silks and spices. Even though the ship had became an object under dispute between the Spaniards and the British, ultimately the British Admiralty in London absolved England of any wrongdoing.

In addition to the seizure of the galleon, the British had also taken a galley carrying more than $30,000 in silver and other valuables. And when the British returned to India at the war's end they brought with them a number of confiscated Spanish sailing ships, boats, cannons and weapons.

Concerning his conduct in Manila, William Draper submitted his reply to the Spanish charges brought against him in 1764 in the form of a letter. It was addressed to the Earl of Halifax and entitled, *Colonel Draper's Answer to the Spanish Arguments, Claiming the Galleon, and Refusing Payment of the Ransom Bills, for preserving Manila from Pillage and Destruction*. The Earl of Halifax, Secretary of State for the Southern Department replaced the Earl of Egremont, who was one of the members at the Admiralty meeting in January 1762, when the Manila invasion campaign was approved in England.

In his statement defending his actions in the Philippines, Draper reiterated Spain's reasons for their presence in the colony. Spain was determined to convert Filipinos to Catholicism and to retain its galleon trade with China and the Americas. He described the invasion of Manila and Cavite and how it was accomplished, as well as the surrender of the colony to the English commanders. He explained the details of the surrender document and the ransom demand of which, only a small portion of the payment had been turned over to the British commanders. He spoke of how the Spaniards managed to hold off paying the entire amount giving a number of excuses for their inability to pay the remaining balance. Ironically, the Spaniards were demanding compensation for the loss of their galleon the *Santissima Trinidad*.

"It was in great hopes, that the good faith, honour, and punctuality of the Spanish nation, would have made this publication unnecessary. But finding, that they have absolutely refused payment of the ransom bills, drawn upon their treasury by the governor of Manila, and do now claim the restitution of the galleon (Santissima Trinidad), I am constrained, for the sake of those brave men, to whom I am obliged and indebted for my success, to assert their rights, in the best manner I am able." 12

However, Draper insisted that the galleon was a legitimate prize taken well before the surrender document was signed. Furthermore, it had been captured too distant from Manila to be claimed as part of the plunder of the city.

When the ransom demand had been made, Archbishop Rojo suggested turning over to the British the Mexican subsidy, which was, transported on the returning galleon, the *Filipino*. Governor Drake was eager to receive the Mexican subsidy, and to facilitate the matter he appointed two Spanish judges and two merchants to bring the subsidy from the galleon to Manila.

The Spaniards delivered an order to the galleon's captain that the silver aboard the ship was to be turned over the bearers of his message. The silver would then be conveyed to Manila and to the British governor. The Archbishop, however, changed his mind about sending the two Spanish judges as his emissaries as he considered that it would be undignified for government officials to participate in the mission. Instead, two Spanish law enforcers, Antonio Conde and Julian Ortuno de Leon, and the two merchants, Fernando Calderon and Francisco Jugo, were selected to carry out the mission. They sailed aboard the British ships the *Argo* and the *Panther* with Captains King and Parker to secure the silver. But the attempt to obtain the silver was overshadowed by the fact that it had already been removed from the ship and delivered to Anda's camp in the provinces.

For three months, the *Argo* and the *Panther* unsuccessfully searched for the *Filipino* galleon. On 25 February 1763, Cornish and the fleet returned to Madras. Meanwhile in Manila, Captain Brereton resumed the search for the missing ship. The vessel was finally located off the coast of Palapag, but by then it had been stripped of all valuables and abandoned by the Spanish captain and crew. Frustrated by not being able to obtain the Mexican silver, Captain Brereton set the ship afire even though if it had been towed to Cavite and then to Canton, the vessel could have been sold for a profit.

As soon as the British realized that the silver had been transported to Anda's camp, an expedition was organized by Captain Thomas Backhouse in a bid to retrieve the treasure. He searched the Laguna-Batangas region where he had been informed than the silver had been taken, but again, all attempts to retrieve the silver failed.

Ultimately, the Spanish government never paid the balance of the ransom. And even though William Draper felt that he had accomplished everything he could to ensure that the ransom was paid. He was also confident that he had acted honorably whilst in Manila and had nothing to feel guilty about. *"As my own character, both as an Officer, and a man of honour, is so wickedly attacked by this unjust accusation, I must beg leave to state the whole affair, in its true light; and do appeal for its veracity to the testimonies of every officer and soldier, who served in the expedition, and to all of the Marine Department."* 13

As far as Draper was concerned, the Spaniards had stopped collecting cash and valuables as part of a partial payment of the ransom once the city was in the possession of the East India Company. He said that the Spaniards no longer felt obligated to pay the ransom despite the fact that the British soldiers could have completely destroyed Manila.

"The destruction that we have occasioned, would have trebled the loss they suffer by the payment of the ransom. The rich churches and convents, the King of Spain's own Palace, with its superb and costly furniture, the magnificent building of every sort, the fortifications, docks, magazines, foundries, cannon, and in short the whole might have been entirely ruined, the Spanish Empire in Asia subverted, and the fruits of their religious mission lost forever, together with the lives of many thousand inhabitants, who were spared by our humanity." 14

When the *Grafton* and the *Lenox*, returned to England they took the *Santissima Trinidad* with them. The three ships sailed into the harbor of Plymouth in June 1764. The galleon was in such a deplorable state that the commanders of the three British vessels were unsure if the Spanish ship would survive the journey. Whilst at Plymouth, the ship became a kind of novelty with many tourists arriving in the city to take a look at one of Spain's largest galleons. The ship was eventually sold, but the amount received in payment was not considered part of the ransom. When Draper and Cornish first captured the galleon, they had estimated that the ship itself was valued at three million dollars, in addition to the 2.5 million dollar cargo. Consequently, it is not clear how much of a share Draper and Cornish received from the capture and sale of the *Santisstima Trinidad*, as well as from the cargo she was carrying when seized.

Draper, Cornish and Drake in the Years After the War's End

On his return to England, William Draper received the praise and recognition of the British Parliament for his role in the invasion of the Philippines. He was elevated to the position of Lieutenant Governor of Great Yarmouth on 13 March 1765. At the same time, he became a colonel of the 16th Foot, as his former unit of the 79th Regiment had been disbanded by then. He was made a Knight of Bath in 1766.

After his first wife died in England, he went on a tour of America. There, he met the lady who was to become his second wife, Susannah Delancey. She was the second daughter of Brigadier General Oliver Delancey, a renowned military commander during the American Revolution. She was also the granddaughter of Stephen Delancey, a member of the New York Assembly from 1702 to 1737.

The Delancey family was one of the most influential and wealthiest families in the city of New York. They owned large tracts of land in the area presently known as lower Manhattan. In 1772, Draper was further elevated in his career with the military to the rank of Major General and then Lieutenant General in 1777. He was appointed Lieutenant Governor of Minorca in 1779 serving in the administration of Governor James Murray. Whilst there, he served during the defense of Fort Philip against the combined French and Spanish offensive of August 1781 to 1782. When he returned to Bristol, England, he lived at his mansion, *Manila Hall*, which was later purchased after his death by a French Catholic nunnery. William Draper died at Bath, England in 1787, where his remains were interred at the Abbey Church.

When Rear Admiral Samuel Cornish returned to England he was a wealthy man. He purchased a large estate and retired to a life of leisure. He was honored by Parliament for his role in the Philippine campaign and was made a Baronet on 9 January 1766. He died a rich bachelor in 1816. His entire estate was left to his nephew, Samuel Pitchford. As a captain with the British Royal Navy, Pitchford had served as the captain of the *America* during the expedition to Manila, which was then commanded by Admiral Cornish, his uncle.

The first British governor of Manila, Dawsonne Drake, faced a number of charges upon his return to Madras in April 1766. One of his accusers, Captain Brereton, charged the governor with participating in a number of inappropriate activities in Manila. His mal-conduct included the fact that he had been protecting an enemy of the British, Cesar Fayette, as well as having created a number of monopolies favoring a few businessmen. He was also accused of receiving money from the Spaniards and the Chinese, which should have been legally entered into the Company's treasury.

In addition to Brereton's accusations, Drake was accused of disobeying East India Company orders and of being continuously involved in disagreements with the officers of the navy, army and civil servants of Manila. The charges brought against Drake included his questionable conduct whilst governor of the colony. The commanders and officers who came into conflict with the governor had forwarded to the king and to the East India Company the charges against him. This led to an investigation of his activities by the East India Company's Madras Council.

The Madras Council, in turn, reported to the President of the Company that Drake had indeed disobeyed the orders sent to him in regard to the Frenchman, Cesar Fayette. The French soldier had become a close acquaintance of Drake's and had acted on behalf of the Spaniards against the British during the invasion where he led soldiers in combat. Drake was also guilty of mismanaging Company funds, not maintaining proper records of cash accounts and carelessness. He was also accused of continuously receiving bribes from members of the Chinese community in the form of cash gifts in return for political favors including, in one case, the setting up of a pork monopoly for the benefit of a select group of businessmen.

Drake was found guilty of several of the charges, and was demoted to a lesser position in the Company. He was also ordered to spend the rest of his life in India, but as he was born in that country and knew very little of England, the sentence was not considered terribly severe. The final court decision by the East India Company's Court of Directors stated,

"Having with great attention read and considered your proceedings upon the inquiry we directed you to make into the conduct of Mr. Dawsonne Drake the Deputy Governor and the Company's other servants at Manila, we find that in the course of their administration there was a great want of harmony among them, discord with His Majesty's Officers, many

irregularities in the management of the farms and much neglect in keeping the accounts, in all which Mr. Drake had too great a share to be passed over without some marks of our disapprobation; you are therefore to let him know it is our opinion he deserves a severe censure for his improper conduct; however in consideration of his long services, we do agree and accordingly direct that his suspension be taken off, and he be again admitted to the Council, but he is to be fixed as the Fourth Member therein, and never rise to an higher rank: and it is our further directions that he shall constantly reside at Madras." 15

Nevertheless, through the intercession of his close associates in government and at the offices of the East India Company, he was eventually reinstated as a member of the Court of Directors of Fort St. George, Madras. There he served as a member of the Governor's Council during the years of 1768 to 1771. He died a wealthy man in 1781. In his possession before his death were a number of Spanish oil paintings taken from the Governor's Palace in Manila. Additionally, a number of rare Spanish maps and charts had been found in his home when an inventory was conducted of his possessions after his death. Many of the Spanish maps and charts are today housed at the British Museum in London.

Governor Dawsonne Drake's successor, Alexander Dalrymple, was also in possession of many important documents and manuscripts looted from Manila during the British occupation. Sotheby's in London sold these in the twentieth century. The collection of looted items included original letters and papers of the Augustinian order and their activities in China; documents describing the Philippines during the seventeenth century; personal correspondence with the religious order, Chinese uprisings, Filipino laborers working on the galleons, and many valuable papers important to the history of the Philippines.

In one particular collection, there were seventy-seven original documents concerning the Spanish garrison in Zamboanga, Mindanao during the years of 1721-28. Thus, the looting was extensive and widespread. Not only did the soldiers in the British army and navy profit through their activities in the Philippines, but the commanders as well were clearly in possession of looted property.

Epilogue

"My silence, perhaps, may be misconstrued; it may be suspected that I have sacrificed the deluded partners of my expedition, to private and base considerations; (for something of a dark and private treaty has been whispered about) but, I thank heaven, my behaviour has been such as will bear the light of day; and the all-searching eye of truth." [1]

General William Draper

There has been some controversy concerning the identity of the mastermind behind the plan to invade the Philippines. Was it Lord Anson's plan or William Draper's or someone else operating behind the scenes? The controversy will, of course, continue as future historians dissect the intricacies of the Seven Year's War, but at the present time all of the available research materials concerning the Manila campaign point to one individual as being the mastermind and this was Brigadier General William Draper.

As a distinguished and experienced military man, William Draper, had come to realize the opportunities a conquest of the Philippines could provide to the British government and its interest in the Southeast Asian region, as well as the effect it would have on the Spanish Empire. Once Spain signed a Family Pact in 1761 forming an alliance with France, the enemy of Britain, it had become an object of war. No doubt, Draper also realized the economic advantages a successfully carried out invasion of the Philippines meant for the East India Company's expansionary plans and commercial growth in the archipelago.

But an added bonus, was the opportunity the venture could provide the Company, the commanders and officers of the expedition to capture a number of valuable prizes, under the guise of an invasion. The possible prizes included the capture of a galleon and other vessels, plundering the seized territories, and imposing a ransom upon the Spaniards to protect their cities, residents and property.

While based in India, Draper had become aware of the Philippines. He was then participating in military action against the French during that portion of the Seven Year's War, which took place in the sub-continent for commercial supremacy. As part of the British forces sent to India to protect the East India Company settlements, he was in a position to learn how the Company operated and of its future expansionary plans in the Southeast Asian area. Much of what he learned about the Philippines was most probably the result of discussions held with Alexander Dalrymple, the East India Company civil servant. Dalrymple's experiences in the Philippines and in particular the Sulu Islands, where he had been attempting to set up a trade post for the East India Company, which was an ongoing work in progress.

During his clandestine journeys to Manila, where Europeans were not welcomed, Dalrymple may have come into contact with a fellow Englishman, Nicholas Norton Nichols. As one of the few Europeans then living in the Philippines, Nichols had become a naturalized Spanish citizen in 1757 whilst in Spain. As such, he was allowed to remain in the Philippine colony. Nichols owned several plantations in Mindanao and had enthusiastically praised the natural resources found on the island. Dalrymple, no doubt, passed this information on to Draper.

Consequently, when William Draper traveled to England and was given a position in 1761-1762 as a Chief of Staff at the Admiralty where he was involved in the planning stages for an attack of the French settlement of Belle Isle which was later scrapped, he was eager for a new challenge. Hence, the approval to wage war against Spain in January 1762, came about whilst Draper was still in England.

It is evident that even before the January 1762 meeting took place between the Admiralty and government officials, where the decision was reached to attack Havana and Manila, that William Draper had been involved in prior meetings with Lord Anson and the Earl of Egremont concerning a possible attack of the Philippines. A document located amongst the papers of the Earl of Egremont, lists the various reasons why such an attack against the Philippines would benefit the East India Company in Madras. When Draper discussed the plans for the Philippines, Lord Anson asked for a detailed report indicating how the invasion could be launched and what benefits the Company could realize through a military campaign of the sort suggested by Draper. It is thought that this particular document in the Earl of Egremont's papers, is the same document prepared by William Draper.

One could say that William Draper was in the right place at the right time. He most likely knew that the government and the Admiralty were planning to attack one of the Spanish settlements in response to the alliance between Spain and France. As someone who was quite familiar with the inner workings of the Spanish colonial government in the Philippines through his associations in Madras, he realized that he could be instrumental in devising a plan to attack another of Spain's colonies other than Havana, and this was namely, Manila.

Lord Anson was also familiar with the archipelago as he had captured a galleon while in the region in his younger years and realized the financial rewards to be gained by attacking one of the galleons or a Spanish settlement. Moreover, he realized that the coffers of the East India Company in Madras were sadly depleted after many years of conflict in India with the French, and an expedition to Manila could provide much needed revenues for the Company's treasury.

Draper was exceedingly enthusiastic about his proposal to attack the Philippines. The report he had submitted to Lord Anson indicates that in many ways he was trying to convince the Admiralty of the soundness and good sense of his plan. He was convinced that he would be successful if given the opportunity to lead the expedition. Several of the reasons he provided to the Admiralty as to why the expedition should be approved, were apparently an attempt to oversell his plan as he was so determined to carry it out one way or the other.

Heading the list of his arguments for the offensive was the retention of Mindanao, which as we now know was not technically a part of the Spanish possession. Nevertheless, the East India Company was interested in setting up a trade post in Mindanao and in the Sulu Islands as evidenced by the activities of Dalrymple in the region. His other reasons included the protection of British ships plying the South Seas if a base could be established in the Philippines for defensive purposes; obtaining new commodities to trade with the Chinese in lieu of always having to pay for exports in silver; and obtaining a source of new revenues by taking prizes to shore up the Company's depleted treasury after the wars it fought against the French settlements in India.

Draper was aware that time was of the essence. He had to act quickly if he was going to take advantage of the brief opportunity to take prizes. Thus, he needed the approval for the venture from the Admiralty, the East India Company and the king in order to return to Madras and immediately prepare the military strategy, ships and soldiers for the campaign. As he was then operating under the assumption that the Philippines was an extremely wealthy country, he expected to seize vast quantities of valuables.

It was also necessary to act quickly as Draper realized that a peace treaty would be signed in either 1762 or 1763 as negotiations were then underway between France and Britain. Any territories he was able to seize during the invasion would surely have to be returned as part of the treaty conditions. But he was aware that if the treaty was signed while he was in the process of sailing to or was already in the Philippines, the news of the war's end would not reach him for many months and during the interval he could take as many prizes as was then possible.

Nevertheless, there had been valid concerns for opposing Draper's plan as being too risky and expensive, but he was very persuasive. As he came from a class in English society, which allowed him to conveniently mix with the hierarchy of the East India Company in London and in India, he was able to develop a number of influential contacts. This enabled him to meet politicians and provided access to the corridors of power at the Admiralty and in government. Through these influential contacts, he was able to present his plan to Lord Anson and the Earl of Egremont.

Consequently, when he returned to India, General William Draper and Admiral Samuel Cornish began organizing the ships and soldiers for the expedition. In comparison to Draper's small military forces and Cornishs' fleet, which had been mobilized for the Philippine campaign, the Admiralty's Havana offensive of July 1762 consisted of a larger contingent of ships and soldiers deployed to the Spanish possession in the Caribbean. The Philippine campaign was obviously not on the same scale nor was it as militarily important to the British government as the Havana campaign. This was a very revealing factor as the Admiralty and the East India Company had no intention of conquering and retaining the entire archipelago. If that had been their objective, the expedition would have been provided with a larger fleet, which was in better condition than the ships they sailed aboard to Manila Bay. Moreover, they would have also been provided with a much larger army to conquer the entire country.

At one point, Draper was on the verge of canceling the expedition. Given the fact that the Company directors had originally approved his plan but were now having second thoughts about it, they offered very little cooperation. Their lack of enthusiasm at this late stage had greatly disheartened him. But then, Draper discovered that the officials of the East India Company in Madras were conducting a private trade with Manila and they were anxious to protect this business. The directors in opposition to Draper's plan viewed the expedition as a threat to their clandestine trade.

Without the support of all of the Company's directors for the expedition, an obstacle Draper found difficult to comprehend, the two commanders of the venture could not hope to gain any additional territories other than capturing Manila and Cavite and a few suburbs of the cities involved. However, as a complete capture of the entire Spanish possession was not part of the original plan and only retaining Mindanao was the main objective, there was no need for a larger invading force. The small army Draper led was adequate enough to successfully seize Manila and Cavite.

At the end of the Seven Year's War and after the British returned Manila and Cavite to the Spaniards in 1764, life returned to normal under the colonial government. The Spaniards picked up where they left off and continued to oppress the Filipinos who were obliged to live under the overbearing regime until the end of the nineteenth century and the advent of the Spanish-American War.

The French soldiers who had deserted the British army settled in the Philippines, as did a number of Indian Sepoys whose descendants can still be found in the country. The Chinese were severely punished for supporting the British and a number of atrocities they had committed such as the burning of towns, plunder, torture and killing of Spaniards. The Spaniards were incensed by the fact that the Chinese had become aligned to the British and could not fathom why they had turned against them.

"'Murderers! Traitors! Apostates! Ingrates!' These are some of the nasty epithets directed against the Chinese in the aftermath of the British Occupation of Manila, 1762-1764. To the Spaniards, it was an intensely emotional issue filled with hatred, revenge and disbelief. How could the sangleyes, the Christian-Chinese in particular, do such a terrible thing! After enriching themselves in the Philippines, they became enthusiastic allies of the English invaders, joined in their military campaigns, set fire to many towns, desecrated the churches, killed several Spaniards, and even tortured a few priests. The Chinese, on the other hand, believed they had legitimate reasons for their disloyalty. They regarded the Spanish government as unbearably oppressive. After suffering discrimination, overtaxation, periodic massacres and expulsions for almost two centuries, they probably considered the arrival of the British as the best thing that ever happened in the Islands." 2

During discussions with the British regarding the return of the seized territories, Simon Anda's emissaries stated that they were against any sort of pardon for the Chinese who supported the British. However, the English negotiator, Captain Backhouse, tried his best to protect the Chinese insisting that the British would remain in the Philippines and not leave as had been agreed to if any Chinese were expelled from the colony. Consequently, when Governor Francisco de la Torre assumed power, he gave in to pressure for an exemption of any charges levied against the Chinese and ordered an amnesty for them. A British proclamation further stated that the Chinese in the Philippines were now under the protection of George III.

Still, the Chinese had their doubts as to the sincerity of the Spaniards. Many individuals decided to sail aboard their own vessels to Mariveles where Alexander Dalrymple was based and had agreed to allow them to travel with his ships, which were first sailing to the Sulu Islands before returning to India. Dalrymple was as good as his word and managed to rescue many Chinese. However, one ship was wrecked off the coast of an area controlled by the colonial government, and the survivors committed suicide rather than face being captured by the Spaniards who they still feared. Some of the Chinese settled in the Sulu Islands and others made their way to Canton, China.

In a letter dated 30 June 1764, to the king of Spain, Simon Anda reported that 3,000 Chinese had fled from the Philippines and suggested that the remaining Chinese in the colony be expelled. The Chinese still residing in Manila and the villages surrounding the capital became the objects of Spanish scorn and hatred. They were forbidden to carry any type of arms under the threat of immediate execution.

By April 1766, Charles III of Spain issued a proclamation ordering the expulsion of all Chinese from the Philippines. Those individuals who fled with the British were permanently exiled from the colony and if they returned, they were to be immediately executed. However, it was stipulated that any Chinese arriving for trade purposes would be allowed to conduct their business in the city in an attempt to continue the economic operations of the colony.

The king's proclamation did not arrive in Manila until 17 July 1767, and was postponed for enactment until two years later. When the first deportations took place, which continued up to 1772, a total of 2,460 Chinese had been deported mainly to China. But by 1781, Chinese were beginning to slowly return to the Philippines. In 1903, there was approximately 41,000 Chinese living in the Philippines with hundreds of thousands of Chinese mestizos residing in the countryside.

While the British commanders had been provided with an opportunity to gain fresh revenues and new territories for the East India Company, as well as personal wealth for themselves, the Spaniards, Filipinos, Chinese and Muslims realized few benefits resulting from the British seizure and occupation of the country. However, it is true that as a result of the invasion, Filipinos experienced a foretaste of the possibilities for independence and freedom from Spain.

To the Filipinos, the invasion and seizure of Spanish territories had suddenly awakened them to the realization that the Spaniards were not as invincible as they had believed they were. Up until that point, the Filipinos had assumed that the Spaniards could never be toppled and that that they had no choice but to endure the hardships imposed upon them by the oppressive colonial regime. Equally important was the factor that not until the advent of the British invasion, were Filipinos able to mobilize a large enough contingent of soldiers to support the British against the Spanish government.

These first stirrings of independence predated those of the later efforts of the well-known and revered Jose Rizal during his independence movement of the nineteenth century. Consequently, even before the advent of Jose Rizal, there was Diego Silang, the first Filipino to organize and raise an army against the Spaniards, as well as to becoming aligned with the British if it meant getting rid of the Spaniards. Unfortunately for the

Filipinos, Silang was killed, as was his wife, Gabriela, who courageously rallied Filipinos to continue her husband's work. Given a different set of circumstances it is possible that Silang could have succeeded if he had not been assassinated. This was a strong possibility as the British had no intention of retaining the Spanish possession and were only interested in Mindanao. An alliance could have been formed with the Filipinos to oust the Spaniards and allow Filipinos to rule their own country, but at the time, this idea was not even contemplated.

After the British evacuation from the Philippines, the country remained, on the whole, in the same neglected state as it was prior to the invasion. The Spaniards only added a few improvements, but these were hardly monumental in scope. They included the expansion of the educational system with a larger number of teachers added to village schools. Moreover, Filipinos were taught to read and write in Spanish. A new postal service was established and some agricultural reforms were instituted to enable Filipinos to grow commodities in an attempt to better their lives. However, Filipinos were still required to pay yearly taxes or tributes to the Spanish government. The British government in Manila had abolished these, but the Spaniards quickly returned to the old system and institutions they had in operation before the invasion.

The Muslims of Mindanao and the Sulu Islands continued to experience a number of conflicts with the Spanish colonial government, which had renewed its campaign to conquer these territories. The Muslims realized that it was easier negotiating with the British than with the Spaniards, and this led to welcoming overtures to the English who were still interested in establishing a trade post in Mindanao. There was an attempt to set up a British trade post with the sultan of the Sulu Islands, but this eventually failed and the Muslims remained independent.

Despite the fact that the Spaniards regained the territories seized by the British, they had endured the loss of tremendous wealth and valuables. Two galleons had been lost as a result of the invasion. The *Santissima Trinidad* galleon was captured by the British and taken to England, whilst the *Filipino* was set afire when the British found that its cargo and silver had been removed. The *Pilar* galley was captured and her cargo and valuables were confiscated. Then there was the looting of Manila. The Spaniards, Filipinos and the Chinese had suffered the physical and psychological aftereffects of an attacked and plundered country. The Spaniards made an attempt to pay a small portion of the ransom demanded by Draper and Cornish, but as a result, they had relinquished large sum of revenues, jewels and other valuables in order to raise funds required for the payment. Ultimately, the ransom balance was never paid once the Seven Year's War had ended.

Many years later, Spain established *The Royal Company of the Philippines* on 10 March 1785 to compete with the trade companies of the British, French and Dutch. But the move came too late and was not as successful as the other foreign trade companies. They had been in operation far longer than the fledgling Spanish Company and proved more successful. However, it was then perceived as providing the colony with some advantages.

"Although a financial failure, the Royal Company was a great help to the Philippine economy. First of all, it opened commercial relations between Europe and the Philippines, ushering in for the first time free trade relations between Manila and Cadiz. Secondly, the Company furnished the Philippines the needed capital to develop its rich natural resources. For instance, from 1785 to 1790 it invested a total of 16,051,000 reales for various agricultural and industrial projects. Finally, the Company encouraged the colony's infant industries. It established textile factories to minimize the importation of textiles from India; it experimented on large-scale production of pepper and spices in Camarines, Cavite, Tayabas, Misamis, and Zamboanga; and it promoted the manufacture of indigo, sugar, and silk." [3]

The Spaniards were beginning to slowly open the doors of Manila to the world and foreign trade. They had kept the Philippines in such an isolated state for so long that they had begun to realize the need to be competitive in trade. Manila became a free port open to commerce and the ships of all nations by 1785. Additional measures had been taken to liberalize trade including the Royal Regulations of 1778, which established free trade eliminating import/export duties on trade between the Philippines and Spain. As the Manila-Acapulco galleon trade ended in 1813, when Mexico gained its independence from Spain, it was necessary to find alternative methods of increasing the colony's revenues.

While the invasion itself was clearly a success for England, the overall mission of the military campaign had not attained its objective of retaining the island of Mindanao. Nevertheless, the East India Company resumed its trade with the Muslims of Mindanao, the Sulu Islands and the Spaniards once they had opened Manila to foreign commercial trade.

However, one point is clearly evident and this is that although Mindanao had not been retained at the end of the Seven Year's War, Brigadier General William Draper, Rear Admiral Samuel Cornish and Governor Dawsonne Drake, had become wealthy men. Not only had the East India Company received a substantial share of prizes taken from the archipelago, but so had the individuals commanding the enterprise and forming the first British government of the Philippines.

Reference Notes

Abbreviations Used
BL – British Library, London
BR – Blair and Robertson, *The Philippine Islands*
PRO – Public Records Office, Kew, England

Chapter One : An Invasion Takes Shape

1. Gregorio Zaide, *Documentary Sources of Philippine History*, King George III to General William Draper, Commander of the British military forces involved in the invasion of the Philippines in September 1762, document 224, pp. 404-408. Also available in PRO CO 77/20.
2. PRO 30/47/20, Earl of Egremont Papers, *Memorial from the Secret Committee of the East India Company Addressed to the Earl of Egremont*, 14 January 1762.
3. PRO 30/47/20, Earl of Egremont Papers, *Reasons and Considerations Upon the Enterprise Against the Philippine Islands,* undated/no signature but generally thought to have been written by General William Draper.
4. Ibid.
5. William Dampier, *Travel Accounts of the Islands 1513-1787*, p. 40.
6. Julian S. Corbett, *England in the Seven Year's War Vol. II : 1759-63*, p. 247.
7. Ministerio de Fomento, Madrid, Spain, *Manila 1571-1898 : The Western Orient,* Exhibition Book Manila.
8. David Syrett, *The Siege and Capture of Havana 1762*, p. viii.

Chapter Two : Preparations for the Invasion Begin in India

1. PRO 30/47/20, Earl of Egremont Papers, The East India Company, *Memorial from the Secret Committee to the Earl of Egremont*, dated 14 January 1762.
2. Geoffrey, Moorhouse, *India Britannica*, pp. 28-29.
3. PRO 30/47/20, Earl of Egremont Papers, The East India Company, *Memorial from the Secret Committee of the East India Company* addressed to the Earl of Egremont and dated 14 January 1762.

4. Gregorio Zaide, *Documentary Sources of Philippine History*, "General Draper's Report to the War Office," dated 2 November 1762, document 233, pp. 450-454. This is also in PRO War Office WO 1/319.
5. LeGentil de la Galaisiere, *A Voyage to the Indian Seas*, chapter 27, p. 147.
6. Ibid. chapter 14, p. 78.
7. Gregorio Zaide, *Documentary Sources of Philippine History*, document 236, pp. 468-480, "Alexander Dalrymple : British Plan to Conquer Southern Philippines : 23 November 1762. The document can also be found at the British Museum London, Department of Manuscripts Add. Mss. 19.298.
8. PRO 30/47/20. Earl of Egremont Papers. This document describes how soldiers were recruited in Mexico for service in the Philippines.
9. LeGentil de la Galaisiere, *A Voyage to the Indian Seas*, Archbishop Rojo's Journal, chapter 30, pp. 176-196. The journal also appears in BR, vol. 49, pp. 101-131. BR provided a translation from the French, which led to some inaccuracies. This was corrected by the newer translation appearing in the LeGentil book, which was translated directly from the Spanish into English.
10. N.A.M Rodger, *The Wooden World : An Anatomy of the Georgian Navy*, p. 257.
11. Nicholas Tracy, "The Capture of Manila," *The Mariner's Mirror*, vol. 55, no. 3, August 1969, Cambridge University Press, pp. 311-323.

Chapter Three : Spain's Contentious Colony

1. LeGentil de la Galaisiere, *A Voyage to the Indian Seas*, Chapter 19, p. 116.
2. F. Landa Jocano, *Filipino Prehistory : Rediscovering Precolonial Heritage*, p. 53.
3. Ibid. p. 54.
4. Nicolas Zafra, *Philippine History Through Selected Sources*, quotes from Antonio Pigafetta's diary of the Magellan journey to the Philippines, p. 12.
5. Ibid. pp. 12-13.
6. Ibid. p. 13.
7. Ministerio de Fomento, *Manila 1571-1898 : The Western Orient*, p. 40.

8. LeGentil de la Galaisiere, chapter 18, p. 114.
9. Ibid p. 115.

Chapter Four : The Endless Cycle of Conflicts

1. LeGentil de la Galaisiere, *A Voyage to the Indian Seas*, Archbishop Rojo's Journal, Chapter 30, pp. 176-196.
2. Ibid. Chapter 13, p. 63.
3. Ibid. p. 65.
4. William Dampier, *Travel Accounts of the Islands 1513-1787*, p. 50.
5. Antonio Morga, *Historical Events of the Philippine Islands*, p. 331.

Chapter Five : Spanish Manila

1. LeGentil de la Galaisiere, *A Voyage to the Indian Seas*, chapter 16, p. 85.
2. Ibid. chapter 14, pp. 74-75.
3. Domingo Abella, *From Indio to Filipino*, p. 18.
4. Joaquin Martinez de Zuniga, *Status of the Philippines in 1800*, chapter 11, p. 182.
5. Ibid. chapter 13, p. 220.
6. H. de la Costa, *Readings in Philippine History*, p. 122.
7. LeGentil de la Galaisiere, *A Voyage to the Indian Seas*, chapter 16, pp. 91-92.
8. H. de la Costa, *Readings in Philippine History*, quote from DeGuignes and his description of society in Manila, chapter 8, p. 124.
9. LeGentil de la Galaisiere, chapter 16, p. 96.
10. Ibid. p. 97.
11. O. D. Corpuz, *The Roots of the Filipino Nation*, vol. 1, chapter 2, p. 101.
12. LeGentil de la Galaisiere, *A Voyage to the Indian Seas*, chapter 27, p. 149.
13. *Manila 1571-1898 : The Western Orient*, p. 138.
14. H. de la Costa, *Readings in Philippine History*, quote from Gamelli Careri, chapter 5, pp. 72-73.
15. Ibid. p. 81, quote from Father Juan Jose Delgado.

Chapter Six : Manila's Neglected Military Defenses

1. LeGentil de la Galaisiere, *A Voyage to the Indian Seas*, Archbishop Rojo's Journal, chapter 30, p. 179.
2. David Syrett, *The Siege and Capture of Havana 1762*, p. viii.
3. Ibid. p. Xxi.
4. Francis Russell Hart, *The Siege of Havana 1762*, p. 12.
5. Santander Investment, *Fernando Valdes Tamon Report*, p. 60.
6. Ibid. pp. 61-62.
7. LeGentil de la Galaisiere, *A Voyage to the Indian Seas*, chapter 14, p. 80.
8. Joaquin Martinez de Zuniga, *Status of the Philippines in 1800*, chapter 21, pp. 180-181.
9. Santander Investment, *Fernando Valdes Tamon Report*, pp. 63-64.
10. LeGentil de la Galaisiere, chapter 14, p. 79.

Chapter Seven : The British Invasion of Manila

1. Gregorio Zaide, *Documentary Sources of Philippine History*, document 224, "War Instructions of King George III of England (1762)" to General William Draper dated 21 January, 1762, pp. 404-408 and also in PRO CO 77/20.
2. BR, *The Philippine Islands 1493-1898*, Draper's Journal, "A Journal of the Proceedings of His Majesty's Forces on the Expedition Against Manila, vol. 49, pp. 81-103.
3. Ibid.
4. Gregorio Zaide, *Documentary Sources of Philippine History*, document 235, "A Participant's Narrative of the British Invasion," authored by Captain William Stevenson of the Engineering Corps and dated 19, November 1762 pp. 458-467.
5. LeGentil de la Galaisiere, *A Voyage to the Indian Seas*, Archbishop Rojo's Journal, chapter 30, pp. 176-196.
6. BR, *The Philippine Islands 1493-1898*, "A Journal of the Proceedings of His Majesty's Forces on the Expedition Against Manila," General Draper's Journal, vol. 49, pp. 81-103.
7. Gregorio Zaide, *Documentary Sources Philippine Sources*, document 235, "A Participant's Narrative of the British Invasion" authored by Captain William Stevenson, Engineering Corps, pp. 458-467.
8. Ibid. Document 226, "British Ultimatum for Manila's Surrender," p. 413.

9. H. de la Costa, *Philippine Studies*, "Texts and Documents : The Siege and Capture of Manila by the British : September-October 1762," vol. 10, 1962, p. 618.
10. BR, *The Philippine Islands*, "A Journal of the Proceedings of His Majesty's Forces on the Expedition Against Manila," General Draper's Journal, vol. 49, pp. 81-103.
11. Ibid.
12. Ibid.
13. LeGentil de la Galaisiere, *A Voyage to the Indian Seas*, Archbishop Rojo's Journal, chapter 30, pp. 176-196.
14. BR, *The Philippine Islands*, "A Journal of the Proceedings of His Majesty's Forces on the Expedition Against Manila," General Draper's Journal, vol. 49, pp. 81-103.
15. LeGentil de la Galaisiere, *A Voyage to the Indian Seas*, Archbishop Rojo's Journal, chapter 30, p. 184.
16. BR, *The Philippine Islands*, General Draper's Journal, vol. 49, pp. 81-103.
17. H. de la Costa, *Philippine Studies*, "Texts and Documents : The Siege and Capture of Manila by the British : September-October 1762," vol. 10, p. 625, General Draper's letter to Archbishop Rojo.
18. Ibid. Archbishop Rojo's letter to General Draper, p. 629.
19. Ibid.
20. Ibid. p. 30.
21. Ibid. pp. 632-633.
22. Ibid. p. 635.
23. BR, *The Philippine Islands*, "A Journal of the Proceedings of His Majesty's Forces on the Expedition Against Manila," General Draper's Journal, vol. 49, pp. 81-103.
24. H. de la Costa, *Philippine Studies*, "Texts and Documents : The Siege and Capture of Manila by the British : September-October 1762," vol. 10, p. 640.
25. BR, *The Philippine Islands*, "A Journal of the Proceedings of His Majesty's Forces on the Expedition Against Manila," General Draper's Journal, vol. 49, pp. 81-103.
26. Ibid.
27. Ibid.
28. LeGentil de la Galaisiere, *A Voyage to the Indian Seas*, Archbishop Rojo's Journal, chapter 30, pp. 176-196.
29. BR, *The Philippine Islands*, "A Journal of the Proceedings of His Majesty's Forces on the Expedition Against Manila," General Draper's Journal, vol. 49, pp. 81-103.

30. LeGentil de la Galaisiere, *A Voyage to the Indian Seas*, Archbishop Rojo's Journal, chapter 30, pp. 176-196.
31. Ibid.
32. BR, *The Philippine Islands*, "A Journal of the Proceedings of His Majesty's Forces on the Expedition Against Manila," General Draper's Journal, vol. 49, pp. 81-103.
33. Ibid.
34. Ibid.

Chapter Eight : The Seizure and Looting of Manila

1. Gregorio Zaide, *Documentary Sources of Philippine History*, "General Draper's Report to the Southern Department," vol. 5, pp. 455-457.
2. BR, *The Philippine Islands*, "A Journal of the Proceedings of His Majesty's Forces on the Expedition Against Manila," General Draper's Journal, vol. 49, pp. 81-103.
3. Le Gentil de la Galaisiere, *A Voyage to the Indian Seas*, Archbishop Rojo's Journal, chapter 30, pp. 176-196.
4. Gregorio Zaide, *Documentary Sources of Philippine History*, Admiral Cornish's report to the British Admiralty London dated 31 October 1762, vol. 5, pp. 436-443.
5. H. de la Costa, *Philippine Studies*, "Texts and Documents : The Siege and Capture of Manila by the British : September—October 1762," vol. 10, p. 647.
6. Martinez de Zuniga, *An Historical View of the Philippine Islands*, chapter 34, p. 188.
7. H. de la Costa, *Readings in Philippine History*, p. 99.
8. Gregorio Zaide, *Documentary Sources of Philippine History*, "Draper's Defense Against Spanish Charges," London 1764, document 242, pp. 510-521.
9. H. de la Costa, *Philippine Studies*, "Texts and Documents : The Siege and Capture of Manila by the British : September-October 1762," vol. 10, pp. 648-650.
10. Antonio M. Molina, *The Philippines Through the Centuries*, p. 196.
11. Gregorio Zaide, *Documentary Sources of Philippine History*, "Admiral Cornish's Report to the British Admiralty," 31 October 1762, document 231, pp. 436-443.
12. Ibid. "The Capture of the Galleon Santissima Trinidad," document 232, pp. 444-448.

13. British Library, "Petition by Don Pedro Calderon Henriquez of the Order of Culatrana dated 25 September 1763."
14. Ibid.
15. Gregorio Zaide, *Documentary Sources of Philippine History*, "Admiral Cornish's Report to the British Admiralty," 31 October 1762, document 231, pp. 436-443.
16. Ibid.
17. Ibid.

Chapter Nine : The Troubled British Government of Manila and Cavite

1. PRO WO 1/319 and Gregorio Zaide, document 233, "Draper's Report to the War Office," pp. 450-454
2. Serafin Quiason, "The East India Company in Manila 1762-1764," *The Culture of the Philippines*, p. 426
3. Ibid. p. 431
4. Ibid. p. 432
5. K. C. Leebrick, "Troubles of an English Governor," in H. M. Stephens and H. E. Bolton, eds., *The Pacific Ocean in History*, Admiral Cornish's comments, p. 200.
6. Ibid. Captain Brereton's letter to Governor Drake, p. 202
7. Ibid. p. 202
8. Ibid. p. 202
9. Gregorio Zaide, *The Pageant of Philippine History*, vol. 2, chapter 1, p. 14
10. Ibid. p. 17
11. LeGentil de la Galaisiere, *A Voyage to the Indian Seas*, chapter 30, p. 199
12. PRO WO 1/319, Draper's comments concerning the French deserters.
13. LeGentil de la Galaisiere, *A Voyage to the Indian Seas*, chapter 31, p. 201

Chapter Ten : The Filipino and Chinese Supporters of the British

1. Joaquin Martinez de Zuniga, *An Historical View of the Philippine Islands*, chapter 36, p.203.
2. LeGentil de la Galaisiere, *A Voyage to the Indian Seas*, chapter 16, pp. 106-107.

3. Gregorio Zaide, *Documentary Sources of Philippine History*, Captain Brereton's letter to Diego Silang, document 238, pp. 498-501 and BR, vol. 49, pp. 160-163.
4. Ibid.
5. Joaquin Martinez de Zuniga, *An Historical View of the Philippine Islands*, chapter 36, p. 207.
6. Eufronio M. Alip, *The Chinese in Manila*, pp. 27-28.
7. Joaquin Martinez de Zuniga, *Status of the Philippines in 1800*, chapter 13, p. 211.
8. Karl C. Leebrick, "Troubles of An English Governor of the Philippine Islands," in *The Pacific Ocean in History*, p. 208.
9. Ibid. p. 203.
10. Ibid.
11. Ibid.
12. Ibid.
13. Ibid. pp. 203-204.

Chapter Eleven : Colony Returned to Spain

1. Joaquin Martinez de Zuniga, *An Historical View of the Philippine Islands*, chapter 37, p. 212.
2. LeGentil de la Galaisiere, *A Voyage to the Indian Seas*, chapter 30, p. 205.
3. Ibid.
4. Ibid. pp. 205.206.
5. Serafin D. Quiason, *The Culture of the Philippines*, "The East India Company in Manila 1762-1764," p. 441.
6. Karl C. Leebrick, "Troubles of an English Governor of the Phiippine Islands," in *The Pacific Ocean in History*, p. 204.
7. Ibid. p. 205.
8. BL notes Claud Russell's letter to Governor Drake and the Manila Council.
9. Ibid.
10. Ibid.
11. Ibid. p. 210.
12. BR, *The Philippine Islands 1493-1898*, vol. 49, pp. 288-295.
13. Gregorio Zaide, *The Pageant of Philippine History*, vol. II, p. 41.

Chapter Twelve : Following the Money

1. Gregorio Zaide, *Documentary Sources of Philippine History*, document 233, "General Draper's Report to the War Office," pp. 450-451.
2. PRO, *Expenses for the East Indies Company Invasion of the Philippines.*
3. Ibid.
4. Ibid.
5. Gregorio Zaide, *Documentary Sources of Philippine History*, document 242, "Draper's Defense Against Spanish Charges," pp. 513-514.
6. Ibid.
7. Ibid.
8. Ibid.
9. Ibid.
10. Ibid.
11. Ibid.
12. Ibid.
13. Ibid.
14. Ibid.
15. Karl C. Leebrick, "Troubles of an English Governor of the Philippine Islands," p. 212.

Epilogue

1. Gregorio Zaide, *Documentary Sources of Philippine History*, document 242, "Draper's Defense Against Spanish Charges," pp. 510-521.
2. Salvador P. Escoto. "Expulsion of the Chinese and Readmission to the Philippines : 1764-1779," *Philippine Studies*, p. 48.
3. Gregorio Zaide, *The Pageant of Philippine Society,* pp. 62-63.

Shirley Fish

Bibliography

England

British Library Oriental and India Office Collections (OIOC), London, England.

Marine Records 1600-1879: L/MAR/A-C, L/MAR/1-9. "List of Marine Records of the Late East India Company and of Subsequent Date, Preserved in the Record Department of the India Office, London," 1896.
Governor Dawsonne Drake's Minutes of the Manila Council, 2 November 1762.
Letter from Captain William Stevenson dated 10 November 1762.
Letter from Claud Russell to Governor Dawsonne Drake.
Rebellion of Don Simon Anda y Salazar.
Petitions of Judge Pedro Calderon Henriquez, Don Francisco Vizente Meylar and Don Juan Francisco regarding the rights of private individuals during the time of war.
Correspondence between Governor Dawsonne Drake and Admiral Cornish at Manila.
Maintenance of Prisoners.
Correspondence between Governor Dawsonne Drake and Members of the Manila Council 25 November to 19 December 1763.
Archbishop of Manila's Draft on the Royal Treasury at Madrid 1764.
Capitulation of Manila October 1762.
Minutes of Deputy Governor Dawsonne Drake and Manila Council 1762 giving the accounts of events that occurred from September and October 1762 when the British invaded Manila.
Letter from Governor Dawsonne Drake to Admiral Samuel Cornish indicating the difficulties he was having in obtaining the 4 million-dollar ransom payment.
Correspondence between Archbishop Rojo and Governor Dawsonne Drake.

Public Records Office: The National Archives, Kew, England

PRO 30/47/20 – Earl of Egremont Papers. Memorial from the Secret Committee of the East India Company Addressed to the Earl of Egremont dated 14 January 1762.
Letter from the Earl of Egremont to the Secret Committee of the East India Company dated 23 January 1762.

Document: Detailing the number of soldiers in the Spanish garrison at Fort Santiago in Manila.
Document: Describing how soldiers are recruited in Mexico for the Manila garrisons.
Document: Reasons and Considerations upon the Enterprise against the Philippine Islands (thought to have been written by William Draper).
WO 1/319: Letter from William Draper dated 27 July 1762 to the War Office prior to the invasion of the Philippines.
Letter from William Draper dated 20 November 1762 to the Secretary of the War Office.
Letter from Major Fell to the War Office dated 28 February 1763.
Document I: "The Memorial of the Court of Directors of the United Company of Merchants of England trading to the East Indies," 28 June 1775.
Document II: "Memorial of the East India Company for Reimbursement of Expenses at Manila 1763," 28 June 1775.
Document III: "Expedition to Manila in account with the East India Company subsequent to the surrender of the Island on the 2 November 1762."
Document: "Expedition to Manila in Account with the United East India Company subsequent to the Surrender of the Island to the Company's Servants on 2 November 1762"
ADM 51/643 Captain's Logs: Expedition to Manila September 1762
Norfolk – Captain Kempenfelt
Panther - Captain George Ourry
Argo – Captain Richard King
PRO 30/20/01 – Dalrymple and trade negotiations with the Sultan of Sulu 28 January 1761.
T1 516 137/A-144A – Reimbursement for the Expense of the Capitulation of Manila 1763.

Philippines

Abella, Domingo. 1978. *From Indio to Filipino and Some Historical Works*. Manila: Abella Family.
Abbott, William. 1969. *Philippine Historical Review*. Manila. International Association of Historians of Asia. Spanish Conquerors of the Philippines from Magellan to Dasmarinas.
Alip, Eufronio. 1993. M. *The Chinese in Manila*. Manila. National Historic Institute.
Ayerbe, Marques de. 1897. *Sitio y Conquista de Manila por los Ingleses en 1762*. Spain. Imprenta de Ramon Miedes.
Bauzon, Leslie E. 1971. *Philippine Historical Review*. Manila. International Association of Asia. Mexican Financial Aid: The Situado.

Blair, E.H., and Robinson, J.A., eds. 1921. *The Philippine Islands*, 1493-1898. Cleveland.

Boxer, Charles R. 1970. *Philippine Studies*. Manila. Ateneo de Manila. Plata es Sangre: Sidelights on the Drain of Spanish-American Silver in the Far East, 1550-1700.

1970. *Philippine Historical Review*. Manila. International Association of Historians of Asia. A Collection of Documents Looted at Manila in 1762-1764.

Beyer, H. Otley. 1979. *Readings in Philippine Prehistory*. Manila. Filipiniana Book Guild. The Philippines Before Magellan. Early History of Philippine Relations With Foreign Countries, Especially China.

Cheong, W. E. 1972. *Philippine Historical Review*. Manila. International Association of Historians of Asia. The Decline of Manila as a Spanish Entrepot.

Chirino, Pedro. 1979. *Readings in Philippine Prehistory*. Manila. Filipiniana Book Guild. Relation of the Philippine Islands.

Corbett, Sir Julian.S. 1918. *England in the Seven Years' War : Vol II: 1759-63*. London. Greenhill Books.

Costa, S.J., Fr. Horacio de la. 1962. *Philippine Studies*. Manila. Ateneo de Manila. The Siege and Capture of Manila by the British, Sept-Oct. 1762.

1965. *Readings in Philippine History: Selected Historical Texts*. Manila. Bookmark.

Corpuz, O.D. 1989. *The Roots of the Filipino Nation*. Quezon City. Aklahi Foundation.

Cushner, Nicholas P. *Landed Estates in the Colonial Philippines*. Connecticut. Yale University Southeast Asia Studies.

1965. *Philippine Studies*. Manila. Ateneo de Manila. Legazpi 1564-1572.

Diaz-Trechuelo, Maria Lourdes. 1963. *Philippine Studies*. Manila. Ateneo de Manila. The Economic Development of the Philippines in the Second Half of the Eighteenth Century.

Escota, Salvador P. 1999. *Philippine Studies*. Manila. Ateneo University Press. Expulsion of the Chinese and Readmission to the Philippines : 1764-1779.

Filipiniana Book Guild XIX, 1971. *Travel Accounts of the Islands 1513-1787*. Manila.

Fox, Robert B. 1979. *Readings in Philippine Prehistory*. Manila. Filipiniana Book Guild. The Philippines in Prehistoric Times.

Flynn, Dennis O. & Giraldez, Arturo. 1996. *Philippine Studies*. Manila. Ateneo University Press. Silk for Silver : Manila-Macao Trade in the 17th Century.

Galaisiere, Jean Baptiste Le Gentil de la. 1779-1781. *A Voyage to the Indian Seas*. Manila. Filipiniana Book Guild. Details Concerning the Capture of Manila and the Archbishop's Journal of the Siege.

Garcia-Abasolo, Antonio. 1996. *Philippine Studies*. Manila. Ateneo University Press. The Private Environment of the Spaniards in the Philippines.

Gardner, Brian. 1971. *The East India Company*. New York. Barnes & Noble Books.

Gatbonton, Esperanza. 1985. *Bastion de San Diego.* Manila. Intramuros Administration.

1983. *Intramuros of Memory.* Manila. Intramuros Administration.

Gradish, Stephen. 1980. *The Manning of the British Navy During the Seven Years' War.* London. Royal Historical Society.

Hart, Francis Russell. 1931. *The Siege of Havana 1762.* London. Houghton Mifflin Company.

Jennings, Francis. 1988. *Empire of Fortune : Crowns, Colonies & Tribes in the Seven Years War in America.* W. W. Norton.

Jesus, Ed. C. de. 1985. *The Tobacco Monopoly in the Philippines : Bureaucratic Enterprise and Social Change 1766-1880.* Manila. Ateneo de Manila.

Jocano, F. Landa. 1975. *The Philippines at the Spanish Contact.* Manila. Punlad Research House.

1998. *Filipino Prehistory : Rediscovering Precolonial Heritage : Anthropology of the Filipino People I.* Manila. Punlad Research House.

Joyner, Tim. 1992. *Magellan.* Maine. International Marine Publishing.

Keay, John. 1993. *The Honourable Company : A History of the English East India Company.* London. Harper Collins.

Leebrick, K.C. 1917. In H. M. Stephens and H.E. Bolton, eds., *The Pacific Ocean in History.* New York. The MacMillan Company. Troubles of an English Governor.

Loarca, Miquel de. 1979. *Readings in Philippine Prehistory.* Manila. Filipiniana Book Guild. Relation of the Philippine Islands.

McNeill, John Robert. 1985. *Atlantic Empires of France and Spain : Louisbourg and Havana 1700-1763.* North Carolina. University of North Carolina.

Mallat, Jean. 1846. *The Philippines : History, Geography, Customs, Agriculture, Industry and Commerce of the Spanish Colonies in Oceania.* Manila. National Historical Institute.

Ministero de Fomento. 1998. *Manila 1571-1898 : The Western Orient.* Madrid. Centro de Publicaciones.

Moir, Martin I. 1970. *Philippine Historical Review.* Manila. International Association of Historians of Asia. Materials in London of the East India Company.

Molina, Antonio M. 1960. *The Philippines Through the Centuries.* Manila. University of Santo Tomas.

Moorhouse, Geoffrey. 1983. *India Britannica.* New York. Harper & Row.

Montero y Vidal, D. Jose. 1894. *Historia General de Filipinas.* Madrid. Desde el Descubrimento de dichas islas hasta nuestros dias.

Morga, Dr. Antonio de. 1609. *Historical Events of the Philippine Islands.* Manila. National Historical Institute.

Patanne, E. P. 1996. *The Philippines in the 6th to 16th Centuries.* Manila. LSA Press.

Pearson, J. D. 1970. *Philippine Historical Review.* Manila. International Association of Historians of Asia. Documents in the British Isles Relating to Southeast Asia.

Plasencia, Juan de. 1979. *Readings in Philippine Prehistory.* Manila. Filipiniana Book Guild. Customs of the Tagalogs.

Pocock, Tom. 1998. *Battle for Empire : The Very First World War 1756-63.* London. Michael O'Mara Books.

Quirino, Carlos. 1960. *The Philippine Historical Bulletin.* Manila. Philippine Historical Association. Anson's Capture of the Manila Galleon.

1967. *Philippine Historical Association Historical Bulletin.* Manila. Philippine Historical Association. Postscript to the British Invasion.

Quison, S.D. 1966. English Country Trade with the Philippines 1644-1765. Manila. University of the Philippines Press.

1965. *Philippine Historical Review.* Manila. International Association of Historians of Asia. The Early Trade of the English East India Company with Manila.

Rashed, Zenab Esmat. 1951. *The Peace of Paris 1763.* Liverpool. Liverpool University Press.

Ray, Dr. S. C. 1970. *Philippine Historical Review.* Manila. International Association of Historians of Asia. Commercial Relations Between India and Southeast Asia in the Early Historic Period.

Rodger, N. A. M. 1988. *The Wooden World : An Anatomy of the Georgian Navy.* London. Fontana Press.

Schurz, William Lytle. 1985. *The Manila Galleon.* Manila. The Historical Conservation Society.

Scott, William Henry. 1997. *Barangay : Sixteenth-Century Philippine Culture and Society.* Manila. Ateneo University Press.

1982. *Cracks in the Parchment Curtain and Other Essays in Philippine History.* Manila. New Day Publishers.

1992. *Looking for the Prehispanic Filipino and Other Essays in Philippine History.* Manila. New Day Publishers.

Story, D. A. 1931. *The De Lanceys : A Romance of a Great Family : With notes on those allied Families who remained loyal to the British Crown during the Revolutionary War.* Massachusetts. Higginson Book Company.

Syrett, David. 1970. *The Siege and Capture of Havana 1762.* London. The Navy Records Society.

1969. *The Mariner's Mirror : The Quarterly Journal of the Society for Nautical Research.* London. Cambridge University Press. The British Landing at Havana : An Example of an Eighteenth Century Combined Operation.

Tamon, Fernando Valdes. 1739. *Report in which, by order of His Catholic Majesty (May God Protect Him), the strongholds, castles, forts and garrisons of the provinces under His Royal Dominion in the Philippine Islands are listed.* Spain. Santander Investment.

Tracy, Nicolas. 1995. *Manila Ransomed.* England. University of Exeter Press.

1969. *The Mariner's Mirror : The Quarterly Journal of the Society for Nautical Research*. London. Cambridge University Press.

Wendt, Reinhard. 1998. *Philippine Studies*. Manila. Ateneo University Press. Philippine Fiesta and Colonial Culture.

Wilkinson, Clennel. 1929. *Dampier Explorer & Buccaneer*. New York. Harper & Brothers.

Young, Robert J. 1972. *Philippine Historical Review*. Manila. International Association of Historians of Asia. The British Company in Southeast Asia.

Zafra, Nicolas. 1967. *Philippine History Through Selected Sources*. Quezon City. Alemar-Phoenix Publishing House.

Zaide, Gregorio F., 1990. *Documentary Sources of Philippine History*. Manila. National Book Store. Document 222 : The Advantages of Direct Trade With Spain. Document 223 : Decision of the East India Company to Support of the British Conquest of the Philippines (1762). Document 224 : War Instructions of King George III of England (1762). Document 225 : War Instructions of the British Admiralty (1762). Document 226 : British Ultimatum for Manila's Surrender. Document 227 : Spanish Reply to the British Ultimatum. Document 229 : British Conditions for Manila's Surrender. Document 230 : Terms of Manila's Surrender to the British. Document 231 : Admiral Cornish's Report to the British Admiralty. Document 232 : The Capture of the Galleon Santissima Trinidad. Document 233 : General Draper's Report to the War Office. Document 234 : General Draper's Reports to the Southern Department. Document 235 : A Participant's Narrative of the British Invasion. Document 236 : British Plan to Conquer Southern Philippines. Document 238 : Captain Brereton's Letter to Diego Silang. Document 242 : Draper's Defense Against Spanish Charges. Document 253 : Bowditch's Visit to Manila in 1796.

1979. *The Pageant of Philippine History : Political, Economic and Socio-Cultural : From the British to the Present*. Manila. Philippine Education Company.British Invasion of the Philippines.Reconstruction After the British Invasion.

1972. *Philippine Historical Review*. Manila. International Association of Historians of Asia. Manila and Acapulco.

Zaragoza, Ramon Ma. 1997. *Old Manila*. New York/Malaysia. Oxford University Press.

Zuniga, Joaquin Martinez de. 1803. *An Historical View of the Philippine Islands*. Manila. Filipiniana Book Guild.

1966. *Status of the Philippines in 1800*. Manila. Filipiniana Book Guild.

****

About the Author:

Shirley Fish is an American Freelance Writer and Researcher working in Asia for the past 23 years. She has lived in Korea, Hong Kong, Indonesia and is currently in Manila, Philippines. Over the years she has been a magazine editor and correspondent with various Asian publications. She has a Master's Degree in Education from the University of Southern California.

Printed in Great Britain
by Amazon.co.uk, Ltd.,
Marston Gate.